ART PROJECTS Plus!

By R. Howard Blount, Jr.
& Martha Venning Webb

Instructional Fair • TS Denison

Dedication

For the illustrators of children's books who add beauty to our lives

R. H. B.
Luke 12:27

For my son, Nathan, who showed me how children devour good books
and
Ms. Posey, my art teacher at Sherwood Forest Elementary who brought art to life

M. V. W.
Philippians 4:8

Credits:
Authors: R. Howard Blount, Jr. & Martha Venning Webb
Original Artwork: Martha Venning Webb
Cover Illustration: Tracy Turner
Graphic Design: Margo De Paulis
Project Director/Editor: Debra Olson Pressnall
Cover Art Direction: Darcy Bell-Myers
Graphic Layout: Deborah Hanson McNiff
Digital Photography: Popular Front Studio

Dear Colleague,

What better way to teach art appreciation than through the very medium by which children are first exposed to creativity! Children's picture books hold many memories dear to us all—times spent together with parents, grandparents, siblings, teachers, and other people we love. As you share the beauty of art and the power of the creative spirit with your students, it is our hope that this handbook will be your guide.

All good wishes,

R. Howard Blount, Jr. & Martha Venning Webb

TABLE OF

CONTENTS

FOREWORD

The Treasure of Diversity in Children's Art

Though any excuse to get children engaged in art-related activities is a good one, I see the great variety of art found in picture books for young readers as an especially good vehicle for beginning to understand that artists are not all the same. They use different media and materials including cut paper, watercolor, pastel, colored pencils, and even oil paint. Each artist has his/her own special interests and area of expertise. Some depict situations in a literal way. Others are good at evoking a sense of time and place. Some artists work in flat color and simple shapes while others use tonal nuances and quality of light to create the appropriate mood. All different, all professional.

One of the thrills of being an illustrator of books for children is walking into an elementary school and discovering that the hall walls are adorned with artwork produced by children. The many different visual interpretations of themes, as with the professionals, are always intriguing and gives evidence to the fact that we are all created with a unique DNA of talents and abilities and ways of seeing, one as valid as the other.

If I were to offer but one bit of advice to teachers, it would be to never compare the children's art one with another, and certainly not with the illustrators. Making a picture can be a courageous act for some children and should be applauded and encouraged. Their worst "mess-up" should be valued as much as those that are perceived to be superior. Creativity at any level of expression is miraculous.

We all know that education is about learning and that learning is a process and not a product. We also know that learning is intensified when we are having fun. So have fun and bathe in the love that making art together generates.

Thomas B. Allen

Thomas B. Allen
Illustration Department Head
Ringling School of Art and Design
Sarasota, Florida

INTRODUCTION

Introducing Art through Children's Picture Books:
An Integrated Approach

PICTURE BOOKS BEYOND THE STORY

Picture books have always been valued as an attractive means to capture the attention of beginning readers. Still, the potential classroom uses of children's picture books have only begun to be discovered. With the educational transformation the whole language movement has effected, you now find picture books used in classrooms K–12.

The quality and diversity of picture book illustrations has increased dramatically even within the last decade. In case you do not remember, take a look back at some of the Caldecott Medal winners from as recent as the 1960s and compare them to the many superior graphic works that today win little or no national attention or recognition.

Several years ago we began using picture book illustrations to teach the basics of art to our students. At first we taught the most obvious elements such as perspective and medium. Now we find opportunity to extend the instruction in many diverse directions.

Our desire is to share with you a way to double the value you currently get from sharing picture books with your students. With a simple, organized approach we want to facilitate the process of introducing art form, media, and technique to your students and help you instill an appreciation for the arts at an early age by using materials that already line the shelves of your classroom storage closets.

PICTURE BOOK BASICS

Very few people both write and illustrate picture books. In fact, it is quite difficult to sell to publishers a book that has already been written and illustrated. A common misconception with new writers is that they must find an illustrator before they can sell their books. On the contrary, editors and publishers want to reserve the right to select an illustrator they believe will do a story justice and make the book a best seller.

Normally, the author and the illustrator of a book never meet or even discuss a book by phone. The merit of this method of book production is controversial in the publishing community, especially with the authors. Many times authors are disappointed with the results; the final illustrations do not look at all like what they had in mind. On the other hand many books may end up even more dazzling than the author imagined.

Unlike novels, the story told through a picture book is a marriage of narrative and illustrations. The best picture books are those where the words and art are mutually dependent to fully communicate the story. It is difficult to imagine a book like *The Stinky Cheese Man and Other Fairly Stupid Tale*s by Jon Scieska and Lane Smith having been published without collaboration between the author, the illustrator, and the book designer. It could not have been done. The three creative minds had to unite for the final product to be the masterpiece that it is.

Often editors will pair a first-time author with an established illustrator, or vice versa, so that at least one name will be known to the buying public. Gloria Houston was still relatively unknown when her picture book manuscript *The Year of the Perfect Christmas Tree* was accepted. Some time later her editor told her that she could not reveal the name yet, but she was negotiating with a two-time Caldecott Medalist to do the illustrations. As it turned out Barbara Cooney was contracted and the rest is history. Barbara Cooney visited Gloria and her parents in Spruce Pine, North Carolina, to conduct research for the illustrations. The rock formations and vegetation on Grandfather Mountain as well as structures such as the Sunny Brook Store and Pine Grove Church are all authentically portrayed in Barbara Cooney's paintings.

If you were to hear the text for Allan Baillie's *Drac and the Gremlin* without a chance to see the illustrations, the story would sound like a basic fantasy adventure. But when the narrative is combined with Jane Tanner's illustrations, it becomes another story indeed. The text for *Tough Boris* by Mem Fox is very simple, with only three to four words on most pages. Although Kathryn Brown's illustrations support the narrative, they also show the reader how there are really two stories in one. Some picture books, like *Time Flies* by Eric Rohmann, have such powerful illustrations that they do not require text. In wordless books the words are those that come to the mind of the reader, making the story new every time the book is "read."

PICTURE BOOK CONSTRUCTION

Virtually all picture books have 32 pages. The reason is that when books go to press they are printed on large sheets of paper with eight pages on each side. The large sheets are folded into booklets called signatures. Two folded signatures are sewn to the endpapers, trimmed, and bound to create a 32-page book. Occasionally, you will find a 40-page or 48-page picture book, but because of an increase in paper costs publishers have begun producing 28-page books, using four of the pages to serve as endpapers.

The pages of most picture books are unnumbered so that extra print does not detract from the story or diminish the beauty of the illustrations. In order to find the examples of picture book pages referred to in this book, you will need to count the pages from the beginning. Disregard the endpaper at the front of the book (usually a different color and texture from the illustrated pages) and count by twos until you reach the target page. Even-numbered pages are always on the left of an open book and odd-numbered pages are on the right.

Copyright pages may be located near the front or in the back of picture books. Regardless of the location of a copyright page, it is always located on one of the 32 pages. Occasionally the copyright notice overlaps an illustrated page, allowing the illustrator to take advantage of as much page space as possible. Editors or book designers will often include a brief statement on the copyright page that tells what media, techniques, and processes were used in the illustrations, a helpful tool for teachers.

The physical dimensions of most picture books are the same. One of the most obvious factors that make them different are the way they open. Picture books that are longer horizontally are called *landscape books,* and books that are longer vertically are called *portrait books.*

ART PROJECT PAGES

The art projects in this collection are directly related to authentic illustrations found in children's picture books. Each activity introduces a medium or highlights a technique used in a focus picture book title. The focus titles were selected for the superior way they model the content covered in each project (yes, we like Thomas Locker). Many focus and related title covers are reproduced to assist visual recognition when you seek them out at a library or bookstore. Included with each lesson is an introductory paragraph, a bibliography of other related picture book titles, the projected number of sessions, the key elements and principles of art, a list of materials needed for the activity, complete directions, and a printed sample of the project.

"Discovering" activities acquaint students with a particular medium or a new way of using the medium. Because the purpose is to become familiar with the medium, the activities do not always result in a displayable work of art.

The introductory paragraph on a project page provides the teacher with background information for the activity, including the history of a particular art form, specifics regarding the use of tools and media, and additional helpful hints. Page numbers in the focus or related titles where illustrators use specific technique or media are frequently included to assist with lesson preparation.

The bibliography of related titles includes additional books by other artists that also provide examples or support for the project. Bibliographies note both author and illustrator unless they are the same.

The projected number of sessions does not include preparation or lesson time. It strictly applies to the actual hands-on project time. Teachers in self-contained classrooms may be able to devote additional time, thereby completing in one session a project that would normally require two or more sessions. With limited blocks of time the teacher will need to divide or modify the recommended session time.

The elements and principles of art identified on the project pages are the ones most readily apparent (see pp. 150–152). Observant teachers and students may be able to recognize additional elements and principles.

Because of variation in group size the materials lists do not state the amounts needed. The lists include recommended materials for the primary activity as well as some extension activities. Teachers may select additional tools or materials to suit their classroom needs.

The directions are very detailed and sequential. To facilitate reading and allow for classroom variation the steps have been diamonded rather than numbered.

Occasionally you will find a section titled "Something Else to Try!" or "Additional Information" at the end of a project page. "Something Else to Try!" suggests ways to modify an activity or recommends additional ways to use the materials. "Additional Information" provides useful suggestions, explanations, or facts to assist the teacher with the completion of a project.

THE ELEMENTS AND PRINCIPLES OF ART

The elements and principles are often difficult to recognize in a work of art, but for the purposes of this book we have tried to identify the more obvious ones for each activity to share with your students. As with any academic subject, art has an established foundation of its own.

So often teachers teach art appreciation but neglect to teach the reasons why a work of art is appealing to the individual. Children will say, "I like the color in that picture," but they have no idea that the artist chose the color to impact the work and the observer's feelings. When students become familiar with the elements of art and the principals that govern them, they will begin to see how the diverse components of a work have become one.

Use the pages that explain the elements and principals of art (see pp. 150–152) as a reference for lessons or duplicate them as handouts for student portfolios.

PLUS PAGES

Several additional art-related sections will further enhance your instruction and extend your students' appreciation of art even more. In direct support of the featured activities we offer a suggested art project sequence that logically and sequentially covers preparation, the lesson, and the activity. You will also find a variety of useful related extensions including The Ten Commandments of Teaching Art to Children, an overview of the elements and principles of art, a proposed curriculum of art basics K–8, and a listing of art resources for students and teachers.

As a bonus feature, we are honored by several illustrators of children's books who have contributed exclusive articles that share a behind-the-scenes look at their particular subjects or styles of illustration.

Art Project Sequence

Preparation

- Read the individual art project description in its entirety.

- Gather the picture book titles you plan to use as models for the art project.

- Collect and prepare all necessary art materials.

- Make a sample of the art project for demonstration purposes and to help eliminate unforeseen complications.

The Lesson

- Read aloud the focus picture book or another related title to your students for pleasure.

- Discuss the story as usual.

- Discuss how the illustrations enhance the story.

- Point out specific art elements, principles, techniques, media, or subject in the illustrations.

- Show students a completed sample of the art project unless it is a discovery activity.

- Explain how the art project relates to the picture book title(s) and share general directions for completing the activity.

- Direct students to plan or sketch their ideas on a sheet of scratch paper.

The Activity

- Have students place their plans or sketches on their desktops.

- Give concise, sequential directions for each step of the activity.

- Distribute materials on an as-needed basis.

- Allow sufficient time to complete the projects.

- Share and display completed projects.

DRAWING MEDIA

DISCOVERING CHARCOAL

FOCUS PICTURE BOOK TITLE
Coerr, Eleanor. *Sadako*. Illus. by Ed Young. Putnam, 1993.

Charcoal is nothing more than black pastel. And planning is the most important step in using charcoal. Knowing where black will be placed is crucial, because once color is applied it cannot be removed. The omission of charcoal on the paper leaves white space. Stroke pressure used with charcoal creates variation in shade and detail. *Sadako* is a picture book adaptation of Eleanor Coerr's 1977 biography entitled *Sadako and the Thousand Paper Cranes*. Notice how white space is as important as the black charcoal on the cover of *Sadako*. Is the illustration penetrating eyes or the wingspan of a whooping crane? The mushroom cloud on the opening sequence morphs to a crane taking flight and ultimately becomes an origami symbol of peace. Likewise, Ed Young's illustrations transform from black and white charcoal to full color pastel.

RELATED PICTURE BOOK TITLES
Bunting, Eve. *Night of the Gargoyles*. Illus. by David Wiesner. Clarion, 1994.
Kovacs, Deborah. *Moonlight on the River*. Illus. by William Shattuck. Viking, 1993.

SESSIONS: 1
ELEMENTS: line, form/shape
PRINCIPLES: informal balance, variety, harmony
MATERIALS:
- charcoal
- paper
- gum eraser

DIRECTIONS:
- This activity is best done when students choose an image or simple scene to imitate, such as the book jacket of *Sadako*.
- Using the charcoal, draw simple lines to establish how the scene will be revealed on the paper. This is best accomplished with the edge of the charcoal, leaving only thin lines.
- Once the scene is outlined, fill in the scene using a variety of charcoal techniques:
  - With the edges of the charcoal, create thick or thin fill lines.
  - Charcoal creates softer images if light pressure is applied when drawing. Heavy pressure strokes will produce bolder images.
  - Fill in small areas with the blunt edge of the charcoal.
  - Fill in wide areas with the broad side of the charcoal.
  - Smudge the charcoal using the side of a finger to soften an area.
  - Blend areas with a gum eraser or fingertip.

DISCOVERING COLORED PENCILS

FOCUS PICTURE BOOK TITLE
Rylant, Cynthia. *The Relatives Came*. Illus. by Stephen Gammell. Simon & Schuster, 1985.

Colored pencils are extremely versatile and children take to them readily. Colored pencils are also inexpensive and available in a wide range of colors. One of the techniques to discover when using colored pencils is the use of sharp and dull points. On pages 14 and 15 of *The Relatives Came*, the clapboard siding offers a perfect example of the use of sharp and dull pencil points. Grass blades in the lower corners of pages 22 and 23 appear to be within grasp and are drawn with a sharper point, in contrast to the soft and delicate background grass that has been drawn with a dull point. On pages 28 and 29 the beams of the headlights appear to have been created by erasing the night sky, while the moon clearly has been left to allow the white paper to shine through. With practice making sharp and dull pencil strokes, you will discover how each point behaves. Once a point is dull, continue to use it and see how delicate an effect can be with colored pencil.

RELATED PICTURE BOOK TITLES
Hoopes, Lyn Littlefield. *Wing-a-Ding*. Illus. by Stephen Gammell. Little, Brown, 1990.
Jensen, Steve. *The Great Alphabet Fight*. Illus. by Joni Eareckson Tada. Questar, 1993.
Levinson, Riki. *I Go with My Family to Grandma's*. Illus. by Diane Goode. Dutton, 1986.

SESSIONS: 1
ELEMENTS: line, color
PRINCIPLES: emphasis, variety, harmony
MATERIALS:
◆ colored pencils
◆ white drawing paper
◆ erasers

DIRECTIONS:
◆ Select as a subject any multi-colored picture from a book or magazine.
◆ Colored pencil works best on white paper. Because you will not be using a white pencil, leave some white areas uncolored. This allows the white to peek through the other colors, or you can attain a similar result by using an eraser.
◆ Encourage the students to experiment with colored pencils having sharp and dull points before selecting a subject to illustrate. Note how different the strokes look.
◆ Direct the students to lightly outline the subject on white paper.
◆ Once the skeleton is created, begin to fill in the image using the various strokes as practiced.

- Continue to color in the image. Be sure to change the direction of the strokes should the subject contain fur, feathers, leaves, bark, grass, etc. Pencil strokes should imitate the subject.
- With an eraser, lightly blend or erase marks made by dark strokes.
- Students should also experiment in line length. Outlining everything is not always necessary, however, a black line can be very dramatic and leaves a clean edge to many objects. Short strokes can be just as effective on more delicate items.
- Caution children not to sharpen colored pencils to a needle point; they will snap right off with the first stroke!

DISCOVERING CRAYON

FOCUS PICTURE BOOK TITLE
Van Allsburg, Chris. *Bad Day at Riverbend*. Houghton Mifflin, 1995.

What art medium is more common in schools today than crayons? They are cheap, easy to use, and clean-up is a snap. Chris Van Allsburg's simplistic illustrations in *Bad Day at Riverbend* demonstrate how illustrated books do not always need to be lavish. And his daughter's work clearly communicates how she is uninhibited by lines. Children begin to work with crayons at home before they even attend school, making the comfort level high for any crayon activity. Children usually have one inborn way of drawing or coloring. They will either apply very light or very heavy pressure to their strokes. Demonstrate light and dark strokes, and encourage the students to use both techniques to achieve more contrast in their drawings. Although this lesson may appear simple, you will be surprised at how difficult it is for your students to practice a technique other than the one they have naturally acquired.

RELATED PICTURE BOOK TITLES
Finchler, Judy. *Miss Malarkey Doesn't Live in Room 10*.
    Illus. by Kevin O'Malley. Walker, 1995.
Myers, Walter Dean. *The Dragon Takes a Wife*.
    Illus. by Fiona French. Scholastic, 1995.
Wahl, Jan. *A Wolf of My Own*. Illus. by Lillian Hoban. Macmillan, 1969.

SESSIONS: 1
ELEMENTS: color
PRINCIPLES: variety
MATERIALS:
- crayons
- duplicated coloring sheets

DIRECTIONS:
- Make and distribute photocopies of any coloring sheet containing large objects.
- Demonstrate using bold strokes made with heavy pressure and light strokes made with light pressure. Explain how to select sections of the coloring sheet to use with each technique.
- Discuss the behavior of the color when different pressure is applied. Encourage the children who usually color with light strokes to apply heavier pressure and vice versa.

DISCOVERING PASTELS

FOCUS PICTURE BOOK TITLE

Hilton, Nette. *The Long Red Scarf.* Illus. by Margaret Power. Carolrhoda, 1990.

Pastels is a fancy name for chalk, a medium so readily available, yet so rarely used in the classroom. Pastels offer a wide range of color, versatility, and beauty to both young and experienced artists alike. The only disadvantage in the classroom setting is the cleanup of dust from tables and hands. Margaret Power uses the nine lines of drawing (see p. 20) very effectively with pastels throughout *The Long Red Scarf.* In *Osa's Pride*, the textures of the colors are soft and allow the color of the background paper to seep through. The selected pastels are very bright and inviting to children. Notice how the illustrations on pages 24 and 25 have bold childlike strokes. The blue background paper's surface, smooth as silky material, becomes the story cloth. Chalks generally work better on slightly grainy paper, but are not to be limited to these surfaces when seeking new ways to use them. The textured paper Thomas B. Allen used for *On Granddaddy's Farm* gives the pastels the illusion of woven canvas.

RELATED PICTURE BOOK TITLES

Allen, Thomas B. *On Grandaddy's Farm*. Knopf, 1989.
Coerr, Eleanor. *Sadako*. Illus. by Ed Young. Putnam, 1993.
Grifalconi, Ann. *Osa's Pride*. Little, Brown, 1990.
Linden, Anne Marie. *Emerald Blue*. Illus. by Katherine Doyle. Atheneum, 1994.
Van Allsburg, Chris. *The Polar Express*. Houghton Mifflin, 1985.
Van Leeuwen, Jean. *Across the Wide Dark Sea: The Mayflower Journey*. Illus. by Thomas Allen. Dial, 1995.

SESSIONS: 1
ELEMENTS: color
PRINCIPLES: emphasis, variety
MATERIALS:
◆ white construction paper
◆ chalk
◆ water
◆ container
◆ paint shirt or smock
◆ hair spray

DIRECTIONS:

◆ Each student should be given sufficient time to experiment and create a picture with chalk or pastels. Demonstrate the following methods of chalk application:
- line drawing
- blending color
- color over color

◆ Experiment with ways artists use chalk:
- dry chalk on dry paper
- wet chalk on dry paper
- dry chalk on wet paper
- chalk on textured surfaces

◆ Hair spray or a spray fixative should be applied to all pictures. A fixative helps prevent unwanted smudges and smearing, which is the nature of chalk. Commercial fixatives work much better, however hair spray is more economical and works well enough for classroom purposes.

Something Else to Try!

◆ Try these combinations of drawing and paint media:
- pen and ink drawings and dry chalk
- tempera, chalk, and pen and ink
- chalk and watercolor
- chalk drawing over paper collage
- chalk and charcoal drawing

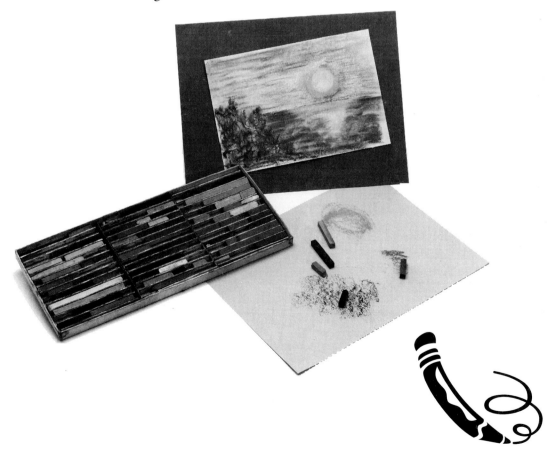

DRAWING WITH THE NINE LINES

FOCUS PICTURE BOOK TITLES

Heavy Pencil

Polacco, Patricia. *Babushka Baba Yaga.* Philomel, 1993.

Light Pencil

Seymour, Tres. *Hunting the White Cow.* Illus. by Wendy Anderson Halperin. Orchard, 1993.

Crosshatching

Steptoe, John. *Mufaro's Beautiful Daughters: An African Tale.* Lothrop, 1987.

Pen and Ink

Macaulay, David. *Cathedral.* Houghton Mifflin, 1973.

Conté Pencil

Van Allsburg, Chris. *Jumanji.* Houghton Mifflin, 1981.

Simply put, there are nine types of drawing lines. They are straight, curved, long, short, thin, thick, zigzag, loop, and dot. Through this lesson, students will be able to demonstrate their ability to utilize these lines and discover how they can create a balanced drawing that is pleasing to look at and fun to create.

There are many recognizable uses of line in the focus titles. Compare Patricia Polacco's use of thick pencil lines in *Babushka Baba Yaga* with Wendy Anderson Halperin's thin lines in *Hunting the White Cow.* In *Cathedral* David Macaulay's pen and ink drawings are composed of many straight lines while curved lines are very prominent in John O'Brien's *Tyrannosaurus Tex.* John Steptoe in *Mufaro's Beautiful Daughters* and Susan Jeffers in *Brother Eagle, Sister Sky* both use crosshatching to create detail. Dots made with pen and ink stand out in Craig Brown's *In the Spring.* In addition to Chris Van Allsburg's use of various lines with conté pencil, it appears that he used eraser to create the effect of fog on page 25 of *Jumanji.*

When purchasing drawing pencils, buy soft lead pencils, usually marked with "B" followed by a number. The higher the number the softer the pencil. The softer the lead, the easier to erase and correct an error. Medium pencils are marked with an "HB" or "F." Pencils with hard lead are marked "H" with a number, higher numbers indicating harder lead. The mark made by hard lead will leave a ridge in the paper, making it difficult to remove.

RELATED PICTURE BOOK TITLES

Birney, Betty G. *Tyrannosaurus Tex*. Illus. by John O'Brien. Houghton Mifflin, 1994.

Brown, Craig. *In the Spring*. Greenwillow/Morrow, 1994.

Enderle, Judith Ross and Stephanie Gordon Tessler. *Six Creepy Sheep*. Illus. by John O'Brien. Boyds Mills Press, 1992.

Graham, Steve. *Dear Old Donegal*. Illus. by John O'Brien. Clarion, 1996.

Isadora, Rachel. *Ben's Trumpet*. Greenwillow/Morrow, 1979.

Kraske, Robert. *The Voyager's Stone*. Illus. by Brian Floca. Orchard, 1995.

Silverstein, Shel. *Where the Sidewalk Ends*. HarperCollins, 1974.

SESSIONS: 1
ELEMENTS: line
PRINCIPLES: balance, variety
MATERIALS:

◆ chisel-tip felt markers
◆ scratch paper
◆ white drawing paper
◆ paper towels

DIRECTIONS:

◆ Precut white drawing paper into 9" x 12" (229 x 305 mm) pieces.

◆ Demonstrate the nine types of lines on the chalkboard or overhead projector.

◆ Direct students to practice making them on scratch paper. The thick line is made by using the broad edge of the marker. Make the thin line with the point of the marker. Instruct students to "dot" carefully so that the points of the markers do not become flattened. When dots are placed on the paper correctly you cannot hear the points being made as you can when they are pounded. Marker points and edges can be "perked-up" with a sharp pair of scissors to cut away frayed material.

◆ Distribute the 9" x 12" (229 x 305 mm) sheets of paper and instruct students to create a doodle picture using the nine types of lines. Each page should demonstrate the use of all nine lines to some degree.

◆ Students should fill up the entire paper with their doodle design.

◆ Students will undoubtedly get marker ink on the heels of their hands. This will result in splotches on their papers if they are not careful. A paper towel placed under the hand as they draw will help prevent unwanted marks.

FELT-TIP MARKERS

FOCUS PICTURE BOOK TITLE
Polacco, Patricia. *The Bee Tree*. Putnam, 1993.

This activity works best when you bring in several copies of Patricia Polacco's books to class. The students will want to work in pairs or trios to have a book for reference. It is not necessary to get several copies of one book, because Ms. Polacco uses her marker techniques in virtually all of her titles. Most marker art is unattractive because students do not take the time to blend and apply the color carefully. *The Bee Tree*, on pages 22 and 23, demonstrates precisely how beautiful marker illustrations can be. Notice the discreet overlapping marker strokes in Mary Ellen's jacket, as well as the smeared looping gray marker stroke tracing the flight pattern of the bee. *How the Sun Was Born*, written and illustrated by students at Drexel Elementary School in Tucson, Arizona, contains bee-u-tiful marker illustrations by third graders.

RELATED PICTURE BOOK TITLES
Murray, Nancy (ed.). *How the Sun Was Born*. Willowisp, 1993. (written and illustrated by third-grade art
  students at Drexel Elementary School, Tucson, Arizona.)
Polacco, Patricia. *Appelemando's Dreams*. Philomel, 1991.
————. *Babushka Baba Yaga.* Philomel, 1993.
————. *Babushka's Doll.* Simon & Schuster, 1990.
————. *Babushka's Mother Goose.* Philomel, 1995.
————. *Just Plain Fancy.* Bantam, 1990.
————. *The Keeping Quilt.* Simon & Schuster, 1988.
————. *Mrs. Katz and Tush.* Bantam, 1992.
————. *My Rotten Red Headed Older Brother.* Simon & Schuster, 1994.
————. *Pink and Say.* Philomel, 1994.
————. *Some Birthday!* Simon & Schuster, 1991.
Thayer, Ernest Lawrence. *Casey at the Bat.* Illus. by Patricia Polacco. Putnam, 1988.

SESSIONS: 1
ELEMENTS: line, color, form/shape
PRINCIPLES: emphasis, variety, harmony
MATERIALS:

◆ paper
◆ felt-tip markers (Patricia Polacco uses Pentel markers.)
◆ pencils

DIRECTIONS:

◆ Allow students to experiment with felt-tip markers using the nine drawing lines (see p. 20) as a warm-up.

◆ Examine the focus title closely with the students, giving specific attention to the blending of colors and the use of line to emphasize a certain area or object in the illustrations.

◆ Allow students to copy their favorite pages, imitating the techniques used by Patricia Polacco.

◆ Add details with pencil in the same manner as Ms. Polacco.

(adapted from pages 8 and 9 of *Babushka Baga Yaga* by Patricia Polacco)

LIGHT & SHADOW

FOCUS PICTURE BOOK TITLE
Dodd, Anne Wescott. *Footprints & Shadows*. Illus. by Henri Sorensen. Simon & Schuster, 1992.

You're getting hot! Now you're getting cold! This activity is great to do in the early morning when the sun is just peeking over the trees at the horizon. On the cover of *Footprints & Shadows* you see a striking change in color as light and shadow break across the roadway. When a shadow takes place on land, as on pages 26 and 27, the shadow is a darker shade than the color of the land. Both a shadow and a reflection result when light hits the surface of water on pages 12 and 13. Note the lack of shadows on several pages where light is dispersed by overcast skies or a canopy of leaves. In *Christmas in the Big House, Christmas in the Quarters* the dramatic effects of firelight from candles, lanterns, and leaping flames add seasonal warmth equally to families regardless of their station in life.

RELATED PICTURE BOOK TITLES
Lewison, Wendy Cheyette. *Going to Sleep on the Farm*. Illus. by Juan Wijngaard. Dial, 1992.
McKissack, Patricia C. and Fredrick. *Christmas in the Big House, Christmas in the Quarters*. Illus. by John Thompson. Scholastic, 1994.
Strand, Mark. *The Night Book*. Illus. by William Péne Du Bois. Potter, 1985.
verDorn, Bethea. *Moon Glows*. Illus. by Thomas Graham. Arcade, 1990.

SESSIONS: several
ELEMENTS: line, color
PRINCIPLES: emphasis, variety
MATERIALS:
◆ white drawing paper
◆ pastels

DIRECTIONS:
◆ Choose a tree in the schoolyard at any time of day and observe how the sunlight falls upon it. Notice shadows and in which direction they lay. Discuss how the sunlight causes the different shades and tints of green. Return to the same tree at different times of day to note how the shadows change and how light plays a part in the color of the tree.
◆ Return to the tree with chairs and drawing materials.
◆ Lightly sketch the outline of the tree.

◆ Fill in the artwork with colored pencils or pastels, using the following suggestions:
  • Cool colors demonstrate shade or shadows. Most artists do not use black to create shadows, but use shades of blue mixed with the original color to create the shadow. Cool colors are greens, blues, and purples.
  • Warm colors are reds, yellows, and oranges. Using the base color in lighter hues demonstrates from where the light is coming. Touching the edges of objects with white, or blending white into the base color at the edges indicates areas that receive direct sunlight—the lighter the color, the brighter the sunlight.

Something Else to Try!

◆ Arrange a still life in the classroom using angles artificial light.

MOVEMENT

FOCUS PICTURE BOOK TITLE
Birchman, David F. *The Raggly Scraggly No-Soap No-Scrub Girl*. Illus. by Guy Porfirio. Lothrop, 1995.

Show your students how to make their artwork come to life with just a few simple techniques. Movement can be demonstrated by the object's shape and placement on the paper, the most common form of movement children use. In *The Raggly Scraggly No-Soap No-Scrub Girl* you know there is movement on pages 5 and 6 by the placement of bubbles extending from the heads and dripping down the tub. The position of the dog shows it is jumping out of the water. Movement can also be shown through special strokes and the use of an eraser. Guy Porfirio demonstrates movement through special strokes on pages 7 and 8. The smudged strokes of the leaves and the curving gray strokes at the door's edge show they are in motion. Splattered paint, another technique, unites movement throughout the book. In the colorful book *Carnival Time*, illustrated by Kazu, rapid speed is shown with long pastel strokes highlighted with white.

RELATED PICTURE BOOK TITLES
Baillie, Allan. *Drac and the Gremlin*. Illus. by Jane Tanner. Dial, 1989.
Hoopes, Lyn Littlefield. *Wing-a-Ding*. Illus. by Stephen Gammell.
    Little, Brown, 1990.
Kiser, SuAnn. *The Catspring Somersault Flying One-handed Flip-flop*.
    Illus. by Peter Catalanotto. Orchard, 1993.
Sathre, Vivian. *Carnival Time*. Illus. by Kazu. Simon & Schuster, 1992.

SESSIONS: 1
ELEMENTS: line, color, space, form/shape
PRINCIPLES: emphasis, movement, rhythm
MATERIALS:
◆ pastels
◆ eraser
◆ white drawing paper

DIRECTIONS:
◆ Brainstorm positions of the human body in motion.
◆ Direct students to draw a person in motion using basic skeletal form. Encourage them to demonstrate movement with billowing clothing and flowing hair. Color the person with pastels.
◆ When using pastels, alternate between dark and light shades of color. With quick, light strokes move the edge of the pastel across the figure to extend slightly beyond the figure.

- Smudge gently along the pastel strokes with a finger or eraser, moving across and away from the figure, thereby creating the illusion of motion. Short strokes indicate slight movement while extended strokes show rapid movement. Details are not needed for a rapidly moving figure and will appear blurred. Be sure to leave some strokes unblended. Note how this method is clearly demonstrated in the focus and related titles.
- With practice your students will be creating action figures everywhere.

(adapted from page 15 of *The Raggly Scraggly No-Soap No-Scrub Girl* by David F. Birchman and Guy Porfino)

Something Else to Try!

- Transition the students from creating movement with the human form to the use of movement with inanimate objects such as carnival rides and race cars.

SCRIBBLE DRAWING

FOCUS PICTURE BOOK TITLE
Van Allsburg, Chris. *Bad Day at Riverbend*. Houghton Mifflin, 1995.

This activity is as fun for the teacher as it is for the student. It requires concentration and attention to detail as well as being fast-paced. The students who feel they have a difficult time in drawing will enjoy "modeling" for the class, and once they see the end results from others, will gladly join in. Students who can always be counted on to volunteer will have an opportunity to shine. Locating a book using scribble drawing was a challenge. The closest example we could find was *Rafiki* by Nola Langner with scribble-painted backgrounds. *Bad Day at Riverbend* and *Harold and the Purple Crayon* are two really cute books with scribbled characters.

RELATED PICTURE BOOK TITLES:
Johnson, Crockett. *Harold and the Purple Crayon*. Harper & Row, 1955.
Langner, Nola. *Rafiki*. Viking, 1977.

SESSIONS: 1 or 2
ELEMENTS: line, space, form/shape
PRINCIPLES: movement, harmony, proportion
MATERIALS:
◆ pencils
◆ newsprint

DIRECTIONS:
◆ Brainstorm easily identifiable body positions such as a quarterback throwing a football. List a few of these positions on the board as a reference.
◆ Distribute newsprint and direct students to fold their papers in half vertically and then horizontally to create four drawing sections.
◆ Tell students they will have three minutes to complete the first drawing. The teacher will be the timekeeper for this activity. Time may be called earlier if all students have finished.
◆ There are two rules for this activity:
    1) Keep the pencil point on the paper at all times. Students may look at the model and then to their paper, unlike the face scribbling activity (see p. 120).
    2) Render the model as tall as possible, filling up the first paper section.

- Ask for a student volunteer to model. If the student model has an idea for a body position, you are on your way. If necessary, assist the child in determining a modeling position that will easily be identified by the students.
- Direct the student to stand on a table in the center of the classroom and strike a pose.
- Using scribble strokes, students are to capture the essence of the model's body position on their papers. Where arms overlap, overlap the scribbles.
- Give the signal for students to begin drawing. Once time has been called, all pencils are to be placed on the desk.
- All student work will not look the same because the students will be drawing the body position from different perspectives—360 degrees around the room.
- The model may call on raised hands to ask artists to name the modeled position. The child who gives the correct response may become the next model or select another student to become the next model.
- Although this activity does not require a formal display, children will find their renderings quite interesting when compared to others. One day of wall display should suffice.

Standing

Bowling

Pitching

TEXTURE RUBBINGS

FOCUS PICTURE BOOK TITLE
Bunting, Eve. *The Wall*. Illus. by Ronald Himler. Clarion, 1990.

Texture rubbing (also called frottage) is a method of transferring an actual pattern to a sheet of paper. Lois Ehlert uses a rubbing of a license plate in her cut-paper collage illustrations on page 19 of *Red Leaf, Yellow Leaf.* When people visit the Vietnam Veterans Memorial in Washington, D. C., they often make rubbings of the names of loved ones. Ronald Himler gives an example on pages 18 and 19 of *The Wall*. Very seldom will you find paint rubbings such as those Marcia Brown uses in her 1983 Caldecott Medal-winning book, *Shadow*.

RELATED PICTURE BOOK TITLES
Brown, Marcia. *Shadow*. Scribner's, 1982.
Ehlert, Lois. *Red Leaf, Yellow Leaf.* Harcourt Brace, 1991.

SESSIONS: 1
ELEMENTS: shape/form, texture
PRINCIPLES: repetition, rhythm, variety
MATERIALS:
◆ newsprint
◆ textured surfaces
◆ crayons, chalk, charcoal

DIRECTIONS:
◆ Lay the newsprint on a textured surface such as brick, burlap, cement, sandpaper shapes, leaves, coins, etc.
◆ Use the side of a peeled crayon (or chalk) and rub the crayon across the paper over the textured surface. Repeat with other colors and textures.

PAINT MEDIA

BLOWN PAINT

FOCUS PICTURE BOOK TITLE

Rosenberg, Liz. *Monster Mama*. Illus. by Stephen Gammell. Philomel, 1993.

The illustrations in *Monster Mama* have been splattered, dripped, blown, slung, propelled, drooled, and oozed onto the pages. But do not be fooled by the violence of the paint patterns in this book. It is truly a love story . . . of sorts. Blown paint provides an authentic texture for wild stringy hair, delicate cobwebs, Spanish moss, dripping fluids, fibrous branches, and roots. Blown paint is also an excellent technique for showing movement.

RELATED PICTURE BOOK TITLES

Aylesworth, Jim. *Old Black Fly*. Holt, 1992.

SESSIONS: 1
ELEMENTS: color, form/shape
PRINCIPLES: informal balance, movement, variety, harmony
MATERIALS:

- tempera paints
- water
- straws
- paper
- containers
- newspaper

DIRECTIONS:

- In addition to visual observation of the focus title illustrations, show pictures or make observations in nature of objects such as trees, grassy meadows, clouds, flowers, hair, or spider webs that can be created using this technique.
- Mix tempera paint in a container with enough water to create a solution the consistency of milk.
- On a flat surface, preferably a sidewalk or any outside area, arrange newspaper as a protective layer. Make sure there is room between students for this activity. It is recommended that students not be placed in a formation facing each other—for obvious reasons!
- After students have made their paper and paint selections, distribute straws.
- Instruct students to fill their straws with paint by dipping the tip of the straw into the paint solution. Do not allow students to inhale the paint into the straw and blow directly from the straw.
- Place only a few drops of paint on the paper, one color at a time, or several colors at once.

- Using the straw, carefully blow the paint in any direction. Continue blowing the paint until the desired effect is reached, preferably until the colors are spread all over the paper.
- Once the blown paint creation has dried, details may be added with brush or pen and ink to give the painting more detail.

DISCOVERING PAINTS: ACRYLIC, OIL, TEMPERA

FOCUS PICTURE BOOK TITLES

Acrylic Paint

Shannon, David. *The Amazing Christmas Extravaganza.* Blue Sky/Scholastic, 1995.

Oil Paint

Johnson, James Weldon. *The Creation.* Illus. by James E. Ransome. Holiday House, 1994.

Tempera Paint

Graham, Ruth Bell. *One Wintry Night.* Illus. by Richard Jesse Watson. Baker, 1994.

In the three lessons for painting, a variety of strokes are used by all of the illustrators. The medium is the only variable. Some of your students may be able to achieve results similar to the focus titles. Look at the rabbit on the last page in *The Amazing Christmas Extravaganza* for a perfect example of simple blending using acrylic paints. The ornamental wreaths that frame the text show the boldness of acrylic colors, another reason acrylics are so popular. Bold colors also abound in *The Creation* as illustrated by James Ransome. The variety of strokes are quite evident when comparing the broad brush-stroked landscape scenes to the intricate strokes used on the faces. The egg tempera paintings in *One Wintry Night*, illustrated by Richard Jesse Watson, were made with a form of the tempera paints commonly used in schools. Your students will feast their eyes upon these masterpieces, the resulting combination of uncommon skill and a very common medium.

Introduce paints using primary and secondary colors. Allow students to experiment with each medium's color wheel. Brushes of different sizes are also recommended and should allow students to discover brush strokes accordingly. Weighted paper specifically designed and created for each paint medium will work more effectively than regular drawing paper. Palettes should be made from a waterproof material such as Styrofoam trays.

Note: School policies need to be reviewed to determine safety procedures for some of these substances, as some are flammable and other safety hazards may be presented if not monitored properly during use.

SESSIONS: 1, 2, or 3
ELEMENTS: color
PRINCIPLES: variety, texture

Students should discover for all three painting media:
- flexibility of use
- ability to replace color
- ability to blend/change color
- texture of paint
- drying time
- use of thinning agents
- differences between paper and canvas

DISCOVERING ACRYLIC

MATERIALS:
- acrylics
- canvas
- paintbrushes
- palettes
- water
- containers
- cleaning cloths
- protective clothes

Allow students to experiment with paint texture and learn the behaviors of the paint. Acrylic paint is very forgiving when a stroke is made and soon thereafter if a correction is needed. The paint may be changed with the addition or blending of another color. Acrylic paints may be changed easily while they are still wet. Depending on the thickness of the applied paint, the color may be changed completely without blending once the material has been allowed to dry approximately 30 minutes to one hour.

During the process of painting with acrylics, students will discover how quickly certain applications dry. They need to experiment with the addition of water to the paint and the painting surface. This will keep the paint "alive" for the continuation of the project. Air conditioning will accelerate the drying process. Keep all moving air to a minimum while painting in order to delay the drying process and allow more "forgiveness" time for the painter, and avoid the overuse of water by inexperienced artists. Acrylic paint develops a film when drying, much like the surface of pudding that has been left out. Once this takes place it is difficult to reverse the paint to a liquid state. After it dries, however, the paint may be easily painted over without changing the color of the newly applied paint.

Keep two containers of water available. One container is kept clear for use with the paints while painting. While students are painting, encourage them to dip the tips of their brushes into the clean water and blend it with the paint on the painted surface. If a palette is used, the mixing should take place there. Students may practice blending on a piece of paper first. They should note that when they place the brush in the water container, the paint does not dissolve in the water as would tempera or watercolor.

The second container of water is for cleaning the brushes. Brushes must be cleaned immediately after use; once the paint has dried on the brush, the brush is dead! Water is all that is needed to clean acrylic paint from brushes. Make sure the paint is removed from the tip of the brush to the bristle attachment. Never leave a brush sitting in the water to clean later. This causes the tips to bend and makes even a clean brush useless.

After cleaning thoroughly with water, blot the brushes with a clean cloth and allow them to air dry. Store brushes in a container with the brush in the air, never bristles down.

The cleanup of acrylics from human skin can be fun. If the paint has dried in a thick layer, just peel it off! Otherwise, soapy water works best. Acrylic paint cannot be removed from material or fabric once it has dried and it is a challenge to remove even when it is wet. Therefore, protective clothing is recommended for all painting projects for children. Spills on carpet should be given immediate attention. Keep plenty of cleanup cloths available as well.

DISCOVERING OIL

MATERIALS:
◆ oils
◆ canvas
◆ paintbrushes
◆ palettes
◆ oil-based blending medium
◆ mineral spirits or turpentine
◆ containers
◆ cleaning cloths
◆ protective clothes

The major differences with the use of oil paint should be explained to the students in the introduction. Students will not use water for thinning or cleanup as with water-based paints. Oil paint is kept pliable and blended with a specialized oil-based medium and cleaned with mineral spirits or turpentine.

Direct students to experiment with mixing paint on a palette and then applying the paint to the painted surface. Paints may be slightly blended for a swirled effect or completely blended to achieve a pure hue. When the paint is wet, paint may easily be blended to discover an array of color with the stroke of a brush. Remember, the thicker the paint application for oils, the longer the drying time, therefore follow-up activities or the continuation of the session may need to be modified. Oils do not have to dry completely between painting sessions. Professional artists seldom wait for complete drying before working again.

A wonderful feature of oil paint, and sometimes acrylic paint, is that the thickness of the substance allows the ability to "build" the paint off the surface. As an extension activity allow the students to discover how the paint behaves when applied with butter knives, or applied liberally with brushes, or manipulated with toothpicks or combs.

Always use oil paints with mineral spirits or turpentine in a well ventilated room. When cleaning the oil paint from the brushes, dispose of the cleaning cloths as per the directions of the cleaning agent. Mineral spirits is a generally acceptable agent for cleaning paint from skin, however you should check your students' records to avoid medical problems. Mineral spirits residue must always be washed from the skin immediately with warm soapy water.

DISCOVERING TEMPERA

MATERIALS:

- ◆ tempera paints
- ◆ paper
- ◆ brushes
- ◆ palettes
- ◆ water
- ◆ containers
- ◆ cleaning cloths
- ◆ protective clothes

Tempera paint is probably the most common paint used in schools today. It is easy to use, simple to clean up, readily available, and inexpensive. When used appropriately and in a timely manner tempera is perfect for most art projects throughout the grades.

Tempera is best mixed on a palette and then applied to the paper or surface to be painted. It is recommended to plan exactly where the paint should be on the surface, because it is not very forgiving once it has been applied. A color may be painted over once it has dried. Although you may use water in the painting process, water thins the texture of tempera making it similar to watercolor.

Tempera paint can be washed from fabric surfaces, but some staining may occur. It will also temporarily stain the skin. Tempera paint may be cleaned with soapy water on nonabsorbent surfaces, brushes, and containers. Immediate attention should be given to removal of tempera from other surfaces.

When considering drying time of paints, an advantage of acrylic paint is its rapid drying time of 30 minutes to one hour. Oil sometimes takes a few days to dry completely. Tempera paint, of course, will dry sooner but it does not allow the flexibility of changing a color by layering the paint.

DISCOVERING SHADES AND TINTS

FOCUS PICTURE BOOK TITLE
Bruchac, Joseph. *Between Earth & Sky*. Illus. by Thomas Locker. Harcourt Brace, 1996.

In Discovering Landscapes, Seascapes, and Skies (see p. 111) we discuss the use of light and dark and how these elements occur in our environment. Our artistic perceptions and the realities of nature are often two different things. In *Between Earth & Sky*, these differences are lessened as we see trees in all shades of green, seascapes in grays, and skies in reds. With shades and tints of a single hue, Thomas Locker, recreates realistic images of nature. Find the paintings in this book that use primarily oranges, blues, and greens. For another interesting discovery, compare *The Dreamer*'s dust jacket illustration with the spread on pages 18 and 19.

RELATED PICTURE BOOK TITLES
Crews, Donald. *Bigmama's*. Greenwillow/Morrow, 1991.
————. *Freight Train*. Greenwillow/Morrow, 1978.
————. *Sail Away*. Greenwillow/Morrow, 1995.
George, Jean Craighead. *The First Thanksgiving*. Illus. by Thomas Locker. Philomel, 1993.
Rylant, Cynthia. *The Dreamer*. Illus. by Barry Moser. Blue Sky/Scholastic, 1993.
Yolen, Jane. *Owl Moon*. Illus. by John Schoenherr. Philomel, 1987.

SESSIONS: 1or 2
ELEMENTS: color
PRINCIPLES: variety
MATERIALS:

- tempera paint: primary colors, black, white
- white drawing paper
- ½" (13 mm) paintbrushes
- containers
- eyedroppers
- scissors
- masking tape
- newspaper

DIRECTIONS:

♦ Cover tables or desks with newspaper.

♦ Designate student pairs or groups to share paint containers.

♦ Distribute the following materials to each group:

- one container of a primary color
- one container of white paint
- one sheet of white drawing paper per student
- one brush per student
- one eyedropper per white paint container

♦ Direct students to fold their papers lengthwise into three equal 4" (102 mm) sections.

♦ Instruct students to position their papers so that the folds run horizontally on their desks before them. Using the white paint first, paint a ½" x 4" (13 x 102 mm) vertical ribbon of white at the upper left hand corner within the top folded section. At the lower right hand corner within the bottom folded section, paint a strip of the pure color.

♦ Add 4–6 drops of color to the white paint, stirring well. Paint a ribbon of tinted white adjacent to the pure white strip of paint. Continue adding drops of color (4–6 at a time) to the tinted paint container and painting ribbons across the top section to the upper right edge. Drop to the middle section and continue the process toward the middle right edge.

♦ Halfway through the middle section, students should assess whether they must increase the drops of color added to the tinted white in order to attain tints closer to the pure color (e.g., 10–15 drops, 15–20 drops).

♦ Finally, the process should continue through the middle section and across the bottom section to meet the original pure color, getting the tinted mixture as close as possible to the original color.

♦ Many students will discover they cannot get to the pure color because they started with white as a base.

♦ When the student papers have dried, they should cut their papers into strips along the horizontal folds. Then they will tape the backsides of the 4" (102 mm) strips sequentially to make one long display.

Note: The directions are provided using white paint for the study of tints. To study shades, replace all references to white paint with black paint.

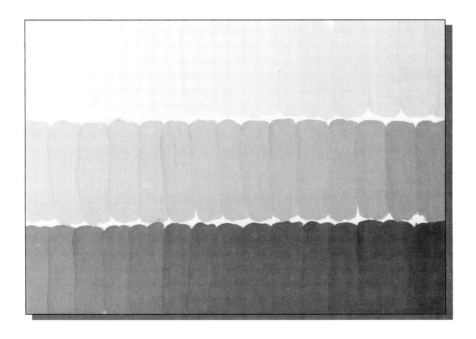

DISCOVERING WATERCOLORS

FOCUS PICTURE BOOK TITLE
Day, Alexandra. *Carl Goes to Daycare*. Farrar, Straus & Giroux, 1993.

Alexandra Day has a way of making watercolors look so easy to use. But the truth is, unless you are a skilled artist, they present quite a challenge. Certain techniques are mastered by children at the first lesson, and others will require much practice. Wet on dry and wet on wet techniques are evident in all of Alexandra Day's books about Carl, a lovable baby-sitting rottweiler who always comes through. The blurred walls on pages 24 and 25 of *Carl Goes to Daycare* were created with the wet on wet technique. Wet on dry, the most common technique used with watercolor, is perfect for more detailed painting such as Carl and the children. Very seldom used, the dry on dry technique is excellent for creating grass blades or distant flower gardens. Remember there is no white watercolor, therefore white areas must be left unpainted.

RELATED PICTURE BOOK TITLES
Wilhelm, Hans. *I'll Always Love You*. Crown, 1985.
Foreman, Michael. *War Game*. Arcade, 1993.
Le Tord, Bijou. *A Blue Butterfly: A Story About Claude Monet*. Doubleday, 1995.

SESSIONS: 1
ELEMENTS: color
PRINCIPLES: emphasis, variety
MATERIALS:
◆ paintbrushes
◆ watercolor paper or white construction paper
◆ watercolors
◆ water
◆ containers

DIRECTIONS:
Wet on Wet
◆ Wet the paper lightly with the paintbrush.
◆ Load the brush with wet paint.
◆ Apply paint to the wet paper.
◆ Notice how the colors bleed together. Colors will dry lighter than they appear when wet. You may use a piece of tissue to blot the wet areas, especially when creating textures or clouds.

Wet on Dry

◆ Begin with dry paper.
◆ Load the paintbrush with wet paint.
◆ Apply paint to the dry paper.

ADDITIONAL NOTES:

◆ You may sketch the picture lightly with a pencil before painting and erase the line with a gum eraser when the painting is complete.
◆ Use the open lid of a watercolor set for mixing colors.
◆ Leave white areas unpainted.
◆ Paint lightest values first. Darker colors will cover light areas, but not vice versa.
◆ When laying one color next to another, make sure the first color is dry. Wet paint next to wet paint tends to bleed.
◆ Change water frequently to avoid muddy colors.
◆ Colors will be lighter when they dry.
◆ Add detail work last.

Something Else to Try!

Dry on Dry

◆ The dry brush method works well for textured effects, especially grass or bushes.
◆ Begin with a dry brush or blot most of the water from a wet brush.
◆ Load a small amount of paint on the brush, blotting on a paper towel if the brush seems too wet.
◆ To create grass, brush upward from the bottom of the grass blade to the top.

Glazing

◆ Glazing is a process of building layers of color to create new colors by overlapping. Wherever one color overlaps another, a new color is made.
◆ Paint individual stripes of six different colors across the length of the paper, leaving white areas between the stripes. Let the paint dry.
◆ Paint the same colors across the width of the paper, overlapping the previous stripes. Notice how the colors change where the overlapping occurs.

POINTILLISM

FOCUS PICTURE BOOK TITLE
Novak, Matt. *Claude and Sun*. Bradbury, 1987.

Cotton swab painting is an easy way for very young children to express their creativity without having sophisticated small muscle coordination. This technique works well when children of older ages choose designs of flowers or plants, where graduated change in color creates depth. Matt Novak imitates techniques of the impressionists Monet, Seurat, and van Gogh in his work *Claude and Sun*. On pages 28 and 29 notice how dots of various color give the illusion of new colors when viewed at a distance. Margaret Neve uses much smaller points very effectively in *More and Better*. The dotting technique is also adaptable for other purposes. *In the Spring* by Craig Brown demonstrates how pen and ink dotting adds detail to pastel illustrations.

RELATED PICTURE BOOK TITLES
Brown, Craig. *In the Spring*. Greenwillow/Morrow, 1994.
Hall, Donald. *Ox-Cart Man*. Illus. by Barbara Cooney. Viking, 1979.
Hulme, Joy N. *Counting by Kangaroos*. Illus. by Betsy Scheld. Freeman, 1995.
Neve, Margaret. *More and Better*. Prentice-Hall, 1977.

SESSIONS: 1
ELEMENTS: line, color, space
PRINCIPLES: movement, rhythm, variety, harmony
MATERIALS:

◆ cotton swabs

◆ tempera paints or watercolors

◆ white drawing paper

DIRECTIONS:

◆ Cut the paper into half- or quarter-sized sheets.

◆ Dip the tip of a cotton swab into the paint.

◆ Dot the paint onto the paper where desired to create a picture.

◆ Continue dotting until the entire paper is covered.

◆ Use a fresh cotton swab for each new color.

◆ Mount the picture on construction paper when dry.

Something Else to Try!

◆ Try this technique using felt-tip markers. Caution students to place dots lightly on the page to prevent beating the marker tips down.

SPLATTER PAINTING

FOCUS PICTURE BOOK TITLE
Aylesworth, Jim. *Old Black Fly*. Illus. by Stephen Gammell. Holt, 1992.

The ancient Aborigines of Australia made splatter designs on rock walls that remain to this day. They used their hands as stencils and blew a white paint-like substance from their mouths to make these primitive paintings. The splatter technique is also found in children's picture books today. What fun Stephen Gammell must have had creating *Old Black Fly*! Chaos under control—a whirlwind of splattered color takes you on a journey with the annoying protagonist from beginning to end. Do not miss the old black fly's demise in the massive pink finale!

RELATED PICTURE BOOK TITLES
Birchman, David F. *The Raggly Scraggly No-Soap No-Scrub Girl*. Illus. by Guy Porfirio. Lothrop, 1995.
Day, Alexandra. *Carl's Masquerade*. Farrar, Straus & Giroux, 1992.
Martin, Rafe. *Will's Mammoth*. Illus. by Stephen Gammell. Putnam, 1989.
Rosenberg, Liz. *Monster Mama*. Illus. by Stephen Gammell. Philomel, 1993.
Wilhelm, Hans. *Tyrone and the Swamp Gang*. Scholastic, 1995.

SESSIONS: 1
ELEMENTS: color, form/shape
PRINCIPLES: movement, rhythm, harmony
MATERIALS:
- stencils
- drawing paper
- watercolors
- markers
- scissors
- toothbrush
- paintbrushes
- pump spray bottles

DIRECTIONS:
- Gather a variety of paint dispensing tools.
- Partially fill bottles and cups with diluted tempera or watercolors.
- Dip the toothbrush into a cup of paint. Flick the paint by rubbing your thumb or finger across the toothbrush bristles toward the paper.
- If you are using a spray bottle direct the paint toward the paper.
- Add details with markers.

Something Else to Try!

◆ Place a stencil on a piece of paper.

◆ Flick or spray paint toward the stencil edges and paper. Allow the paint to dry.

◆ Move stencils to different locations on the paper and repeat the process with a variety of colors.

WOOD VENEER

FOCUS PICTURE BOOK TITLE
Isaacs, Anne. *Swamp Angel*. Illus. by Paul O. Zelinsky. Dutton, 1994.

Swamp Angel, a 1995 Caldecott Honor title features oil illustrations on cherry, maple, and birch veneer. The wood grain backgrounds give the book an early American flavor and act as frames for these folksy illustrations. Use the solid wood panels on the opening pages to teach your students to recognize the rich shades of dark maple, red cherry, and light birch. Illustrator Stefano Vitale uses woodgrain panels to his advantage. The natural patterns of the stained woodgrain create breathtaking skies as backdrops for *Christmas Lullaby*. Though the paintings for *King Bidgood's in the Bathtub* were done in oil on pressed board, they could just as well have been done on any background because no wood grain texture shows through. It is still a delightful book!

RELATED PICTURE BOOK TITLES
Jewell, Nancy. *Christmas Lullaby*. Illus. by Stefano Vitale. Clarion, 1994.
Wood, Audrey. *King Bidgood's in the Bathtub*. Illus. by Don Wood.
    Harcourt Brace, 1985.
Zolotow, Charlotte. *When the Wind Stops*. Illus. by Stefano Vitale.
    HarperCollins, 1995.

SESSIONS: 2 or 3
ELEMENTS: color, texture
PRINCIPLES: variety, harmony
MATERIALS:
◆ wood paneling
◆ scrap lumber
◆ fine sandpaper
◆ spray varnish
◆ acrylics
◆ paintbrushes
◆ water
◆ wood stain (optional)
◆ oils (optional)
◆ blending medium (optional)
◆ mineral spirits (optional)

DIRECTIONS:

◆ Direct students to collect scrap pieces of wood paneling, plywood, and lumber. Although thin pieces of paneling will work best for this project, any clean scrap lumber will do.

◆ Allow students to select their own pieces of wood for the background.

◆ Begin by sanding the wood panel on the top surface to remove any roughness.

◆ Stain the surface of the wood panel if desired and allow it to dry.

◆ Sketch in a design or image in light pencil on the stained surface.

◆ Spray the wood panel with a spray varnish and allow it to dry. Repeat the sanding and varnishing process if needed.

◆ When the final coat of varnish has dried, begin painting by following the pencil sketched design or image that will still be visible through the varnished coating.

PAPER

GRAPH PAPER DESIGNS

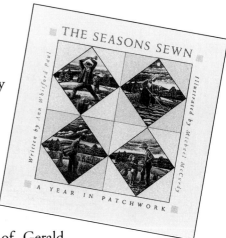

FOCUS PICTURE BOOK TITLES
McDermott, Gerald. *Arrow to the Sun*. Viking, 1974.
Paul, Ann Whitford. *The Seasons Sewn: A Year in Patchwork*. Illus. by
    Michael McCurdy. Browndeer/Harcourt Brace, 1996.

In man's earliest artistic attempts he adorned walls, weapons, weaving,
and virtually anything he touched with geometric patterns. More
recently, geometric design was evidenced in the diverse art forms of
both nineteenth century natives and pioneers of the American West.
Those designs have spanned the years and made their way into the
illustrated pages of children's books. The illustrations in many of Gerald
McDermott's books, such as *Arrow to the Sun*, replicate Native American geometric images that
emerge from his study of folklore and mythology. *The Season's Sewn* recounts the history of American quilt-
making. It is illustrated by Michael McCurdy with actual geometric quilt patterns accompanied by the unique
stories behind them.

RELATED PICTURE BOOK TITLES
Charles, Donald. *Chancay and the Secret of Fire*. Putnam, 1992.
Kismaric, Carole. *The Rumor of Pavel and Paali: A Ukrainian Folktale*. Illus. by Charles Mikolaycak. Harper
    & Row, 1988.
McDermott, Gerald. *Coyote*. Harcourt Brace, 1994.
————. *The Voyage of Osiris*. Dutton, 1977.
————. *Zomo the Rabbit*. Harcourt Brace, 1972.

SESSIONS: 1
ELEMENTS: line, color, space, form/shape
PRINCIPLES: proportion, variety, harmony
MATERIALS:
◆ graph paper
◆ markers, crayons, or pencils
◆ rulers
◆ background paper (optional)

DIRECTIONS:

◆ Discuss the geometric designs located in the focus titles, such as the centerfold page in *Arrow to the Sun* where Boy is fitted to his bow and becomes a special arrow by Arrow Maker. Examine the quilt patterns in *The Seasons Sewn*.

◆ Note the various geometric shapes, their relationship to each other, and background space. Notice how certain shapes use only half of a square on the graph paper and other shapes have curves within the square.

◆ Brainstorm geometric shapes. Record these shapes on the chalkboard or overhead projector and draw a representational image for student reference throughout the activity.

◆ Triangles can be created by using a ruler and drawing a line diagonally across the square from corner to corner. Rectangles can be created by coloring in two or more squares with one color.

◆ Decide whether to create Native American designs or to make a quilt pattern. ½" (13 mm) graph paper works well for Indian patterns while 1" (25 mm) graph paper lends itself easily to designing quilts.

◆ Using markers, crayons, or colored pencils begin to color in the graph paper according to the planned geometric design.

◆ Mount drawings on a piece of construction paper.

MIRROR IMAGING

FOCUS PICTURE BOOK TITLE
Jonas, Anne. *Round Trip*. Greenwillow/Morrow, 1983.

The text in *Round Trip* is unique because the book is read front to back, then upside-down and back to the front. The illustrations follow the text in both directions, a challenge we are sure. However, your students will find this project much simpler than the book. The contrasting images in *Round Trip* resemble the look of negative film, a natural connection to understanding the symmetry involved with mirror imaging. Though the illustrations are not mirror images, there is an element of almost-perfect symmetry on page 7 where half of the car appears to have been cut from one edge of black paper resulting in white reflections on the street. One of the four illustrated sub-stories in David Macaulay's *Black and White* also demonstrates a strong use of contrast where everything may not be what it first appears to be. There is an absence of symmetry in the black and white illustrations, but two images frequently share the same line much like the shared edge of the cow and the burglar on page 21.

RELATED PICTURE BOOK TITLE
Macaulay, David. *Black and White*. Houghton Mifflin, 1990.

SESSIONS: 1
ELEMENTS: color, space, form/shape
PRINCIPLES: formal balance
MATERIALS:
◆ black construction paper
◆ white construction paper
◆ scissors
◆ glue

DIRECTIONS:
◆ Teach a math lesson on symmetry and/or a language arts lesson on opposites.
◆ Identify together examples of symmetry and positive/negative design in the illustrations of the focus title.
◆ Show the included sample illustration of mirror imaging or share a teacher-made sample.
◆ Distribute a black and a white sheet of construction paper to each student. Set one piece of construction paper aside for the background color. Cut the other sheets to 6" x 12" (152 x 305 mm) with a paper cutter so the edges will be clean. The dimensions of the two sheets of paper may be adjusted to suit your needs, however, sizes smaller than 4" x 9" (102 x 229 mm) become difficult to use.

- Students should plan the symmetrical figures they will cut. The cut shapes should be perfect halves of the images they wish to create. Encourage students to experiment with the use of symmetrical letters.
- Sections of the original cutouts may also be cut and reversed (e.g., eyes, mouth).
- When students have finished cutting their shapes, instruct them to position the original 6" x 12" (152 x 305 mm) paper in the center of the 12" x 18" (305 x 457 mm) paper. Then, arrange the cutouts along the edges of the 6" x 12" (152 x 305 mm) piece. Be sure to check for hangovers.
- Glue the centered 6" x 12" (152 x 305 mm) piece down first, then flip the cut-out pieces and glue them opposite the spaces of the original cuts.

Something Else to Try!
- Create mirror imaging pictures with contrasting and complimentary colors.

Papermaking

FOCUS PICTURE BOOK TITLE
Smith, Lane. *The Happy Hocky Family*. Viking, 1993.

This papermaking activity introduces children to the actual process used to manufacture paper. The collage illustrations created by David Diaz in *Smoky Night* feature homemade paper of various types and textures. Examine the opening pages in particular to determine what type of original paper and additives were used in the various pulps. In recent years recycled paper has been used for paper products of all kinds, making trees and people all over the nation very happy. *The Happy Hocky Family* by Lane Smith is printed on authentic recycled paper, giving it a distinctive textured appearance. "I have a piece of recycled paper. Do you have a piece of recycled paper? I have a piece of recycled paper." Read the book and you will understand.

RELATED PICTURE BOOK TITLES
Bunting, Eve. *Smoky Night*. Illus. by David Diaz. Harcourt Brace, 1994.
Young, Ed. *Seven Blind Mice*. Philomel, 1992.

SESSIONS: 1
ELEMENTS: texture
PRINCIPLES: variety
MATERIALS:
◆ aluminum baking pans
◆ screen or netting
◆ scissors
◆ clothespins
◆ tissue
◆ newspaper
◆ old paper of any kind
◆ blender
◆ measuring cup
◆ water
◆ dishpan

DIRECTIONS:
◆ If you do not have a papermaking mold, you can make one from aluminum baking pans. Cut out the bottom of two aluminum baking pans. Cut a sheet of screen or netting larger than the openings in the two pans, allowing an overhang. Sandwich the screen tightly between the two pans and clip them together with clothespins.

◆ Tear paper scraps into 1" (25 mm) pieces.

◆ Combine a handful of scrap paper and three cups (237 ml) of water in the blender to make the pulp. Blend for about two minutes.

◆ Place the mold inside the dishpan. Pour the pulp into the mold, taking care to cover the screen well. Lift the mold and shake it gently to allow excess water to drain.

◆ Undo the clothespins and remove the screen. Lay it between two absorbent dishcloths or paper towels. Apply gentle pressure to blot the excess water.

◆ Allow the paper to dry for a few hours and then peel the recycled paper from the screen.

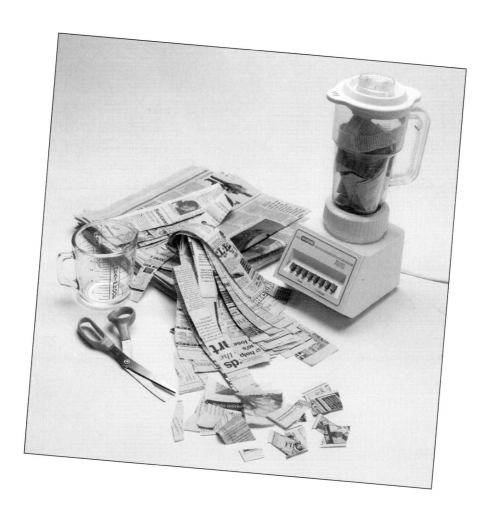

SILHOUETTES

FOCUS PICTURE BOOK TITLE

Noyes, Alfred. *The Highwayman*. Illus. by Neil Waldman. Harcourt Brace,
1990.

Before the advent of photography, making shadow portraits was practically
the only way to create a lasting image of a loved one. And every elementary
teacher has made silhouettes of students at least once or twice in their career.
Teachers were making them when we were in elementary school, and per-
haps you still have the one your teacher made of you in third grade. (Yes, we still have ours,
too). Seldom, however, have you seen silhouettes created using subjects other than heads. Well, stand back,
get your scissors ready, and consider these new twists to an old activity.

RELATED PICTURE BOOK TITLES

Brown, Marcia. *Shadow*. Scribner's, 1982.
Fleischman, Paul. *Shadow Play*. Illus. by Eric Beddows. Harper & Row, 1990.
Lyon, George Ella. *A B CEDAR: An Alphabet of Trees*. Illus. by Tom Parker.
    Orchard, 1989.
Munari, Bruno. *The Circus in the Mist*. World, 1969.
Rankin, Laura. *The Handmade Alphabet*. Dial, 1991.
Riggio, Anita. *A Moon in My Teacup*. Boyds Mills, 1993.
Root, Phyllis. *Aunt Nancy and Old Man Trouble*. Illus. by David Parkins.
    Candlewick, 1996.
Yolen, Jan. *Piggins*. Illus. by Jane Dyer. Harcourt Brace, 1987.

SESSIONS: 1
ELEMENTS: line, form/shape
PRINCIPLES: emphasis, harmony, proportion
MATERIALS:
◆ white construction paper
◆ black construction paper
◆ pencil
◆ scissors
◆ glue
◆ overhead or filmstrip projector
◆ masking tape

DIRECTIONS:

- ◆ Create an arrangement of artificial flowers in a vase.
- ◆ Place a projector on a table so it projects light onto a flat wall surface, and allow ample space to place the flower arrangement on a separate table against the wall.
- ◆ Tape a sheet of black construction paper on the wall directly behind the arrangement.
- ◆ Turn on the projector, and slide the arrangement toward or away from the wall to adjust the silhouette size.
- ◆ Trace around the silhouetted shape with a pencil.
- ◆ Cut out the silhouette and place it on a background of white paper.
- ◆ Repeat the process with several arrangements of artificial flowers.
- ◆ Glue each silhouetted image pencil side down to a white construction paper background with liquid glue or glue sticks.

Something Else to Try!

The process can be modified to create any number of silhouetted shapes. Don't let your head get in the way! Try several of these silhouette variations:

- • Experiment with silhouetted positions of the human body using a G. I. Joe or Gymnastic Barbie.
- • Trace coffee table knickknacks, what-nots, animal figurines, leaves, and other objects that would create an interesting silhouette.
- • Create a silhouetted finger spelling alphabet using a different child's hand for each letter.

STENCILS

FOCUS PICTURE BOOK TITLE
Macaulay, David. *Black and White*. Houghton Mifflin, 1990.

Purchase commercially manufactured stencils, save stencils you have created from die plates, or allow your students to invent stencils of their own. Then, try the methods below to make stencil designs of all kinds. David Macaulay does not use stencils to create the illustrations for *Black and White*, but the art for the "Udder Confusion" substory provides a good model for the cow stencil activity. Though we were unable to locate any picture books where the artist used stencils as the primary medium, we are sure that somewhere there is a single title we overlooked. Please, write us and tell us what it is.

SESSIONS: 1
ELEMENTS: color, form/shape, space
PRINCIPLES: rhythm, variety, harmony
MATERIALS:
◆ stencils
◆ crayons, pastels, paints
◆ paintbrushes
◆ white construction paper
◆ black construction paper
◆ poster paper
◆ manila file folders (optional)

DIRECTIONS:
◆ To create a stencil, select a simple outlined shape. Trace the object onto a sheet of poster paper or a manila file folder.
◆ To create a positive stencil, cut out the shape. To create a negative stencil, cut out the inside of the shape.
◆ Place the stencil on a sheet of construction paper. If using a light sheet of construction paper, dark paint works best for your stencil. If you select a dark sheet of construction paper, light paint will create a more distinct image.
◆ Splatter paint lightly along the positive or negative stencil edges with a toothbrush. Be careful not to smear the wet paint, and avoid overlapping unless you plan to wait for paint to dry between each stencil.
◆ When using crayons or pastels, feather the edges of the stencil, shading enough of the background paper to reveal the outline of the image. Move the stencil and repeat the process.
◆ As a variation, overlap some of the stencils and notice what happens to the colors as they combine.

Something Else to Try!

◆ To create Holstein cow images resembling the illustrations in the focus title, use the reproducible pattern on page 58 to make negative stencils.

◆ Lay a cow stencil on a white sheet of construction paper. Using a black piece of chalk or a black crayon, shade patterns across the stencil edges intermittently to reveal the shape of the cow. Leave other areas unshaded so that they blend in with the background paper.

◆ For a reverse effect, follow the same steps using black construction paper for a background and color with a white piece of chalk or a white crayon.

◆ This activity works well with a panda pattern also.

PATTERN

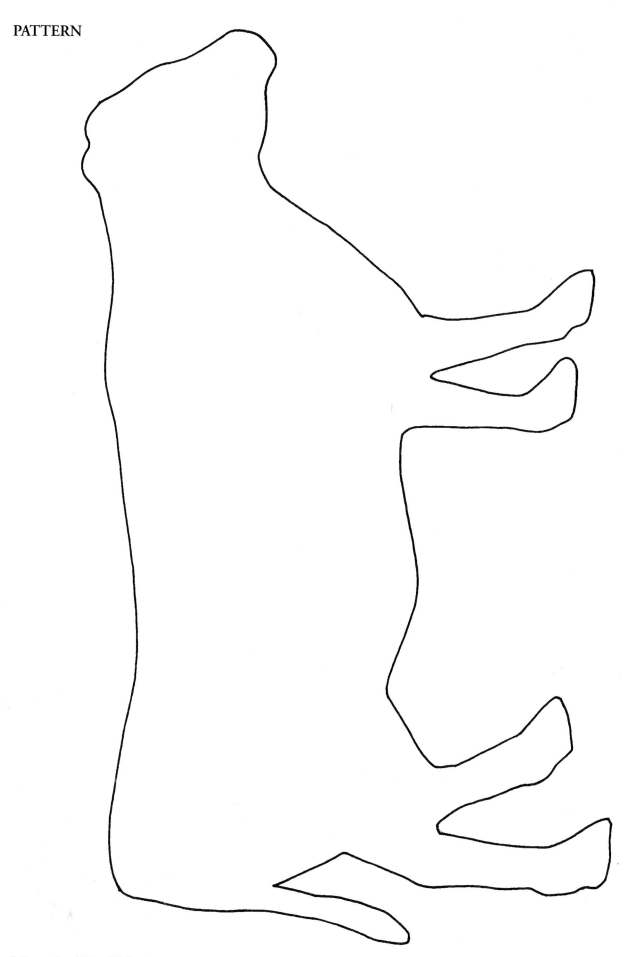

COLLAGE

CUT PAPER COLLAGE:
SIMPLE, DETAILED, & RELIEF

FOCUS PICTURE BOOK TITLES

Simple Paper Cut

Lowery, Linda. *Twist with a Burger, Jitter with a Bug.* Illus. by
    Pat Dypold. Houghton Mifflin, 1995.

Detailed Paper Cut

Wisniewski, David. *Sundiata: Lion King of Mali.* Clarion, 1992.

Paper Relief

Hopkins, Lee Bennett. *Ragged Shadows.* Illus. by Giles Laroche.
    Little, Brown, 1993.

Twist with a Burger, Jitter with a Bug offers perfect examples of simple cut paper.
The challenge is to make the artwork fit together once the items have been cut.
The cut paper may be as detailed as your skill allows. Notice the intricacy and
overlapping of the overhanging trees, umbrella, and the people in *Sundiata* on
pages 6 and 7. Simple and detailed cut-paper collage activities offer a perfect springboard for
paper relief artwork such as those in *Ragged Shadows* (see p. 135 for Giles Laroche's discussion of paper relief).
Students will readily move from securing their objects to the paper with glue to using the double-sided tape
required for paper relief. The results, after having perfected simple and detailed cut-paper collage, will wow
your colleagues!

RELATED PICTURE BOOK TITLES

Ehlert, Lois. *Red Leaf, Yellow Leaf.* Harcourt Brace, 1991.

Field, Rachel. *A Road Might Lead to Anywhere.* Illus. by Giles Laroche. Little,
    Brown, 1990.

Field, Rachel. *General Store.* Illus. by Giles Laroche. Little, Brown, 1988.

Lenski, Lois. *Sing a Song of People.* Illus. by Giles Laroche. Little, Brown, 1987.

Linscott, Jody. *Once Upon A to Z: An Alphabet Odyssey.* Illus. by Claudia Porges
    Holland. Doubleday, 1991.

Wisniewski, David. *The Wave of the Sea-Wolf.* Clarion, 1994.

Wisniewski, David. *Rain Player.* Clarion, 1991.

SESSIONS: 2

ELEMENTS: color, form/shape, space

PRINCIPLES: informal balance, proportion, variety, harmony

MATERIALS:

- ◆ colored construction paper
- ◆ scissors
- ◆ glue
- ◆ spongy double-sided tape

DIRECTIONS:
SIMPLE AND DETAILED PAPER CUT
- Precut colored construction paper into halves and quarters for easier handling by students.
- Discuss interesting pages from the focus titles.
- After distributing materials, direct students to begin cutting items out of the paper. Monitor how the cut items relate in size, shape, and color to other items on the paper.
- Save large paper scraps in a central location for other students to use.
- Little direction is needed for cutting simple shapes. But when objects with rough, jagged, or uneven edges are desired, you will need to direct students how to remove the scissors from one side of an object and approach it from another angle.
- As a challenge, some students may want to experiment with cutting out negative, or inside, spaces in order to reveal the background paper. By gently folding and cutting a slit in the designated space, the scissors can easily be inserted. Begin cutting at the slit and continue around the inside area until the section is removed.
- Arrange each cut item on the background paper. Where the objects will be placed is important so that simple objects will lay down easily and be overlapped without problem.
- Glue the background objects in place first. Overlapping objects should be glued last. If using white glue remind students that a little bit of glue is sufficient and that this is definitely a situation where more is not better. Great globs of glue do not allow items to lie flat and will result in bulges and wrinkles.
- It is a personal preference to glue down the edges of cutouts or allow them to raise slightly from the paper.

PAPER RELIEF COLLAGE
- Instruct students to create their cutouts using the directions above. The more detailed the cutouts are, the more dramatic the final effect will be. Encourage students to cut feathered edges, curves, leaf shapes, clothing creases, facial features, etc. as in the focus titles.
- Assemble the artwork by placing the background pieces down first and then laying the foreground objects on top. Have the students move their objects about to emphasize their subjects.
- Secure the background objects with glue.
- Build the middle ground objects using one layer of double-sided tape. Cut the tape to match the sizes of the cut paper. Peel the paper backing from the side to be attached to the cut object. After it is attached, peel the backing from the other side of the tape and gently press it onto the artwork.
- Apply a double or triple layer of double-sided tape to the foreground objects that should extend farthest from the page. Caution students that when applying the final foreground objects to gently press them in place. Too much pressure may flatten the middle ground objects.

DIE-CUT COLLAGE

FOCUS PICTURE BOOK TITLE
Ehlert, Lois. *Red Leaf, Yellow Leaf.* Harcourt Brace, 1991.

The interchangeable plates of a die-cut machine have razor-sharp blades. Although it may appear to be a simple machine, even older children should be monitored carefully if allowed to operate. It is strongly recommended that all die cutting be done by the teacher. Lois Ehlert's *Red Leaf, Yellow Leaf* uses die-cutting in two ways. The inside front cover and first page replicate a floor of positive die-cut scattered leaves and a negative die-cut first page made during book construction. *Color Zoo,* a Caldecott Honor book, uses simple overlapping die-cut shapes to cleverly create zoo animals. You will enjoy the metamorphosis that occurs with the turn of each page.

RELATED PICTURE BOOK TITLE
Ehlert, Lois. *Color Zoo.* Lippincott, 1989.

SESSIONS: 1
ELEMENTS: color, form/shape, space
PRINCIPLES: informal balance, proportion,
    variety, harmony
MATERIALS:
◆ colored construction paper
◆ glue
◆ paper cutter

DIRECTIONS:
◆ Check out the school die-cut machine and plates to use in the classroom.
◆ Precut colored construction paper into 4" (102 mm) strips.
◆ Show students the variety of plate patterns available for the activity.
◆ Brainstorm pictures to be created.
◆ Begin by die cutting multiple basic patterns of various colors, and allow students to select their own pieces. Later on, when all students are working, you may die cut additional patterns for students as needed. Usually the die-cut plates will cut through three or four layers of paper successfully. Too many paper layers will cause the plates to make only partial cuts.
◆ Place die-cut pieces on construction paper and arrange them in an attractive way. Overlapping of items may create positional perspective.
◆ When the final arrangement of pieces has been determined, glue them to the construction paper, working from background to middle ground to foreground.

FOUND OBJECT COLLAGE

FOCUS PICTURE BOOK TITLE
Bunting, Eve. *Smoky Night.* Illus. by David Diaz. Harcourt Brace, 1994.

This project not only teaches an art form, it allows students to discover that materials can serve more than one purpose. At first glance the collage illustrations in *Smoky Night* look like David Diaz just raided the nearest dumpster (actually, he probably did). A closer look reveals how appropriately the found objects in the illustrations match the story, which is precisely why Caldecott Medals are awarded. Cereal kibbles are strewn across the page that tells how Kim's market is looted. Spent wooden matches are an element bordering the text describing the apartment fire. What found objects did David Diaz use as collage elements on other pages? Found object collage is both ecologically beneficial and fun.

SESSIONS: 2 or 3
ELEMENTS: space, texture, form/shape
PRINCIPLES: variety, harmony, informal balance
MATERIALS:
- poster board, corrugated board, or wood panel
- staple gun
- hot glue gun
- hot glue cartridges
- wood glue
- white glue
- found objects

ADVANCE PREPARATION:
- Begin the process of found object collection on a Friday in order to provide children a full weekend to find their objects. Discuss handling of found objects and specific materials to exclude from the activity. During the construction of this project, it would be helpful to have parental involvement in the classroom for assisting in the use of hot glue guns, staple guns, or other fastening tools.

DIRECTIONS:
- Discuss the various materials used in the illustrations of the focus title and what materials students will supply for themselves as well as share with their classmates.
- Direct students to collect found objects at home and bring them to class. Categorize the materials by placing them in shoe boxes or large containers. This will help students to discover if they should bring in more of one material as well as give them additional ideas for their projects. Students may also store objects in their desks for their own collages.
- Review the focus title and discuss the use of materials in creating a found object collage.

- Cut and distribute the backboards. The dimensions of the backboard are irrelevant, but large, heavy objects are better mounted on corrugated board or wood panels than poster board. Backboards may be painted or left natural.
- Allow students to take turns selecting the objects for their collages.
- Once enough objects have been distributed, instruct children to arrange objects on their backboards.
- Before securing objects to the backboard, students should remove them from the arrangement in an orderly manner. Remove top objects and place them away from the board and allow objects directly touching the backboard to remain in place. Begin attaching objects to the backboard while reconstructing the artwork until all pieces have been secured.
- Cleanup should continue the ecological concept by recycling leftover materials.

MAGAZINE COLLAGE

FOCUS PICTURE BOOK TITLE
Aylesworth, Jim. *McGraw's Emporium*. Illus. by Mavis Smith. Holt, 1995.

Mavis Smith used 432 magazines and three pairs of scissors, as well as watercolors, colored pencils, and an airbrush to create the fun multimedia collage illustrations for *McGraw's Emporium*. The most prominent feature is the use of magazine pictures combined in a new setting. For example, on the cover illustration the bay window has been modified to become a storefront window. Visit the emporium and find the Saturday Night Fever record, Velveeta from the 1950s, the NBC peacock, Madeline dolls, the lava lamp, and the Energizer bunny.

RELATED PICTURE BOOK TITLE
Scieska, Jon. *The Stinky Cheese Man and Other Fairly Stupid Tales*. Illus. by Lane Smith. Viking, 1992.

SESSIONS: 1
ELEMENTS: line, color, form/shape, space
PRINCIPLES: harmony
MATERIALS:

- construction paper
- scissors
- glue
- old magazines

DIRECTIONS:

- Choose a construction paper background.
- Cut out various items from magazines to combine in a new arrangement.
- Glue in place.

MOSAICS

FOCUS PICTURE BOOK TITLE
Sabuda, Robert. *Saint Valentine.* Atheneum, 1992.

Mosaic-making is an ancient art that flourishes in many different forms today. One of the earliest known examples of mosaics dates back to 2600 B. C. At that time mosaic ornamentation was used on drinking vessels, wands, and other small objects. Throughout the centuries, the art of mosaics made its way to the walls and floors of burial tombs, outside pavements, and to today's kitchens and bathrooms. Robert Sabuda's marbleized and hand-painted paper mosaic illustrations in *Saint Valentine* give the appearance of authentic tile. Mr. Sabuda creates realistic images by using shades and tints of a single hue and by shaping and arranging the "tiles." In addition to the distorted mosaic-like images portrayed in *The Boy with Square Eyes,* ask your students to find examples of real world mosaics. The geometric designs in the Gerald McDermott titles are excellent models for mosaic patterns.

RELATED PICTURE BOOK TITLES
Charles, Donald. *Chancay and the Secret of Fire.* Putnam, 1992.
McDermott, Gerald. *Arrow to the Sun.* Viking, 1974.
———. *Coyote.* Harcourt Brace, 1994.
———. *The Voyage of Osiris.* Dutton, 1977.
———. *Zomo the Rabbit.* Harcourt Brace, 1972.
Snape, Juliet & Charles. *The Boy with Square Eyes.* Prentice-Hall, 1987.

SESSIONS: 2 or 3
ELEMENTS: line, color, form/shape
PRINCIPLES: proportion, harmony, rhythm
MATERIALS:
◆ colored construction paper
◆ white drawing paper
◆ glue
◆ pencil (optional)
◆ scissors (optional)

DIRECTIONS:
◆ Precut the colored construction paper into ½" (13 mm) strips. Precut the white background paper to 6" x 9" (152 x 229 mm) or 9" x 12" (229 x 305 mm).
◆ Lightly sketch a picture with pencil on background paper. Students who have difficulty with drawing may design their pictures as they work.

- Cut ½" (13 mm) squares from the strips of construction paper. Caution students that a few squares go a long way—they should not cut up an entire strip of one color all at once. Rather, cut squares only as needed.

- Arrange the small squares on top of the background paper according to the design. This is an important step for the students to really see what their pictures will look like. They may modify the picture if necessary before permanently affixing the squares.

- Glue the squares to the paper. Given the size of the squares, it is generally easier to dot glue in rows on the paper and affix the squares in small areas, rather than putting the glue on the back of each square. Leave spaces between the squares to simulate real mosaic tile.

- Here is a trick that makes handling the tiny squares easier. Squirt some glue on a scrap piece of paper. Dip just the tip of your finger into the glue. Place your glued finger on a square—it will lift right up. Use your other hand to flip the square over and position it on the paper.

- Spray a couple of coats of clear varnish on the paper to protect the mosaic.

- To help your design really stand out, make sure there is plenty of contrast (light versus dark) in the mosaic. Make the background squares much lighter (or darker, for a different effect) than those you choose to use in the design itself.

- You may also use colored paper to create a more subtle mosaic. Cut plenty of paper in various shades of the main colors of your picture. Suggest the roundness of forms in the mosaic by going from light to dark, with the darker shades giving the appearance of shadow.

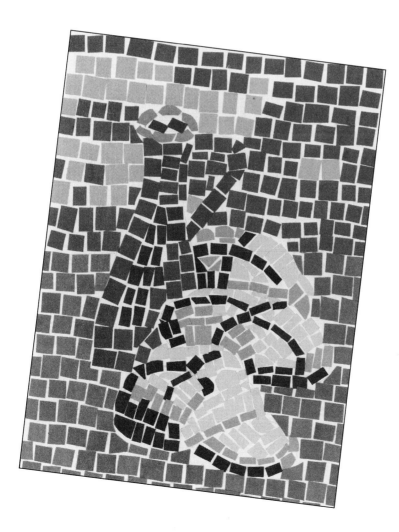

SHADOW COLLAGE

FOCUS PICTURE BOOK TITLE
Brown, Marcia. *Shadow.* Scribner's, 1982.

Marcia Brown uses a clever technique to show shadow in her multimedia collage illustrations for this Caldecott Award-winning title. The silhouetted characters in the illustrations are frequently backed by a duplicate cutout as a method of creating a shadow. The cut-outs are occasionally enlarged or altered to make distorted shadows. The same shadow effect has been created electronically in the illustrations for *A B CEDAR*. With an ounce of ingenuity the shadowing technique is easily adaptable to the classroom setting.

RELATED PICTURE BOOK TITLE:
Lyon, George Ella. *A B CEDAR: An Alphabet of Trees.* Illus. by Tom Parker. Orchard, 1989.

SESSIONS: 1
ELEMENTS: color, form/shape
PRINCIPLES: emphasis, harmony, proportion, rhythm
MATERIALS:

- scissors
- magazines
- pencils
- black construction paper
- construction paper
- glue
- markers or other coloring medium

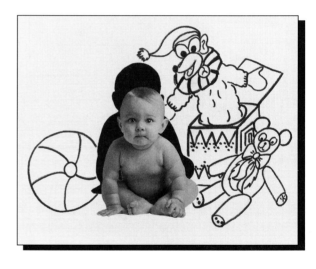

DIRECTIONS:

- Look through magazines for objects, people, buildings, or anything large enough to make a shadow and cut them out.
- Select a cutout, trace its pattern on black construction paper, and cut the shadow out.
- Place the magazine cutout directly over the shadow on a light colored background paper. When the cutouts are positioned, gently slide the magazine cutout to the left or right of the shadow.
- Repeat this process with other cutouts to create a picture.
- Once the items and shadows are in place, secure them with glue.
- Fill in the background with markers or another medium.

TISSUE PAPER COLLAGE

FOCUS PICTURE BOOK TITLE
Fox, Mem. *Hattie and the Fox.* Illus. by Patricia Mullins. Bradbury, 1986.

Tissue paper is fun to work with and provides a new art dimension for young children to experience. The collage illustrations of *Hattie and the Fox* and *Shoes from Grandpa* are made with torn tissue paper. Where the paper overlaps or has been layered it creates new shades and colors, such as the horse on pages 6 and 7 of *Hattie and the Fox.* Details are added with a fine-tipped felt pen for the hairs, eyes, and mouth of the pig on page 5. On page 8 Patricia Mullins has added water to the tissue paper to create a camouflage effect for the fox in hiding. Students should try these techniques when creating tissue paper illustrations of their own.

RELATED PICTURE BOOK TITLES
Carle, Eric. *The Very Quiet Cricket.* Philomel, 1990.
Fox, Mem. *Shoes from Grandpa.* Illus. by Patricia Mullins. Macmillan, 1986.
Martin, Jr., Bill. *Brown Bear, Brown Bear, What Do You See?* Illus. by Eric Carle. Holt, 1983.

SESSIONS: 1
ELEMENTS: color, form/shape
PRINCIPLES: informal balance, proportion
MATERIALS:
◆ tissue paper
◆ white construction paper
◆ glue
◆ scissors
◆ paintbrush

DIRECTIONS:
◆ Some students may want to lightly sketch their designs prior to the application of the tissue paper.
◆ Glue the cut or torn tissue paper shapes to the background paper. A blanket application of glue will ensure that the edges of the paper will not roll up.
◆ *Note:* Wait until the glue is dry before stacking the artwork.

Something Else to Try!
Tissue Paper Painting
◆ For tissue paper painting, apply the torn or cut tissue paper as before using water instead of glue.
◆ When the artwork has dried, remove the tissue paper to reveal the painted image below.

Rolled Paper Technique

◆ Cut tissue paper into small rectangular shapes with a paper cutter.

◆ Roll each piece into a tiny ball, making several of one color at a time.

◆ Using liquid glue, outline or fill in a small area of the design. Apply paper balls closely together, taking care to fill in all blank space.

Fluffy Paper Technique

◆ Cut the tissue paper into small squares or circles.

◆ Place a dull pencil point in the center of a cut tissue paper piece. Twist paper around the point of the pencil.

◆ Press the tissue paper point to the glued area. Carefully remove the pencil from the center of the tissue paper, leaving it attached to the background paper. The tissue paper will "stand up."

◆ Flat, rolled, and fluffy tissue paper techniques may be combined into one work.

TORN PAPER COLLAGE

FOCUS PICTURE BOOK TITLE
Say, Allen. *Grandfather's Journey.* Houghton Mifflin, 1993.

Leo Lionni uses torn paper collage throughout his book *Alexander and the Wind-Up Mouse.* Note the teddy bear on page 9, the tree trunks on pages 20 and 21, and the ground on page 26. (As a matter of fact, the copy of this book from the Plant City Public Library has very authentic torn paper!) *Grandfather's Journey* is illustrated in magnificent watercolor, but the desert rock sculptures on page 8 lend themselves perfectly for a torn paper scene. The mountain range on page 11 offers a lovely landscape to copy using purple, blue, and gray shades of construction paper. Art does not get any simpler than this.

RELATED PICTURE BOOK TITLES
Lionni, Leo. *Alexander and the Wind-Up Mouse.* Random House, 1969.
Walsh, Ellen Stoll. *Mouse Paint.* Harcourt Brace, 1989.

SESSIONS: 1
ELEMENTS: form/shape, space, texture
PRINCIPLES: proportion
MATERIALS:
◆ construction paper
◆ glue

DIRECTIONS:
◆ Distribute picture books with landscapes and seascapes for students to peruse.
◆ Demonstrate tearing paper into the shape of mountains, hills, clouds, trees, waves, boulders, or seashores. Direct students to do the same.
◆ Arrange the torn objects on a construction paper background, gluing the background landforms first, then the middle ground objects, and finally the foreground details.

Something Else to Try!
◆ Tear a teddy bear from colored construction paper. Tear a bow to match.

WALLPAPER COLLAGE

FOCUS PICTURE BOOK TITLE

Lionni, Leo. *Alexander and the Wind-Up Mouse.* Random House, 1969.

It is time for you to become friends with the owner of a wallpaper store. Every season store owners discard discontinued wallpaper pattern books. Store managers will hold the books for you and even call you to help clear their shops. Ezra Jack Keats uses print wallpaper primarily for the walls and floors in his book *Peter's Chair.* Leo Lionni, however, in *Alexander and the Wind-up Mouse,* takes the use of wallpaper a step further by creating cut-out characters and other objects for his collage illustrations. *Glorious Angels* features Victorian wallpaper designs as frames for the poetry opposite the antique photographs. The uses of wallpaper are many. Have fun!

RELATED PICTURE BOOK TITLES

Keats, Ezra Jack. *Peter's Chair.* Harper & Row, 1967.
Myers, Walter Dean. *Glorious Angels.* HarperCollins, 1995.

SESSIONS: 1
ELEMENTS: form/shape, space, texture
PRINCIPLES: proportion, variety, harmony
MATERIALS:

- wallpaper samples
- glue
- construction paper
- scissors

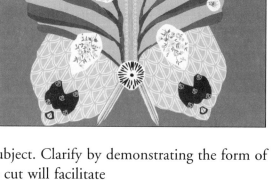

DIRECTIONS:

- In preparation for this activity, cut closely along the gutter with a case cutter to remove the wallpaper samples from the binders.
- Discuss how cut wallpaper patterns may not relate to the subject. Clarify by demonstrating the form of a cat or dog cut from a wallpaper sample. The shape of the cut will facilitate recognition.
- Some students will want to make simple flowers and vases from the wallpaper. Encourage them to create scenes with animals, trees, houses, mountains, etc.
- Students should choose patterns of wallpaper that compliment each other, selecting from a variety of patterns, colors, and textures.
- Cut the wallpaper into the shapes that will create the picture and glue them to the construction paper.

PRINTS

ENGRAVINGS

FOCUS PICTURE BOOK TITLE
Osborne, Mary Pope. *American Tall Tales.* Illus. by Michael McCurdy. Knopf, 1991.

Most children's picture books that are illustrated with engravings are made with wood blocks or linoleum that require detailed and often dangerous cutting. Michael McCurdy uses wood engraving for the illustrations in *American Tall Tales,* but he is equally proficient using scratchboard. Compare this focus title with one of his scratchboard-illustrated titles (see p. 123) to see how similar the final products are. Children can obtain a similar effect and create a design more safely by using a softer medium such as potatoes, soap, or gum erasers. They will be able to design letterheads, seal envelopes, make wrapping paper, or create decorative borders for their work. They may also design the stamps around a focus title and illustrate the entire story with home-made prints. If students share their stamps they will be able to enjoy an even greater variety of prints.

RELATED PICTURE BOOK TITLES
Carrick, Carol. *Whaling Days.* Illus. by David Frampton. Clarion, 1993.
Emberley, Barbara. *Drummer Hoff.* Illus. by Ed Emberley.
    Prentice-Hall, 1967.
MacLachlan, Patricia. *What You Know First.* Illus. by
    Barry Moser. HarperCollins, 1995.
Pomeroy, Diana. *One Potato: A Counting Book of Potato Prints.*
    Harcourt Brace, 1996.

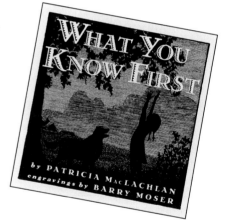

SESSIONS: 1 or 2
ELEMENTS: form/shape
PRINCIPLES: emphasis
MATERIALS:
◆ craft knives
◆ soap, soft wood, gum erasers, or potatoes
◆ pencil
◆ paint
◆ paper
◆ flat paint containers or sponges

DIRECTIONS:
◆ Cut the potato in half, making sure the surface is perfectly flat. This will ensure a design that will print properly on a paper surface. Shave the large edge of the soap to achieve the same effect. Gum erasers come with flat sides.

- Using a pencil lightly draw a design on the flat surface of the material to be carved.
- Carefully cut away the negative sections leaving a positive design elevated on the surface.
- When using potatoes this process is best done in one session because the potato will loose moisture over time, thereby distorting the impression. Erasers or soap, on the other hand, can be carved in one session and the stamping may take place on another day.
- Pour the printing paint into a flat container, such as a plate, or soak a sponge in paint. If using tempera, thin it slightly with water to avoid cracking of prints.
- Press the engraving into the paint or sponge much like you would use a stamp pad, making sure you cover the design completely.
- Press the stamp onto a piece of paper, being careful to remove the stamp in an upward motion to avoid the print being smudged or distorted. It may be possible to make more than one print before re-inking.

Something Else to Try!

- Instead of a potato, try printing with pieces of Styrofoam. Just trim off the curved edges of a Styrofoam tray. Lightly draw a design or scene on the tray and then retrace it by pushing down on the pencil to etch the image into the Styrofoam. Using a brayer facilitates the inking process. Be creative! Your beautiful prints can be used to make greeting cards.

FINGERPRINTING

FOCUS PICTURE BOOK TITLE
Emberley, Ed. *Ed Emberley's Great Thumbprint Drawing Book.* Little, Brown, 1977.

Although this is not an illustrated picture book, we could not bypass this adorable activity. A simple thumbprint when detailed by any combination of the nine drawing lines (see p. 20) can become virtually any character or image you want, such as a lion, a mouse, a spider, a house, a skyscraper, King Kong, or a millipede a thousand thumbprints long!

SESSIONS: 1
ELEMENTS: line, color, form/shape, texture
PRINCIPLES: variety, harmony, rhythm
MATERIALS:
◆ white drawing paper
◆ ink pad
◆ fine-tip felt marker

DIRECTIONS:
◆ Cut paper to 9" x 12" (229 x 305 mm) pieces or smaller.
◆ Firmly press thumb or fingertip flatly to an ink pad.
◆ Gently press the inked finger to a piece of paper. You should be able to clearly see the striations of the fingerprint in the impression. Make one or two more prints as desired, then re-ink.
◆ Create a single print of the finger or develop a pattern using multiple fingerprints. Single prints are great for faces, while multiple prints can create a grouping such as a bunch of grapes.
◆ Use a fine-tip felt marker to add details to the fingerprints.

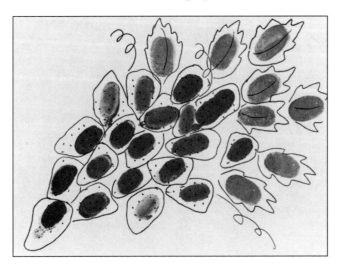

LEAF PRINTS

FOCUS PICTURE BOOK TITLE

Wahl, Mats. *Grandfather's LAIKA.* Illus. by Tord Nygren. Carolrhoda, 1990.

Leaves play supporting roles in the illustrations of *Free Fall* and *A Tree's Tale,* and they take on a major role in *Red Leaf, Yellow Leaf.* But the golden paint prints and rubbings of birch leaves in *Grandfather's LAIKA* have a special significance beyond mere aesthetic quality. Discuss the surface qualities of prints and rubbings with your students. Then ask them to examine the leaf art carefully on the opening pages, pages 7, 14, 15, and 32 of *Grandfather's LAIKA,* and to distinguish between the two techniques. How are birch leaves different from the leaves of "foolhardy" willows? Your students will be sure to agree that regardless of their role, simple leaves are minute masterpieces by nature's design.

RELATED PICTURE BOOK TITLES

Carrier, Lark. *A Tree's Tale.* Dial, 1996.
Ehlert, Lois. *Red Leaf, Yellow Leaf.* Harcourt Brace, 1991.
Sohi, Morteza E. *Look What I Did with a Leaf!* Walker, 1993.
Wiesner, David. *Free Fall.* Lothrop, 1988.

SESSIONS: 1
ELEMENTS: color, form/shape, space, texture
PRINCIPLES: rhythm, informal balance, variety, harmony, emphasis
MATERIALS:

- leaves
- tempera paint
- paintbrushes
- black construction paper
- string

DIRECTIONS:

- One day before the planned activity, direct the students to collect leaves of various sizes and shapes.
- Cover tables or desks with newspaper. Distribute one sheet of black construction paper to each student, and space tempera paint bottles intermittently around the room to provide access to all students.
- Students begin by blending small amounts of paint to create fall colors. You will be amazed at the vivid magentas and dusky blues that emerge in the discovery part of this activity.

- When a desired color has been achieved, paint the underside of the leaf (where the veins are located) to make the most detailed print.
- Lay the painted leaf on the black paper and then press it firmly and evenly to ensure that a complete print is made.
- Continue making leaf prints with a variety of colors until the paper is full. Some overlapping of prints adds a natural look. Students should share their new colors if excess paint remains.
- Dip a yard-long (100 cm) length of string into a container of white tempera. Use a brush to make sure the string is completely covered in paint. Remove the string from the container and lay it in random loops across the surface of the leaf prints, then remove it. The black background, the leaf prints, and white string design give the project a three-dimensional effect.
- Splattering with white tempera gives the illusion of snow.

MISCELLANEOUS PRINTS

FOCUS PICTURE BOOK TITLE
Smith, Lane. *Glasses—Who Needs 'Em?* Viking, 1991.

Prints can be made using virtually any solid medium. One of the latest trends in interior house painting has been creating wall texture by using sponge and rag prints. The same techniques are used in children's books. Lane Smith uses a multimedia approach for his illustrations in *Glasses—Who Needs 'Em?* His use of miscellaneous prints, however, is evident particularly for the rims of the glasses on each page. He also prints hair, lips, teeth, and noses. Before Sharon McGinley-Nally painted the illustrations for *Django,* she sponged several layers of an all natural beverage to create a textured pattern on her watercolor paper. Use your imagination to discover new ways of using old materials when creating miscellaneous prints.

RELATED PICTURE BOOK TITLES
Cech, John. *Django.* Illus. by Sharon McGinley-Nally. Four Winds Press, 1994.
Lionni, Leo. *Swimmy.* Pantheon, 1963.

SESSIONS: 1
ELEMENTS: color, space, texture
PRINCIPLES: rhythm, variety, harmony
MATERIALS:
- found objects
- sponge pieces
- cloth rags
- paper
- tempera
- shallow dishes

DIRECTIONS:

Found Object Printing
- Direct students to collect a variety of found objects, such as bottle caps, cardboard tubes, and kitchen utensils, that have an enclosed shape.
- Sketch and color two or three faces on a sheet of paper, or photocopy a large portait photograph.
- Dilute several colors of tempera paint to the consistency of milk and pour them into shallow dishes.
- Press the edges of the found objects into paint and make prints over the eyes of the faces to make the shape of frames for glasses.
- Draw the bridges and arms of the glasses to connect to the printed frames.

Sponge Printing

◆ Collect a variety of natural, synthetic, or cellulose sponges.

◆ Tear the sponges to manageable sizes.

◆ To create an ocean scene similar to the one in *Swimmy*, blend several shades and tints of blue and green tempera. Dilute them to the consistency of milk.

◆ Beginning with darker shades, press the sponge pieces into the paint, then make repetitive, overlapping prints across the paper as desired.

◆ Allow the first layer of sponge prints to dry to the touch, then continue layering prints progressing from dark layers to light layers.

◆ Draw undersea plant and animal life.

◆ For a variation on the theme, try making prints with wadded rags or crumpled paper.

RUBBER STAMPING

FOCUS PICTURE BOOK TITLE
Keats, Ezra Jack. *Whistle for Willie*. Viking, 1964.

Rubber stamping is very popular with children. You may be surprised at how many rubber stamps your students already own. Ezra Jack Keats used rubber stamps for the graffiti wall on pages 20 and 21 of *Whistle for Willie*. Mr. Keats also used rubber stamps to create snow patterns in his 1963 Caldecott Medal-winning book *The Snowy Day*. Two decades later, Lane Smith used this same technique on pages 7, 17, 24, and 27 of his book *Glasses—Who Needs 'Em?* Glasses, however, are not required for this activity.

RELATED PICTURE BOOK TITLES
Keats, Ezra Jack. *Snowy Day*. Viking, 1962.
Lionni, Leo. *Swimmy*. Pantheon, 1963.
Smith, Lane. *Glasses—Who Needs 'Em?* Viking, 1991.

SESSIONS: 1
ELEMENTS: color, form/shape, space
PRINCIPLES: rhythm, variety, harmony
MATERIALS:

- water-soluble ink pads
- rubber stamps
- white drawing paper
- shallow dishes
- water
- paper towels

DIRECTIONS:

- Direct students to bring in rubber stamps, while you solicit rubber stamps of letters, characters, animals, shapes, and objects from your colleagues. Or you could use your classroom budget and purchase a kit.
- If the stamp is new, you will need to press it into the pad several times to condition the stamp before using it. Stamp it on a piece of paper several times to assure successful printing.
- Identify the stamps for your students. Brainstorm how they would fit into or create a story. List these ideas on the chalkboard.
- Arrange ink pads of varying colors on tables around the classroom. If the students use the stamps with more than one color, it is important to clean the stamps on damp paper towels before using another color.
- Create a graffiti wall like the one in *Whistle for Willie*.
- Students may choose to create a wordless story book by stamping on small sheets of folded paper. Or students may make a rebus by writing a short story and using stamps to take the place of certain words within the text.

String Prints

FOCUS PICTURE BOOK TITLE
Ness, Evaline. *Sam, Bangs and Moonshine.* Holt, 1966.

String works well for creating printed designs such as spider webs, grass, or rope and nets for ships. The illustrations in the 1967 Caldecott Medal winner *Sam, Bangs and Moonshine* use a multimedia approach, including three-color preseparated art of Japanese pen and wash, printer's ink, roller, and string. Although this multimedia approach may be a bit sophisticated for your classroom, students can create interesting designs by looping, drooping, and swooping strings.

SESSIONS: 1
ELEMENTS: line, form/shape
PRINCIPLES: emphasis, formal/informal balance
MATERIALS:

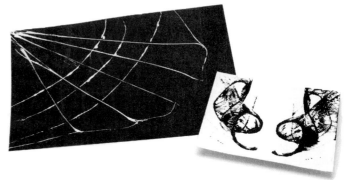

- ◆ white drawing paper
- ◆ string
- ◆ poster paint
- ◆ shallow containers
- ◆ chalk

DIRECTIONS:
- ◆ Place a length of string in paint, covering all but 2" (51 mm) of one end with paint so that your fingers will remain free of paint.
- ◆ Lay the string on the paper in a web, rope, or net pattern.
- ◆ Remove the string and allow the paint to dry.
- ◆ Add details to complete the project.

Something Else to Try!
- ◆ Place string in paint, completely covering it with paint as before.
- ◆ Fold a sheet of paper in half. Open the paper and place the string in any pattern on one side of the folded paper, leaving about 1" (25 mm) of the string hanging from the outer edge.
- ◆ Fold the paper, enclosing the string within the two halves.
- ◆ Place one hand on top of the paper, applying slight pressure.
- ◆ Grip the inch of string extending from the folded paper and pull.
- ◆ View the resulting pattern and use it as a catalyst for your art.

MISCELLANEOUS

CLIP ART & PHOTOCOPY CREATIONS

FOCUS PICTURE BOOK TITLE
Schneider, R. M. *Add It, Dip It, Fix It: A Book of Verbs.* Houghton Mifflin, 1995.

A variety of cut papers and other media are combined in the collage illustrations of *Add It, Dip It, Fix It,* with each page's featured verb acting on the word "it." Hand-colored photocopies of magazine photographs are prominently displayed. Note how the poor quality of the photocopies actually creates a unique shading effect and how the simplistic illustrations on each page allow the reader to focus on the verb action at hand. *Flyaway Girl* by Ann Grifalconi features multimedia collage using color xerography for the photocopied components. The cut paper collage illustrations in *My House* by Lisa Desimini uses patterned magazine photographs to create new shapes. Introducing children to the world of clip art, cut and paste, and photocopying will not only serve as a creative outlet for the artistically challenged, but it will provide them with a necessary job skill that can be utilized in virtually any office setting.

RELATED PICTURE BOOK TITLES
Desimini, Lisa. *My House.* Holt, 1994.
Grifalconi, Ann. *Flyaway Girl.* Little, Brown, 1992.

ANOTHER RESOURCE
Fleischman, Paul. *Copier Creations.* Illus. by David Cain. HarperCollins, 1993.
(A manual on creating photocopied products of all kinds.)

SESSIONS: 1 or 2
ELEMENTS: form/shape, space
PRINCIPLES: balance, proportion, variety, harmony

MATERIALS:

- clip art books
- magazines
- copy machine
- copy paper
- construction paper
- scissors
- glue stick
- correction fluid
- clear adhesive tape
- bulletin board letter stencils
- textured papers (optional)
- die cut machine (optional)

DIRECTIONS:

◆ Brainstorm with the class a list of common action verbs not used in the focus title.

◆ Assign or direct each student to select a verb to use for illustrating its action on the word "it."

◆ Plan or sketch what the action verb will do to the word "it" and how the final collage should look.

◆ Students will select clip art images or magazine photographs to be photocopied. Demonstrate how photocopying does not destroy the original.

◆ Make photocopies of the selected pages.

◆ Direct students to cut out the photocopied images.

◆ Choose colored or textured paper and cut out the letters "i" and "t" using stencils or a die cut machine. If stencils are to be used, the teacher may want to make duplicate stencils from poster paper or manila folders so that students do not become impatient waiting to use one set of letters.

◆ Use any other media as needed to color the photocopies, distort the letters, or add dimension.

◆ Arrange all pieces on a sheet of white copy paper and glue them in place.

Something Else to Try!

◆ Create personal stationery or greeting cards using clip art.

COMMUNITY MAPS

FOCUS PICTURE BOOK TITLE

San Souci, Robert D. *Kate Shelley: Bound for Legend.* Illus. by Max Ginsburg. Dial, 1995.

Max Ginsburg uses two maps to show the setting for *Kate Shelley: Bound for Legend.* The larger map details the vicinity of Moingona, Iowa, in 1881, and gives a bird's-eye view of the Des Moines River, Moingona's city blocks, the Chicago & North Western Railroad, and the washed-out Honey Creek Bridge where Kate Shelley averted disaster. The inset map shows the state of Iowa and the midwestern states on its borders. On page 20 of *Have You Seen Birds?* Barbara Reid gives a very realistic representation of a neighborhood map. Although *Stepping on the Cracks* is a novel, it contains a community map frontispiece for the reader's information. *The Monument,* another novel, offers the reader a vivid written description of the fictional town of Bolton, Kansas, making it an ideal model for a community map. With this activity your children can replicate their own community or neighborhood to share with each other.

RELATED PICTURE BOOK TITLES

Hahn, Mary Downing. *Stepping On the Cracks.* Clarion, 1991.
Hartman, Gail. *As the Roadrunner Runs: A First Book of Maps.* Illus. by Cathy Bobak. Bradbury, 1994.
Oppenheim, Joanne. *Have You Seen Birds?* Illus. by Barbara Reid. Scholastic, 1986.
Paulsen, Gary. *The Monument.* Delacorte, 1991.

SESSIONS: 2 or 3
ELEMENTS: line, form/shape, space
PRINCIPLES: proportion, harmony
MATERIALS:

◆ pencil
◆ drawing paper
◆ coloring medium

DIRECTIONS:

◆ Direct children to draw their houses and yards on a piece of paper from a bird's-eye perspective. Only the roof of the house should be seen, as well as the tops of trees and shrubs.
◆ From the same perspective, sketch the layout of the road.
◆ Add other houses and trees, birdbaths, driveways, sidewalks, mailboxes, and telephone poles in the area.
◆ Add a compass rose and identify landmarks in a legend.
◆ Color the neighborhood map.

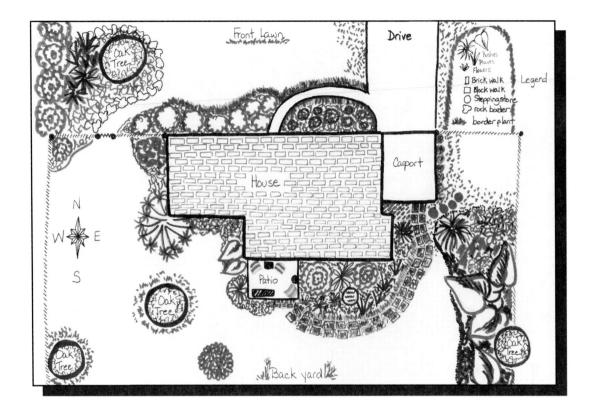

Something Else to Try!

The Monument, a novel by Gary Paulsen, tells the story of a young, crippled, biracial adoptee whose life is transformed when an eccentric artist comes to design a war memorial for the town of Bolton, Kansas. Chapter three describes in detail Bolton's boundaries, landmarks, and various micro-settings. As they read, have students jot descriptive story passages in their journals. Then direct them to use the information to draw a town map the way they visualize the locale. Display the maps for reference as reading continues. At the end, discuss how accurately the maps reflected Gary Paulsen's written description of the town.

CONTINENTAL MAPS

FOCUS PICTURE BOOK TITLE

Kraske, Robert. *The Voyager's Stone.* Illus. by Brian Floca. Orchard, 1995.

One of the annual geography assessments conducted at the middle school level in our school district is the drawing of the world map from memory. Maps are assessed according to a number of criteria with the highest scores given only to those students who draw with precise accuracy to coordinates on the global grid. Brian Floca's pen and ink world map on pages 6 and 7 sets the stage for *The Voyager's Stone.*

As the message-carrying bottle travels around the world, specific regions are enlarged to provide further detail. What better way to prepare elementary students for the future than by having them sketch and label the seven continents and four oceans?

RELATED PICTURE BOOK TITLES

Krupinski, Loretta. *Bluewater Journal: The Voyage of the Sea Tiger.* HarperCollins, 1995.
Musgrove, Margaret. *Ashanti to Zulu: African Traditions.* Illus. by Leo and Diane Dillon. Dial, 1976.
Schuett, Stacey. *Somewhere in the World Right Now.* Knopf, 1995.
Stanley, Diane. *The True Adventure of Daniel Hall.* Dial, 1995.

SESSIONS: 3–5
ELEMENTS: line, form/shape, space
PRINCIPLES: proportion, harmony
MATERIALS:

- white drawing paper
- graph paper (optional)
- pencils
- colored pencils
- black fine-tip felt pens
- a global grid for drawing the continents
- large classroom world map

DIRECTIONS:

- Display a large pull-down classroom world map or project an overhead transparency of a world map. Discuss the basic shapes and locations of the continents and oceans.
- Distribute your choice of drawing paper, graph paper, or duplicated global grid.
- Looking at the classroom world map or a textbook map, have each student lightly sketch a basic outline of the seven continents. When the outline is complete, draw a darker outline to add more detail.
- Trace over the final pencil outline with a black fine-tip felt pen.
- Color each continent with a different colored pencil. Using a blue colored pencil, feather a ¼" (7 mm) border along the outside perimeter of the continents to indicate the oceans.

◆ Label the continents and oceans.

◆ Draw a compass rose in one corner and label north (N).

◆ For younger students or basic classes you may choose to focus on each continent individually before drawing the world map. Advanced classes may draw rivers and mountains, identify countries, capital cities, and regions, label major cities, and create a legend for their continental maps.

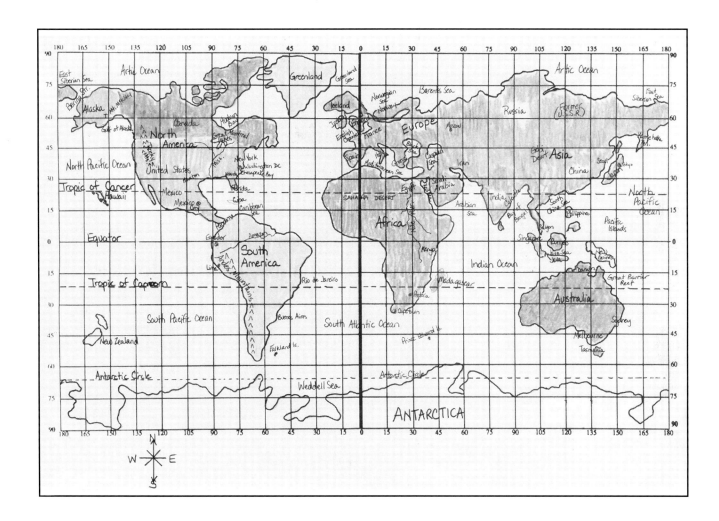

DECORATIVE LETTERING

FOCUS PICTURE BOOK TITLE

Thomas, Elizabeth. *Green Beans.* Illus. by Vicki Jo Redenbaugh. Carolrhoda, 1992.

In *Green Beans,* Vicki Jo Redenbaugh has drawn the title letters to look like bean pods, complimenting them with twining vines. Trina Schart Hyman uses thematic decorative lettering on the cover and title page of *St. George and the Dragon.* Children, too, can design creative lettering of their own.

RELATED PICTURE BOOK TITLE

Hodges, Margaret. *St. George and the Dragon.* Illus. by Trina Schart Hyman. Little, Brown, 1984.

SESSIONS: 1
ELEMENTS: line, form/shape
PRINCIPLES: variety, harmony
MATERIALS:
◆ paper
◆ pencils
◆ colored pencils

DIRECTIONS:
◆ Direct students to lightly write their names in 1" (25 mm) uppercase letters.
◆ Draw around the letters to give them a serpentine body shape.
◆ Draw heads with forked tongues or flaming nostrils. Add wings, legs, and scales.
◆ Color the letters.
◆ Now try making decorative letters from a variety of motifs, such as knotted rope, flowers, vegetables, trailing vines, animals, etc.

DISCOVERING COMPUTER-GENERATED ART

FOCUS PICTURE BOOK TITLE

Coman, Carolyn. *Losing Things at Mr. Mudd's*. Illus. by Lance Hidy. Farrar, Straus & Giroux, 1992.

The illustrations, typesetting, and design of *Losing Things at Mr. Mudd's* were entirely produced on a Macintosh computer with Adobe Illustrator and Adobe Photoshop, along with many other high tech applications and peripherals. Look closely at the illustrations for examples of gradient shading, scanned photographs, fill technique, and altered scannings to share with your students. The similar illustrations in *A B CEDAR* were first drawn with India ink, then color was applied photo-mechanically. Don and Audrey Wood's *Bright and Early Thursday Evening* features highly-detailed illustrations executed with state-of-the-art digital technology. Although only a few computer-illustrated picture books have been produced to date, undoubtedly there will be many more on the horizon as visual technology expands.

RELATED PICTURE BOOK TITLES

Lyon, George Ella. *A B CEDAR: An Alphabet of Trees*.
  Illus. by Tom Parker. Orchard, 1989.
Wood, Audrey. *Bright and Early Thursday Evening: A Tangled Tale*.
  Illus. by Don Wood. Harcourt Brace, 1996.

SESSIONS: 1 or 2
ELEMENTS: color, space, form/shape
PRINCIPLES: variety, harmony, proportion
MATERIALS:
◆ computers
◆ electronic draw & paint application
◆ color printer
◆ computer paper

DIRECTIONS:
◆ Schedule the school computer lab and verify that a draw & paint application has been installed in each computer. Familiarize yourself with the application or ask the computer teacher to conduct the activity. Most students already know computer basics and have experience working with a mouse or other drawing peripherals.
◆ Direct students to locate the drawing and painting tools on pull down windows, tool bars, or icon palettes. Identify select tools and explain how they are used. Allow students to experiment with the tools and then clear the page before proceeding to the next tool.

◆ Be sure to include the following tools: pencil, paint, airbrush, fill, eraser, rectangle, oval, as well as any application-specific features.

◆ When students have had time to experiment with the focus tools, tell them they will have a set time (15-20 minutes) to draw and paint a page.

◆ Instruct students on how to save their documents on the computer hard drives or on a single class diskette.

◆ Print the students' work with a color printer and then distribute the copies.

Something Else to Try!

◆ Allow students to experiment with computer clip art. Many designs can be enlarged, reduced, flipped, colored, altered, and warped to the delight of young electronic illustrators.

◆ There are several story-writing and book-making applications at varying levels of difficulty that allow children to create their own stories, illustrate them, and publish them within a single application. If your computer lab is networked with such an application, it would be a snap to have an entire class produce individual books simultaneously.

Discovering
Separations

FOCUS PICTURE BOOK TITLE
Heller, Ruth. *Color.* Putnam, 1995.

All hues, shades, and tints are created with black and the three primary colors: yellow, magenta (red), and cyan (blue). Ruth Heller's book *Color* clearly demonstrates the process used by color printers. It seems almost impossible that all the magnificent color found on the pages of this book emerged from various combinations of these four layers. Page 18 shows how small dots of the primary colors and black create the optical illusion of a new color when viewed at a distance. The book *Color* also features two sections that use colored acetates to demonstrate how four-color printing works. *A Book Takes Root* details the creation of a picture book from the original illustrations to the completion of the four-color printing process. Today computers separate the color of original picture book illustrations. Years ago artists had to create their own separations by layering the primary colors and black. William Joyce explains the process on pages 90 and 91 of *Talking with Artists Volume Two.*

RELATED PICTURE BOOK TITLES
Cummings, Pat (ed.). *Talking with Artists Volume Two.* Simon & Schuster, 1995.
Kehoe, Michael. *A Book Takes Root: The Making of a Picture Book.*
    Carolrhoda, 1993.

SESSIONS: 1
ELEMENTS: color
PRINCIPLES: emphasis
MATERIALS:

- clear acetates
- white paper
- overhead pens

- colored transparencies: yellow, magenta (red), cyan (blue)
- overhead projector

DIRECTIONS:

- Cut the transparencies into strips approximately 1" (25 mm) wide.
- Distribute one acetate strip of each hue and a sheet of white paper to every student. List the primary colors on the board or overhead projector.
- Direct students to overlap the strips in various combinations using the white paper as a backdrop, then elicit responses from their discoveries. List the secondary colors.
- Direct students to form pairs and to combine their strips to discover even more hues. Discuss and list the tertiary colors students discover.
- If you are unable to acquire colored transparencies, modify the activity by using clear acetates with yellow, red, and blue overhead pens.

DRAWING HANDS

FOCUS PICTURE BOOK TITLE
Polacco, Patricia. *Pink and Say.* Philomel, 1994.

Hands in the pockets, hands under shawls, hands behinds backs, hands around a pole—but you never see hands in the open! Why? Children are not taught to draw hands, so they don't know how. It is very easy to include hands when teaching children to draw. Hands appear larger than life in *Pink and Say* by Patricia Polacco. They portray helping hands on page 8, tender hands on page 16, inquisitive hands on page 24, hands joined in spiritual unity on page 26, comforting hands on page 30, and grieving hands on page 35. In the closing sequence on pages 42 and 43, hands portray the eternal struggle to overcome hate with love. In *The Dreamer,* Barry Moser paints the creative hands of the very first artist at work. What better model than the Master?

RELATED PICTURE BOOK TITLES
Lawrence, Jacob. *Harriet and the Promised Land.* Simon & Schuster,
    1968, 1993.
Lyon, George Ella. *A B CEDAR: An Alphabet of Trees.* Illus. by
    Tom Parker. Orchard, 1989.
Rylant, Cynthia. *The Dreamer.* Illus. by Barry Moser.
    Blue Sky/Scholastic, 1993.

SESSIONS: 1
ELEMENTS: line
PRINCIPLES: emphasis, proportion
MATERIALS:
◆ pencil or charcoal
◆ white drawing paper
◆ gum eraser

DIRECTIONS:
◆ Give each student a piece of paper large enough for a hand to be traced without extending off the edge.
◆ Place the hand on the paper with all fingers extended from the palm, comfortably separated.
◆ Trace the hand, using light pencil pressure to leave a faint outline.
◆ Place the hand palm down on the table beside the paper, recreating the position of the traced hand.
◆ Note the various skin wrinkles around the knuckles, between the fingers, at the joints, and around the wrist.

- With light and heavy strokes draw the lines on the traced outline. Shadow in the areas where the lines are darker and blend.

- Notice how the veins are slightly raised on the surface of the hand. Draw the veins, using the edge of the pencil lead to create the raised surface of the hand.

- Students with dark or medium skin coloring will find this extremely interesting as they attempt to closely match their hand color using shades of gray. Children who have very light-skin coloring will find this activity most challenging because they need to use very little or no gray in their drawings.

- Make sure students include scars, freckles, moles, hairs or other identifying marks.

- Allow students to practice redrawing their hands, tracing if necessary, and eventually drawing their hands from memory. Soon there will be hands everywhere!

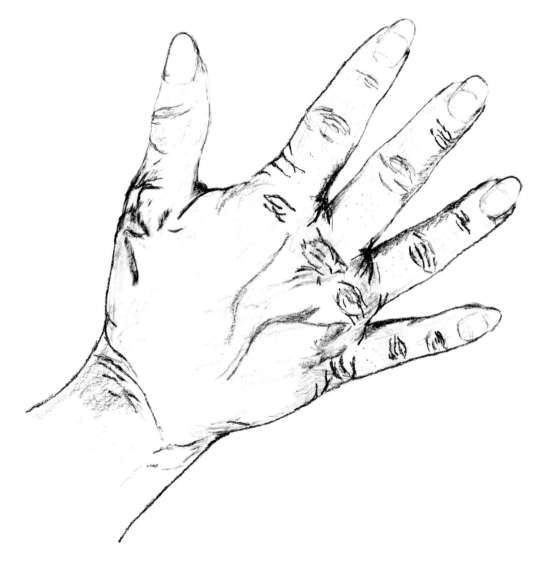

FABRIC ART

FOCUS PICTURE BOOK TITLE
Bolton, Janet. *Mrs. Noah's Patchwork Quilt.* Andrews and McMeel, 1995.

The multimedia collage illustrations in *Rainsong Snowsong* use both fabric and color photocopies of fabric. Fabrics that keep their shape and do not unravel were actually used in the illustrations. Photocopies were made of knitted fabrics in order to create the illusion of smooth edges. In *Mrs. Noah's Patchwork Quilt,* animals are created with a variety of natural fiber fabrics. The colors in the fabric give each animal its character. When creating any artwork with cloth, consider the texture, weight, and color of the fabric and how each element will fit into the overall piece. Making a quilt is a terrific undertaking for a year-long project, so you may want to start with something simple, like a bookmark.

RELATED PICTURE BOOK TITLES
Koralek, Jenny. *The Boy and the Cloth of Dreams.* Illus. by James Mayhew. Candlewick, 1994.
Kraus, Robert. *Strudwick: A Sheep in Wolf's Clothing.* Viking, 1995.
Sturges, Philemon. *Rainsong Snowsong.* Illus. by Shari Halpern. North-South, 1995.
Roth, Susan L. *Creak, Thump, Bonk! A Very Spooky Mystery.* Simon & Schuster, 1995.

SESSIONS: 2 or 3
ELEMENTS: texture, space, color
PRINCIPLES: emphasis, variety, harmony
MATERIALS:

- needle
- pinking shears
- tissue paper
- thread
- cotton cloth
- straight pins
- embroidery thread
- underfacing
- paper

DIRECTIONS:
- Trace a bookmark size image from a coloring book or picture book on tissue paper, or design your own image.
- Cut out the paper design for the pattern.
- Place the pattern on a piece of fabric and cut the pattern out leaving a ¼" (6 mm) margin.

- Cut two pieces of fabric the size you want for a bookmark. Cut one piece of underfacing the same size as the bookmark fabric. Be sure to add ¼" (6 mm) margin to all pieces.
- Pin the pattern into place on the front side of one of the pieces of fabric, tucking under the margin of the design.
- Sew the design into place with a running stitch or hem stitch using embroidery thread of contrasting or neutral color.
- Place underfacing on backside of the second piece of fabric and baste stitch together along the margin.
- Pin front sides of bookmark together. Sew together with a running stitch along all sides leaving a one inch opening.
- Using the eraser end of a pencil, turn the bookmark inside out. Manipulate the material into proper bookmark shape. Use an iron to press the bookmark flat.
- Sew the opening, concealing margins and stitches as well as possible. Iron the bookmark again.
- Options: Adorn the bookmark with a tassel or piping. Prior to sewing the two bookmark sides together, stitch names onto one side of the bookmark with decorative thread or embroidery thread.

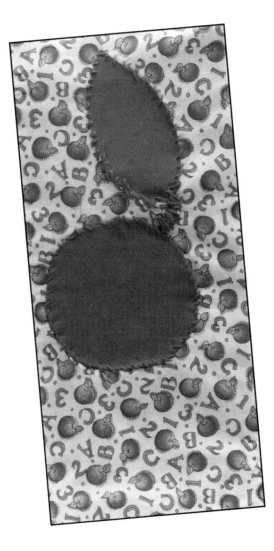

Something Else to Try!

- Use fabric pieces as collage elements. Fabric pieces can be attached with fabric glue or hot glue. Spray starch will make the fabric pieces more manageable.

FAUX STAINED GLASS

FOCUS PICTURE BOOK TITLE
Sabuda, Robert. *Arthur and the Sword*. Atheneum, 1995.

This is a wonderful activity to use not only as a springboard from the focus title, but also if you are conducting a thematic unit on the Middle Ages. Though classroom teachers have used the crayon resist or paper batik method for years, the activity takes on a very authentic look if it is done with stained glass designs and a black tempera wash. Although many stained glass windows in churches contain single colored panels, most of the individual panels in *Arthur and the Sword* are marbled. *Arthur and the Sword* was made to order at the request of many librarians, using stained glass secrets Robert Sabuda learned from his Aunti Joni. Ed Young uses oil pastels and a wash that create a resist effect in *The First Song Ever Sung*. Isn't the baby monkey on page 31 ir-RESIST-ible?

RELATED PICTURE BOOK TITLES
Andersen, Hans Christian (retold by Amy Ehrlich). *The Wild Swans*.
    Illus. by Susan Jeffers. Dial, 1981.
Macaulay, David. *Cathedral*. Houghton Mifflin, 1973.
Melmed, Laura Krauss. *The First Song Ever Sung*. Illus. by Ed Young.
    Lothrop, 1993.
Myers, Walter Dean. *The Dragon Takes a Wife*. Illus. by Fiona French,
    Scholastic, 1995.

SESSIONS: 2 or 3
ELEMENTS: color, form/shape, texture
PRINCIPLES: emphasis, variety, harmony
MATERIALS:
◆ white construction paper
◆ pencils
◆ crayons
◆ black tempera
◆ paintbrushes
◆ small container
◆ water

DIRECTIONS:
◆ Study the stained glass designs in the focus title, and research other designs in clip art books and nonfiction titles about gothic architecture.

- Instruct students to sketch a stained glass design, leaving a ¼" (6 mm) border between each section.
- Color each section with a heavy, dark coating of wax crayon. A marbled appearance can be created by layering complimentary or contrasting colors of crayon.
- When all sections have been colored, crumple the paper into a ball and then flatten it out again.
- Paint the entire paper with a coating of black wash (thinned tempera). The crayon will resist the tempera, but the white borders, between the colored sections will absorb the wash. The crumpling will also create wrinkled sections that absorb the wash, leaving a black veining effect.
- If needed, hold the paper under running water to remove excess wash from the colored sections. Place the paper between layers of newspaper to absorb excess water. A heavy textbook or dictionary placed on the newspaper layers for a few hours will flatten the paper nicely.

Something Else to Try!
- Research the look of Tiffany lamps or use commercially produced stencils of stained glass patterns.

Floor Plans

FOCUS PICTURE BOOK TITLE
Couture, Christin. *The House on the Hill.* Farrar, Straus & Giroux, 1991.

Although your students will not design their homes to conform to the National Model Building codes, this activity may spark an interest in some students to consider drafting or architecture as a career choice. When designing a home or recreating a bedroom, you can add or cut square footage in a plan and rearrange the space to meet your needs. Encourage your students to consider traffic patterns, easy access for windows and doorways, as well as space requirements for furniture. You will be surprised at the development of budding architects. For this project, your students will adapt the side views of rooms in *The House on the Hill* to an aerial view.

RELATED PICTURE BOOK TITLE
Anno, Mitsumasa. *Anno's Counting House.* Philomel, 1982.

SESSIONS: 2 or 4
ELEMENTS: line, form/shape, space
PRINCIPLES: harmony, proportion
MATERIALS:
◆ ¼" (6 mm) graph paper
◆ pencils
◆ erasers
◆ rulers
◆ templates (optional)

DIRECTIONS:
◆ Establish the scale or legend to be used in this activity. For simplicity, one square may represent a 1' x 1' (30.48 x 30.48 m) area. Therefore a 15 square outline would represent a 15' x 15' (457.2 x 457.2 cm) room.
◆ Direct students to draw the outline of a room or dream house.
◆ Once the room or house is drawn, students can draw furniture scaled to the size of the room on colored paper. The furniture can be cut out, manipulated around the rooms, then glued in place.

ADDITIONAL INFORMATION:
◆ Using blue-lined graph paper will enable you to photocopy the students' drawings onto white paper and give the students a clean copy of the design.

- Following are some standard drafting points you may wish to share with advanced students:
  - Interior doorways are 3' (91.44 cm) wide. Exterior doorways can be up to 4' (121.92 cm) wide. Students may show the direction the doors open with an arrow.
  - Interior doorways without doors are indicated with a double-dashed line.
  - Exterior and solid interior walls are shaded in when drawn on the diagram. Indicate hollow interior walls on the diagram with double-solid lines. Exterior walls are approximately 10" (25.4 cm) thick. Interior walls are approximately 4" (10.16 cm) thick.
  - Standard windows are 3' (91.44 cm) wide.
  - Bathrooms begin with a 5' x 8' (152.4 cm x 243.84 cm) room. A bathtub is 5' (152.4 cm) long.
  - Hallways are 3' (91.44 cm) wide.
  - Closets are usually 3' (91.44 cm) wide.
  - Plumbing is best utilized on a common wall. Two bathrooms usually back up to each other.
  - Building codes specify that the refrigerator and stove be on one wall with the kitchen sink on another.
- You may be able to contact a contractor, draftsman, or architect for discarded blueprints to share with students. These professionals also make great guest speakers.

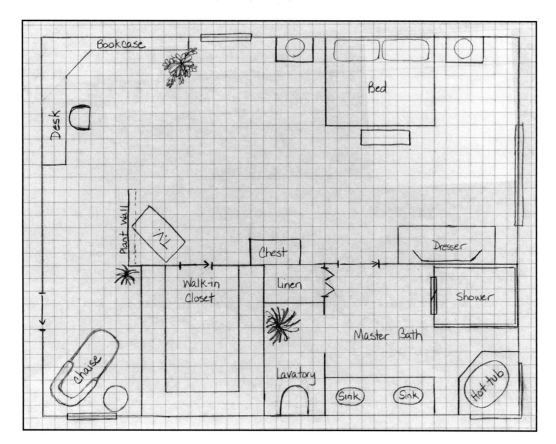

FOUR SEASONS

FOCUS PICTURE BOOK TITLE
Locker, Thomas. *Sky Tree: Seeing Science through Art.* HarperCollins, 1995.

The subject of Thomas Locker's *Sky Tree* is a single tree on a hill. Mr. Locker takes the reader on a journey through a year in the life of that tree. The fourteen tree paintings illustrate not only seasonal changes, but also changes in weather, light, and sky. In an ever-changing environment, the lone tree remains a constant. A highlight of this book are the accompanying background notes where Mr. Locker explains how he portrayed science through art in each painting. Thomas Locker says in his introduction to the book, "I have spent most of my life learning to paint trees against the ever changing sky. After all these years I still cannot look at a tree without being filled with a sense of wonder. . . . Through storytelling, art appreciation, and scientific exploration, *Sky Tree* attempts to reach both the heart and the mind." In this project your students can replicate story, art, and science as their sky trees weather four seasons of change.

SESSIONS: 1
ELEMENTS: color, line, form/shape
PRINCIPLES: emphasis, variety, harmony, proportion
MATERIALS:
◆ white drawing paper
◆ paper cutter
◆ pencils
◆ colored pencils

DIRECTIONS:
◆ Cut the 12" x 18" (304 x 457 mm) drawing paper into 4½" x 6" (114 x 152mm) pieces. Give each student four pieces. *Note:* One 12" x 18" (304 x 457 mm) sheet will supply enough paper for two students.
◆ Instruct students to sketch a leafless tree on a small hill much like the tree on the cover of the focus title on each of the four sheets of paper.
◆ Using the focus title, direct your students' attention on the following illustrations: The Summer Tree, The Autumn Tree, The Cloud Tree, and The Bud Tree. These trees most closely match the four seasons and work well with white paper. Instruct students to copy Thomas Locker's illustrations as closely as possible, paying attention to the detail of leaves and skies.
◆ Mount the four seasons on a colored construction paper background.

FRAMES & BORDERS

FOCUS PICTURE BOOK TITLE

Shelby, Anne. *Homeplace.* Illus. by Wendy Anderson Halperin. Orchard, 1995.

Frames and borders can enhance virtually any piece of artwork. In fact the appropriate frame is essential to many of the museum masterpieces in order to fully appreciate the work. Several illustrators of children's books, such as those featured in the focus and related titles, include decorative borders for many of their picture books. Wendy Anderson Halperin and Jan Brett typically add detail and dimension to the central illustrations in their books by showing simultaneous or sequential scenes in the decorative borders of titles such as *Homeplace* and *The Mitten.* The frames and borders of *St. George and the Dragon* surround both the illustrated and text pages. The frames around the illustrated pages give the illusion of looking out the glass of a window while the matching borders on text pages are decorated with story-related images such as flowers, fairies, and unicorns. Children, too, should discover how selecting frames or borders can add or detract from their own pieces of art. Rather than focus on a single method like most of the art projects in this book, this section offers a variety of frame and border techniques for young artists to try.

RELATED PICTURE BOOK TITLES

Brett, Jan. *The Mitten.* Putnam, 1989.

Hodges, Margaret. *The Kitchen Knight.* Illus. by Trina Schart Hyman. Holiday House, 1990.

————. *St. George and the Dragon.* Illus. by Trina Schart Hyman. Little, Brown, 1984.

SESSIONS: 1

ELEMENTS: color, line, space

PRINCIPLES: harmony, emphasis, informal/formal balance

MATERIALS:

- ◆ paper
- ◆ pencils
- ◆ rulers
- ◆ coloring media

DIRECTIONS:

♦ Probably the simplest way to frame a piece of artwork is to mount it on a larger sheet of construction paper. For a 1" (25 mm) frame, measure the length and width of the artwork and add 2" (51 mm) to each measurement. Select a complimentary color of construction paper and cut it to the new dimensions. Center and glue the artwork to the background paper.

♦ The reverse of mounting an illustration on background paper is to make an actual paper frame. Measure the original artwork and add 2" (51 mm) to the measurements. Cut the framing paper to the new dimensions. To create the inside edges of the frame measure 2½" (64 mm) from each side of the background paper and lightly draw the border. Cut out the inside of the frame. Place the frame over the artwork and attach it by gluing the overlapping edge.

♦ When working with watercolor, measure and lightly sketch a pencil border around the inside perimeter of the paper. Paint as usual within the pencil border. It is not necessary to have perfect straight edges with this technique. Slightly overlapping the penciled border creates an informal, yet dramatic effect.

♦ Measure and draw a 1" (25 mm) border around the inside perimeter of the paper. This time make the pencil marks heavy and straight. Allow the border lines to intersect at the ends, creating squares in all four corners of the paper. Color the top, bottom, and side panels one color and then fill in the corner squares with a complimentary color. This method is similar to the frames used on the front cover illustration and back cover of this book, *Art Projects Plus*.

♦ As before, measure and draw a border approximately 2" (51 mm) wide around the inside perimeter of the paper. Be sure to make the lines heavy and straight. Divide the top, bottom, and side panels into smaller sections. Sketch elements within the sections that complement the central illustration, or draw images that show simultaneous or sequential action much like a comic strip.

♦ Select a rubber stamp or design a potato cut and print a single repetitive border around a sheet of stationery or class assignment.

A GLOWING CHRISTMAS TREE

FOCUS PICTURE BOOK TITLE
Houston, Gloria. *Littlejim's Gift*. Illus. by Thomas B. Allen. Philomel, 1994.

Thomas B. Allen has illustrated three of Gloria Houston's books for young readers. He illustrated the text pages with pencil drawings and designed cover illustrations in pastel for the novels *Littlejim* and *Mountain Valor*. But in our opinion the pastel illustrations for Gloria's picture book *Littlejim's Gift* are Mr. Allen's finest work. Gloria Houston has said that Thomas Allen captured her daddy—the real Littlejim—on paper in these fine illustrations. The original cover art from *Littlejim's Gift* now adorns a wall of Gloria's mountain home. In the early 1900s Christmas was a special time for the Appalachian Mountain people of North Carolina. Families would gather in the community churches to celebrate the birth of the Savior with drama, singing, and a visit from St. Nick. Electricity had not yet made its way up the hills and hollows so the churches were ablaze with firelight and the radiant candles that decorated the trees. Your students can easily recreate the glowing tree depicted on the cover illustration and on page 25 of *Littlejim's Gift*.

RELATED PICTURE BOOK TITLES
Reed, Lynn Rowe. *Pedro, His Perro, and the Alphabet Sombrero*. Hyperion, 1995.
Van Allsburg, Chris. *The Polar Express*. Houghton Mifflin, 1985.

SESSIONS: 1
ELEMENTS: line, color, form/shape
PRINCIPLES: informal balance, variety, harmony, emphasis, proportion
MATERIALS:
◆ black construction paper
◆ chalk or pastels
◆ paper cutter (optional)

DIRECTIONS:

◆ Cut black construction paper to any size easily manipulated by your students.

◆ Distribute black paper and chalk.

◆ Direct students to draw a straight, vertical brown line in the center of the page for a tree trunk or draw only the part that shows beneath the tree.

◆ Draw the shape of the Christmas tree and fill in with green and blue branches and pine needles.

◆ Dot the entire tree with multicolored Christmas lights.

◆ Smear each light in a small circular motion and notice how the tree begins to glow.

Something Else to Try!

◆ Use the same effect to create the glowing lights of a city skyline at night such as those in *The Polar Express.*

HORIZONTAL PERSPECTIVE

FOCUS PICTURE BOOK TITLE

Paulsen, Gary. *The Tortilla Factory*. Illus. by Ruth Wright Paulsen.
Harcourt Brace, 1995.

To give landscapes a feeling of depth or distance as well as making them appear realistic use perspective. Draw objects and lines the way they appear rather than the way they really are. Objects appear smaller the farther away they are. They also usually appear higher on the paper the farther away they are. The oil paintings in *The Tortilla Factory* by Ruth Wright Paulsen show horizontal perspective in the rows of corn, the city block, and the inside of a warehouse. When viewing pages 12 and 13 it is easy to understand how the vanishing point of the corn row extends far beyond the edge of the page. On pages 16 and 17 you may need to convince your students that though the street appears to dead-end the vanishing point also extends off the paper.

RELATED PICTURE BOOK TITLES

Brown, Craig. *Tractor*. Greenwillow/Morrow, 1995.
Van Allsburg, Chris. *The Polar Express*. Houghton Mifflin, 1985.

SESSIONS: 1
ELEMENTS: line, space
PRINCIPLES: emphasis, rhythm, harmony
MATERIALS:

- drawing paper
- pencil
- ruler
- colored pencils (optional)
- pastels (optional)
- markers (optional)

DIRECTIONS:

- Draw a line across the paper horizontally, approximately one-fourth of the way down the paper for beginners. For experienced artists a horizontal line anywhere on the paper will work.
- Place a point on the line at any location, preferably at the center of the paper for beginners. This is called *the vanishing point*. Everything drawn will emanate from this point.
- Draw lines angling out and down from the vanishing point as guidelines for a street, sidewalk, path, fencerow, cornfield, etc.

- Draw a continuous row of objects such as trees, buildings, power poles, fence posts, along one or both sides of the road. Begin drawing the sequential objects in the foreground, making each successive object smaller until they eventually disappear into the vanishing point.
- A vanishing point may be created to extend off the paper by placing another paper under and above the paper on which you are working. This will allow objects drawn on the artwork to be larger as they are added to the background, and still remain in proper perspective to foreground objects.
- Color the drawing with pencils, pastels, or markers.

THE HUMAN BODY

FOCUS PICTURE BOOK TITLE
McKissack, Patricia C. and Fredrick L. *Christmas in the Big House, Christmas in the Quarters.* Illustrated by John Thompson. Scholastic, 1994.

All sizes, all shapes, all angles, all colors, all positions, so diverse, yet so much the same. There is a simple formula to use when drawing any human body because man was created in the image of God with more in common than disparate. The similarities and differences between people are masterfully illustrated by John Thompson in *Christmas in the Big House, Christmas in the Quarters*. The characters in this book are so real you expect them to move at any moment. You feel that you know them or have seen them before. Your students can begin by drawing people they know, and soon they will be successful—with lots of practice, and a formula. The related titles listed below offer perfect examples of the human body in motion. Check them out!

RELATED PICTURE BOOK TITLES
Alexander, Lloyd. *The Fortune-Tellers.* Illus. by Trina Schart Hyman. Dutton, 1992.
Babbitt, Natalie. *Bub or the Very Best Thing.* HarperCollins, 1994.
Catalanotto, Peter. *The Painter.* Orchard, 1995.
Hamilton, Virginia. *Drylongso.* Harcourt Brace, 1992.

SESSIONS: 1–3
ELEMENTS: line, form/shape
PRINCIPLES: informal balance, harmony, proportion
MATERIALS:

- white drawing paper
- pencil
- ruler
- tempera paint
- crayons
- butcher paper
- scissors
- wire hangers
- transparent packaging tape

DIRECTIONS:
HUMAN BODY PATTERNS
- Create a human body pattern sheet (see diagram) and distribute it to your students.
- Cut out the 14 pattern pieces for each human body.
- Direct the students to arrange the pattern pieces in the following positions to show the human form in motion: running, riding a bicycle, dancing, swimming, playing volleyball, handstanding, etc. Allow students to experiment with the patterns by creating other positions.

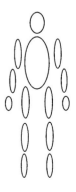

BUBBLE PEOPLE
◆ Using the human body pattern pieces as examples, direct students to draw the human body in motion using circles and ovals.

CLONING
◆ Measure each child's height, and distribute white butcher paper in that length to the student.
◆ Pair students. Place the length of paper on a smooth floor. One student will lay on the length of paper while the other student traces the body onto the butcher paper with a pencil.
◆ Students will cut out their own body forms and write their names on the back sides.
◆ Color in the body form of the clone with tempera or crayons. Students will need to recall the clothing they wore during the tracing session so it will match their shapes.
◆ Open a wire hanger and attach with clear tape to the back side of the clone.
◆ Sit the clones in the student chairs, bending the wire hangers to conform to the seats. Display at open house and ask visiting parents to find their cloned children.
◆ Cut the tape and remove the wire hangers before sending the clones home.

DRAWING THE HUMAN BODY
◆ Distribute a sheet of white drawing paper and a ruler to each student.
◆ Draw nine horizontal lines on paper spaced 1" (25 mm) apart. Number the sections 1–8.
◆ Follow these guidelines:

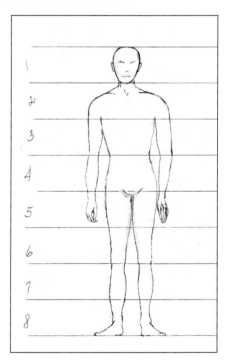

Section #1: Draw an egg-shaped head with the crown of the head touching the top line and the tip of the chin touching the bottom line.

Section #2: Draw neck, shoulders, and top of chest.

Section #3: Draw arms from shoulders to elbows and bottom of chest to the waistline.

Section #4: Draw arms from elbows to just above the wrists. Draw abdomen and hips.

Section #5: Draw wrists, hands, and upper thighs.

Section #6: Draw lower thighs to bottom of kneecaps.

Section #7: Draw upper shins and calves.

Section #8: Draw lower shins and calves, ankles, and feet.

ADDITIONAL INFORMATION:
The human body at any age can be divided into sections. If you count the head as one unit, an adult figure is about seven heads tall. A one-year old is four heads tall; a four-year old is five heads tall; a nine-year old is six heads tall. A young child's arms may be about two heads long, but a full grown man's arms are easily three heads long. When the arms hang at the sides, the tips of the fingers reach halfway between the hips and knees.

LANDSCAPES, SEASCAPES, AND SKIES

FOCUS PICTURE BOOK TITLE
George, Jean Craighead. *The First Thanksgiving.* Illus. by Thomas Locker. Philomel, 1993.

"Trees are not green, water is not blue, and neither is the sky!" With these words you may create a chaotic response from your students. Classroom teachers have taught that trees are green, water is blue, and clouds are white for so long that students actually believe it. The cover of *The First Thanksgiving* shows landscapes, seascapes, and skies—all in one, and demonstrates the realistic use of color perfectly on page 25. The sky is purple and salmon, the water is pink, and the grass is yellow. The beauty of nature is its diversity, and it should not be limited by the boundaries of traditional instruction. Display all of the Thomas Locker books you can get your hands on, and free students from those elementary concepts of color. "Yes, trees can be red!"

RELATED PICTURE BOOK TITLES
Armstrong, Jennifer. *King Crow.* Illus. by Eric Rohmann. Crown, 1995.
Locker, Thomas. *Anna and the Bagpiper.* Philomel, 1994.
————. *Sailing with the Wind.* Dial, 1986.
————. *The Boy Who Held Back the Sea.* Dial, 1987.
————. *Where the River Begins.* Dial, 1984.
Nakawatari, Harutaka. *The Sea and I.* Farrar, Straus & Giroux, 1990.

SESSIONS: 1
ELEMENTS: line, form/shape, color, space
PRINCIPLES: variety, harmony, proportion
MATERIALS:
◆ pencils
◆ white drawing paper
◆ coloring medium (preferably pastels)

Note: To simplify the activity, we recommend using pastels. Thomas Locker's illustrations are done in oil, but your students may achieve pleasing results with the use of acrylics on canvas.

DIRECTIONS:
◆ Pass out the picture books illustrated by Thomas Locker. Encourage students to record in their journals the colors they see and how they apply to the subject matter. Discuss how Thomas Locker's paintings show nature the way it truly is.
◆ After class discussion, pass out paper and coloring medium.

- Using illustrations from picture books, magazines, or photographs as models, begin sketching with pencil any landscape. Remind students that the sketches are informal lines, not dark, not detailed, and only catch the essence of the landscape.

- Using the Thomas Locker books as a reference, begin to add color to the landscape to achieve the desired time of day, season, light, and weather conditions.

- Discuss various strokes and techniques used with pastels. Explain how some strokes are soft and appear smudged. Some strokes are dark and definite, as used in outlining or defining an object.

- Clouds are blended with the edge of the finger, revealing the sky color through the edge of the cloud. The sky offers a complete palette of color from pink to lavender to gray. Water reflects the color of the objects around it. White is used as an accent to emphasize rushing water or where the sunlight directly touches an object. Trees have a multitude of color from the lightest of yellows to blue to brown and yes, even green.

- All trees are not the same shape, nor are they all straight as you can see in *Where the River Begins* and *The Boy Who Held Back the Sea.*

- Remember that water reflects whatever is above it. Tall objects are reflected further into the water, while short objects may not even appear in the reflection. Put some color of the surrounding area into the water, giving special consideration to the sky.

- The further away an object is from the viewer the lighter the color. Note how the trees become less detailed and the colors muted as they fill in the background. Their shapes are also less defined as can be clearly seen in *The Mare on the Hill.*

- Darker colors are used to denote shadows, and objects become less defined when this technique is used as in *Where the River Begins.* Caution students to determine where the sun is in their artwork, making the light come from the same direction.

- Practice the use of color demonstrated in *Snow Toward Evening.* The sky blasts with reds, yellows, teals, and purples. "Red at night sailors delight, red in the morning sailors take warning." In this activity, the sky is not the limit.

MASQUERADE MASKS

FOCUS PICTURE BOOK TITLE
Heller, Ruth. *Behind the Mask.* Putnam, 1995.

Much of a culture's beliefs and state of development can be determined by the masks they have left behind. Paintings and carvings of masks have been found dating back to the Stone Age. Creating masks is an enlightening activity to help students understand different cultures. The exquisite feathered and sequined masks on the front and back covers of Ruth Heller's *Behind the Mask* make it a perfect model for this project.

RELATED PICTURE BOOK TITLES
Charlip, Remy. *Harlequin and the Gift of Many Colors.* Illus. by Burton Supree. Parents' Magazine Press, 1973.
Day, Alexandra. *Carl's Masquerade.* Farrar, Straus & Giroux, 1992.

SESSIONS: 1
ELEMENTS: color, shape/form, texture
PRINCIPLES: balance, variety, harmony, proportion
MATERIALS:

- poster board
- paints
- crayons
- markers
- craft sticks
- glue
- glitter
- feathers, pom-poms, buttons, sequins, yarn (optional)

DIRECTIONS:

- Fold a piece of poster board—approximately the size of a finished mask with details—in half so the mask will be symmetrical.
- Using imagination or pattern, cut the shape of half of the mask from the poster board, allow space for decorative add-ons before cutting. Unfold the mask form.
- Mark eye holes on poster board and cut them out.
- Add decorative details using paints, crayons, markers, or extra materials such as yarn, feathers, pom-poms, buttons, sequins, glitter, etc. You are limited only by your imagination.
- When front is dry, glue a craft stick, painted or unpainted, to the side of the mask.

Something Else to Try!

Aluminum Foil Masks

Materials:
- five sheets of foil 15–20" (38–51 cm) long for each student
- scissors
- spray paint
- tempera
- glue
- eyeglass frames
- construction paper, felt, yarn, sequins, glitter (optional)

Directions:
- Tear off five pieces of foil that are longer than each student's head.
- Place the pieces of foil in a stack, making sure they are all turned the same way. Bend the edges slightly to hold the foil together.
- Lift the stack of foil and place it in front of the student's face. Very gently press the foil around the head. Mold the foil around the eyes, nostrils, brow, nose, mouth, and chin.
- Remove the foil from the student's face.
- Cut out openings for the eyes, nostrils, and mouth.
- Reshape the mask if it has become distorted during cutting, and roll under the sharp edges.
- Decorate the mask.
- Attach the mask to an old pair of eyeglass frames.

Hopi Kachina Mask

In the Hopi culture, the spirits of the people are called Kachina. There are more than 250 Kachina spirits altogether. The Polik Mana, or corn maiden, mask is used for the Corn Dance ceremonies.

Materials:
- black crayon
- black, yellow, red, and blue tempera
- paintbrush
- feathers
- construction paper
- scissors
- glue
- hole punch
- string

Directions:
- Prepare a basic mask.
- Paint geometric designs on the mask with black, yellow, red, and blue tempera. Students may choose to cut out geometric shapes (triangles, circles, squares) from scrap paper and apply them to the masks.
- Add feathers.
- Punch holes on the sides of the mask and attach a length of string to each hole.

Multimedia Illustration

FOCUS PICTURE BOOK TITLE
Scieszka, Jon. *The Stinky Cheese Man and Other Fairly Stupid Tales.* Illus. by Lane Smith. Viking, 1992.

Lane Smith does not limit his media when illustrating children's books like his Caldecott Honor title *The Stinky Cheese Man and Other Fairly Stupid Tales.* For starters, Lane Smith lays down a textured background created by the natural resistance of spray acrylic and spray varnish. Then, he incorporates a plethora of media including oils, rubber stamps, fingerprints, fabric, clip art (because he does not draw ducks well), found objects, U.S. currency, and of course, oil and vinegar. When your students have completed several of the art projects using paints, prints, and collage, they will be able to create a multimedia illustration much like the ones in *The Stinky Cheese Man.*

RELATED PICTURE BOOK TITLE
Bunting, Eve. *Smoky Night.* Illus. by David Diaz. Harcourt Brace, 1994.

SESSIONS: 2 or 3
ELEMENTS: line, color, space, form/shape, texture
PRINCIPLES: variety, harmony, emphasis
MATERIALS:

◆ construction paper
◆ paint medium
◆ print materials
◆ collage pieces
◆ glue
◆ scissors
◆ clear spray sealer

DIRECTIONS:
◆ Determine the number of media to be used in the illustration, making sure to include at least one paint medium, one print method, and one type of collage.
◆ Decide the order in which the media will create the successive layers.
◆ Begin with the background layer and build up with each of the selected media.
◆ Spray completed illustration with a clear sealer.

Natural Inks

FOCUS PICTURE BOOK TITLE
Cech, John. *Django.* Illus. by Sharon McGinley-Nally. Four Winds Press, 1994.

Before the advent of synthetic inks, scribes all over the world had no choice but to make inks from natural sources. Some artists of children's books have included natural products in the creation of their illustrations. To give readers a feeling for the woods, Sharon McGinley-Nally sponged layers of an all-natural beverage containing malt, chicory, rye, figs, and beet roots as a background for her illustrations in *Django*. In addition to the products listed below, seek out new and unique sources for natural ink.

SESSIONS: 1
ELEMENTS: color
PRINCIPLES: variety
MATERIALS:

- natural food products
- salt
- vinegar
- sieve
- bowls
- fountain pens (optional)
- paintbrushes (optional)
- sponges (optional)

DIRECTIONS:

- Direct students to bring to class a variety of natural food products such strawberries, blackberries, beet roots, blueberries, raspberries, elderberries, mulberries, boysenberries, cherries, etc.
- Press ½ cup (118.5 ml) berries through a sieve to extract the juice. Discard the remaining seeds and pulp.
- Stir in ½ tsp. (2.46 ml) vinegar and ½ tsp. (2.46 ml) salt.
- Choose from a variety of ink activities:
  - Write names with fountain pens using the natural ink.
  - Use a paintbrush to paint a name or scene.
  - Sponge paper to give a textured or antiqued look for other illustrations.
- Store remaining ink in a closed container.

Something Else to Try!

- Experiment with coffee, tea, green vegetables, red onions, and flowers.
- Use milk or lemon juice to make invisible ink.

PHOTOGRAPHY:
SEPIA TONE, COLORIZED, COLOR

Photography is a visual medium that is often overlooked in classroom art activities. With the advent of automatic 35 mm cameras, it is now possible for anyone, including children, to take great pictures. The following three activities were inspired by the sheer beauty of the photographs in these focus titles.

SESSIONS: 3–5
ELEMENTS: color
PRINCIPLES: emphasis

ACTIVITY 1: SEPIA TONE PHOTOGRAPHY

FOCUS PICTURE BOOK TITLE
Myers, Walter Dean. *Brown Angels: An Album of Pictures and Verse.* HarperCollins, 1993.

Students will enjoy the antique look of the pictures in *Brown Angels* and many other nonfiction titles such as Russell Freedman's photobiographies. If you are conducting a thematic unit on the Civil War, the Wild West, or Pioneers, an antique photography activity will add a unique dimension to the study.

MATERIALS:
◆ 35 mm cameras
◆ Ilford black and white 35 mm film
◆ period costumes

DIRECTIONS:
◆ Acquire at least one 35 mm camera.
◆ Purchase as many rolls of black and white film as you will need.
◆ Examine the clothing from the time period you are studying and direct students to collect and bring in similar pieces.
◆ Take pictures of students dressed in period costume. Explain how most people during the early days of photography did not smile for the camera because they had to freeze in position while the film was exposed. Any movement would result in a blurred photograph.
◆ Develop film by Process C-41, specifying that it is to be developed in sepia (brown) tone and not black and white.

ACTIVITY 2: COLORIZED PHOTOGRAPHY

FOCUS PICTURE BOOK TITLE

McMillan, Bruce. *Grandfather's Trolley.* Candlewick, 1995.

In the years prior to the advent of color photography it was only natural for artists to tint black and white or sepia tone photographs by hand, in an attempt to achieve a natural, colored look. Today students can experience what it must have been like to create color photographs in the "good ol' days."

MATERIALS:

◆ antique photographs
◆ ivory or beige copy paper
◆ copy machine
◆ colored pencils

DIRECTIONS:

◆ Instruct students to bring in old black & white or sepia tone photographs from home, with parent permission of course. 8" x 10" (20 x 25 mm) photographs will work best, but other sizes may be enlarged or reduced.
◆ Make photocopies of the antique pictures on ivory or beige copy paper. The photo quality feature on many copy machines will produce a more authentic-looking print.
◆ Using colored pencils, students will begin to colorize the print. Instruct them to color lightly and to smoothe and blend the colors with their fingertips.

ACTIVITY 3: COLOR PHOTOGRAPHY

FOCUS PICTURE BOOK TITLE

Yolen, Jane. *Water Music.* Photography by Jason Stemple. Wordsong/Boyds Mills Press, 1995.

Certainly color is the most common type of photography we use today. Many picture books such as *Water Music* illustrate how uncommonly beautiful professional photographers can make their work, especially when combined with lovely poetry.

MATERIALS:

◆ disposable cameras (optional)
◆ cameras
◆ film
◆ white copy paper

DIRECTIONS:

◆ Instruct students to go out and take pictures of nature. Look for a variety of plant and animal life and weather. Those students who do not own cameras can team with other children.
◆ Develop the film and bring the color prints to class.
◆ Direct students to allow the pictures to inspire poetry. Write simple free verse or haiku for each of the selected pictures.

◆ Write the final draft of each poem neatly on a sheet of copy paper, or type on a classroom computer and generate a printed copy.

◆ Glue the accompanying color photo to each page.

RELATED PICTURE BOOK TITLES

Cech, John. *Jacques-Henri Lartigue: Boy with a Camera.* Four Winds, 1994.

Cornelissen, Cornelia. *Music in the Wood.* Photography by John MacLachlan. Delacorte, 1995.

Freedman, Russell. *Immigrant Kids.* Dutton, 1980.

———. *Indian Chiefs.* Holiday House, 1987.

———. *Lincoln: A Photobiography.* Clarion, 1987.

Myers, Walter Dean. *Glorious Angels: A Celebration of Children.* HarperCollins, 1995.

———. *One More River to Cross.* Harcourt Brace, 1995.

Stanley, Jerry. *Children of the Dust Bowl.* Crown, 1992.

OTHER RESOURCES:

Clark Laboratories processes film by mail with processing centers in major cities across the nation. Their prices on film, developing, and enlarging are very economical. Their 5" x 7" (127 x 178 mm) prints are an exceptional value. Prints are usually returned within one week. For mailing envelopes write to:

Clark Color Laboratories, P.O. Box 96300, Washington, DC 20090

PORTRAITS

FOCUS PICTURE BOOK TITLE
Melmed, Laura Krauss. *The Rainbabies*. Illus. by Jim LaMarche. Lothrop, 1992.

The focus of a portrait is the face, and the face is the door to the soul. The best way to become proficient at drawing people and their faces is through practice. It's like playing the piano—the best way to get better is to practice. Before drawing, study faces in the mirror, in the classroom, in magazines, and in picture books. Here are a few faces not to be missed: the expression of joy on the faces of the husband and wife on pages 6 and 7 of *The Rainbabies;* the widow McDowell and son Thomas on page 33 of *The Christmas Miracle of Jonathan Toomey*; the beautiful African faces on page 19 of *The Fortune-Tellers*; the Native American faces in *Brother Eagle, Sister Sky*; Asian faces on page 36 of *Turandot*; the precious faces on any page of *Baby Angels*; and the diversity of all God's children on pages 28 and 29 of *The Dreamer*.

RELATED PICTURE BOOK TITLES
Alexander, Lloyd. *The Fortune-Tellers*. Illus. by Trina Schart Hyman. Dutton, 1992.
Cowen-Fletcher, Jan. *Baby Angels*. Candlewick, 1996.
Jeffers, Susan. *Brother Eagle, Sister Sky*. Dial, 1991.
Locker, Thomas. *Miranda's Smile*. Dial, 1994.
————. *The Young Artist*. Dial, 1989.
Mayer, Marianna. *Turandot*. Illus. by Winslow Pels. Morrow, 1995.
Mochizuki, Ken. *Baseball Saved Us*. Illus. by Dom Lee. Lee & Low, 1993.
Rylant, Cynthia. *The Dreamer*. Illus. by Barry Moser. Blue Sky/Scholastic, 1993.
Shepard, Aaron. *The Baker's Dozen*. Illus. by Wendy Edelson. Atheneum, 1995.
Wojciechowski, Susan. *The Christmas Miracle of Jonathan Toomey*. Illus. by P. J. Lynch. Candlewick, 1995.

SESSIONS: 1
ELEMENTS: line, form/shape
PRINCIPLES: proportion, harmony
MATERIALS:
◆ white drawing paper
◆ pencil

DIRECTIONS:
SCRIBBLE FACES
◆ Set up students in pairs. Students may decide who will draw first and who will be the model for the first session.
◆ Distribute a sheet of newsprint to each student, directing them to fold it vertically in half.

- There are two rules for this activity:
    1) Drawers must keep their eyes on the models at all times.
    2) Pencils must remain touching the paper until time is called.
- With a single continuous line, the drawer will scribble the face including hair, ears, neck, and all facial features on the paper.
- Allow approximately two minutes of scribbling time.
- Record the name of each model directly below the rendering and the illustrator's name in the lower right hand corner of the paper.
- The drawers and models will exchange roles and repeat the procedure.

Martha by Howard

Howard by Martha

DRAWING FACES
- Draw an egg-shaped head with the narrow end as the chin.
- Divide the oval into quarters by drawing one horizontal line and one vertical line.
- Draw ears with top edges beginning slightly above the horizontal line.
- Draw eyes on the horizontal lines, equally spaced from the vertical line.
- Draw another horizontal line connecting the lobes of the ears.
- Draw the nose on the vertical line, beginning between the eyes and extending to the horizontal line connecting the ear lobes.
- Draw a third horizontal line halfway between the bottom of the nose and the tip of the chin.
- Draw a mouth with the lower lip placed on the third horizontal line.
- Draw eyebrows above the eyes and hair on the head.

ADDITIONAL INFORMATION:
The following explanations may be helpful:
- eye level line–the first horizontal line that divides the head in half
- central axis–the vertical line that divides the head in half
- distance between eyes–divide eye level line into fifths and draw eyes within the second and fourth sections
- edge of nostrils–line up with the inside corners of the eyes
- outside corners of mouth–line up with the center of the pupils
- width of neck–as wide as jaw directly in front of ears
- hair line–approximately one-third of the way down from the top of the head to the eyes

POSITIONAL PERSPECTIVE

FOCUS PICTURE BOOK TITLE
Van Allsburg, Chris. *The Polar Express*. Houghton Mifflin, 1985.

The size and placement of objects in an illustration can greatly affect the viewer's perception. Look at Santa Claus in the sleigh soaring above the elves on pages 24 and 25 of *The Polar Express*. We know people around the world are relatively the same size, however, from this picture Santa appears normal and the elves below are mere dots. This demonstrates the use of positional perspective. One's position in the picture determines the actual surface size. In *The True Adventure of Daniel Hall* by Diane Stanley, the ships appear to be the same size as the boys' heads on page 35, then turn the page and suddenly the ship's portholes are larger than the heads of the men. The opening scene on pages 4 and 5 of *Flight* shows how the size and position of images on the page give the illusion of distance. Put it in perspective!

RELATED PICTURE BOOK TITLES
Burleigh, Robert. *Flight*. Illus. by Mike Wimmer. Putnam, 1991.
Stanley, Diane. *The True Adventure of Daniel Hall*. Dial, 1995.

SESSIONS: 1
ELEMENTS: space
PRINCIPLES: proportion, rhythm, emphasis
MATERIALS:
◆ paper
◆ charcoal or pencil
◆ colored pencils (optional)
◆ pastels (optional)

DIRECTIONS:
◆ Direct students to choose any subject they feel comfortable drawing as a set of three, such as boats on the sea, trees in a meadow, or horses in a pasture.
◆ Direct students to draw a horizon line within the top quarter of the paper.
◆ In the lower portion of the paper, students are to draw their three objects with the first in the foreground as the largest, the second in the middle ground half the size of the first, and the third object in the background the smallest of all.
◆ Fill the scene with additional objects, allowing some larger objects to overlap other smaller objects.
◆ Color if desired.

SCRATCHBOARD

FOCUS PICTURE BOOK TITLE
Pinkney, Andrea Davis. *Dear Benjamin Banneker*. Illus. by Brian Pinkney.
Gulliver/Harcourt Brace, 1994.

Crayons are very accessible to children and usually they are the tools that most children feel comfortable using. Because of this it is very important to show children new and exciting ways to create pictures with crayons, such as homemade scratch-boards. Brian Pinkney (see p. 138) purchases ready-made scratchboard, which is a white board covered with black ink. First he scratches a simple line drawing into the scratchboard, revealing the white board underneath. Then, he scratches away the background and adds the details. Finally, he rubs oil pastels into the scratches and finishes his work with oil paints. The scratchboard drawings in *When I Left My Village* are in black and white, while the illustrations in *Dear Benjamin Banneker* have been colorized with oil paints. Compare Michael McCurdy's scratchboard style in *Lucy's Summer* with Brian Pinkney's approach.

RELATED PICTURE BOOK TITLES
Hall, Donald. *Lucy's Christmas*. Illus. by Michael McCurdy.
Browndeer/Harcourt Brace, 1994.
———. *Lucy's Summer*. Illus. by Michael McCurdy.
Browndeer/Harcourt Brace, 1995.
Hughes, Langston. *The Dream Keeper and Other Poems*.
Illus. by Brian Pinkney. Knopf, 1994.
Kennedy, X. J. *The Beasts of Bethlehem*. Illus. by
Michael McCurdy. Macmillan, 1992.
Paul, Ann Whitford. *The Seasons Sewn:*
A Year in Patchwork. Illus. by Michael McCurdy.
Browndeer/Harcourt Brace, 1996.
Pinkney, Brian. *Max Found Two Sticks*. Simon & Schuster, 1994.
Schur, Maxine Rose. *When I Left My Village*. Illus. by
Brian Pinkney. Dial, 1994.

SESSIONS: 1
ELEMENTS: line, color, form/shape, texture
PRINCIPLES: variety, harmony
MATERIALS:
- white drawing paper
- black tempera paint
- crayons
- toothpicks or paper clips
- black oil pastel

DIRECTIONS:

◆ Cover desks with newspaper to catch the crayon residue that comes from creating the scratchboard.

◆ Cover the entire surface of sturdy paper with a heavy coat of brightly colored patches of crayon. Do not use black crayon in this step. Young children may tire of the continued pressure needed to cover the paper with color, so use smaller pieces of background paper.

◆ Using a dark oil pastel or tempera, completely cover the bright colors with a smooth coating until no original colors show through. Black, brown, or dark purple work best.

◆ Use a toothpick or opened paper clip to scratch the design revealing the colors underneath.

SCULPTURED ILLUSTRATIONS

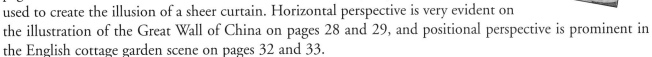

FOCUS PICTURE BOOK TITLE

Bogart, Jo Ellen. *Gifts*. Illus. by Barbara Reid. Scholastic Canada Ltd., 1994.

The delightful illustrations in *Gifts* and the related titles below were created using a sculpting medium called Plasticine. Similar illustrations can be made by following a simple recipe for homemade dough. Unlike Plasticine, the dough will harden so your creations will last. The illustrations in *Gifts* reveal how diverse this activity can be. Objects can be made with detail as minute as buttons and tassels or as simple as the wall covering a large area on pages 20 and 21. On the dedication page, what tools does Barbara Reid use to create the surfaces of the grandmother's dress, sweater, purse, and hair? On page 16 notice how the combination of Plasticine and acrylic paint was used to create the illusion of a sheer curtain. Horizontal perspective is very evident on the illustration of the Great Wall of China on pages 28 and 29, and positional perspective is prominent in the English cottage garden scene on pages 32 and 33.

RELATED PICTURE BOOK TITLES

Chase, Edith Newlin. *The New Baby Calf*. Illus. by Barbara Reid. Scholastic, 1984.
Oppenheim, Joanne. *Have You Seen Birds?* Illus. by Barbara Reid. Scholastic Canada Ltd., 1986.
Reid, Barbara. *Playing with Plasticine*. Morrow, 1988.
———. *Two by Two*. Scholastic, 1992.

SESSIONS: 2 or 3
ELEMENTS: texture, form/shape, space
PRINCIPLES: emphasis, variety, harmony, proportion
MATERIALS:

- flour
- salt
- water
- medium-size bowls
- rolling pin
- containers
- kitchen utensils
- paint
- paintbrushes
- clear spray sealer

DIRECTIONS:

◆ Display pages 10 and 11 from *Gifts*. The large images should be fairly easy for students to use as a model for their work.

◆ Each student will need to make two batches of dough, one for the background and one for the designs. Assist students in making the first batch of the dough recipe. Additional batches can be made on an as-needed basis.

◆ Combine 1 cup (237 ml) flour, 2 tsp. (9.86 ml) salt, and 2 cups (480 ml) water in a medium-size bowl. Knead the dough until it reaches a smooth, firm consistency.

◆ With a rolling pin, roll the first batch into a flat rectangle to create a background surface for the project.

◆ Make a second batch of dough to create designs to place on the flat dough surface. Use a variety of kitchen utensils and other tools to create texture in the objects.

◆ Attach dough art to the flat dough surface by creating a glue sludge with water and the dough mixture. If you are planning to hang the illustrations, you will need to implant small hooks into the back of the plaque or you may use adhesive hangers once it has dried.

◆ Allow the dough to dry overnight. Any piece that does not stay attached may be reattached with glue.

◆ Paint the project with acrylics for a glossy finish or use tempera for a matte finish.

◆ After the paint has dried thoroughly, spray all sides with a clear sealer. This will discourage damage by pests in later years.

Something Else to Try!

◆ Make a world map similar to the one on the endpapers of *Gifts* with homemade dough. What tool was used to create the equator and polar circles in the focus title?

THE STARRY NIGHT

FOCUS PICTURE BOOK TITLES

Pilkey, Dav. *'Twas the Night Before Thanksgiving.*
    Orchard, 1990.

Pinkney, Andrea Davis. *Dear Benjamin Banneker.*
    Illus. by Brian Pinkney. Gulliver/Harcourt Brace,
    1994.

The myth persists to this day that budding artists should not trace or copy the works of others. Actually the reverse is true. Even talented illustrators of children's books copy the works of the masters for various reasons. This procedure is called artistic parody. It parallels literary parody in that it reproduces for the purpose of humor or familiarity a well-known work. *'Twas the Night Before Thanksgiving* has "parody" written all over it. The delightful text is an obvious parody of Clement Moore's "A Visit from St. Nicholas." But be sure to find in the illustrations the artistic parodies of "American Gothic" and Vincent van Gogh's "The Starry Night." Who knows? The observant one may find others. The reproduction of "The Starry Night" in *Dear Benjamin Banneker* demonstrates that not all artistic parody is humorous. Not only did Brian Pinkney mimic van Gogh's work in the two scenes where Benjamin Banneker and Thomas Jefferson are writing each other, he actually researched the weather and phases of the moons so they would be accurate for the actual dates in 1791. Young artists have the opportunity to acquire an unlimited wealth of knowledge, particularly about technique and style, when they study or reproduce the works of other artists. Remember: Imitation is the highest form of flattery.

RELATED PICTURE BOOK TITLES

Barrett, Mary Brigid. *Sing to the Stars*. Little, Brown, 1994.

Crews, Donald. *Bigmama's*. Greenwillow/Morrow, 1991.

Hort, Lenny. *How Many Stars in the Sky?* Tambourine/Morrow, 1991.

SESSIONS: 2 or 3
ELEMENTS: line, color, space
PRINCIPLES: emphasis, harmony, proportion
MATERIALS:

- white drawing paper
- watercolors
- tempera
- chalk
- crayons
- colored pencils
- felt markers
- copy of Vincent van Gogh's "The Starry Night"

DIRECTIONS:

◆ Display a transparency, slide, filmstrip frame, or print of Vincent van Gogh's "The Starry Night."

◆ Note the dimensions of the cypress tree, the village, and of course the swirling stars.

◆ Lightly sketch the scene on white drawing paper.

◆ Point out the shades of blue, gray, green, and yellow that are used in the original painting.

◆ Apply color to the pencil sketches with the medium of choice.

STILL LIFE

FOCUS PICTURE BOOK TITLE
Flournoy, Valerie. *Tanya's Reunion*. Illus. by Jerry Pinkney. Dial, 1995.

Jerry Pinkney has infused the illustrations for *Tanya's Reunion* with still life scenes. The title page has a still life of utensils and ingredients for a cake recipe. The dedication page has a still life of a glowing oil lamp. On pages 24 and 25, when Tanya discovers Aunt Kay's sitting parlor, she finds a room filled with furniture, frames, lamps, blankets, baskets, and books. Turn the page and you will find another large room still life, this time in the kitchen. Though perspective is a prominent element in *The Tortilla Factory*, there is a simple still life opposite the copyright page accompanying the epigraph, as well as a two-page tabletop spread on pages 24 and 25. Explain to your students that although hands appear in this scene, the term "still life" refers to inanimate objects.

RELATED PICTURE BOOK TITLES
Flournoy, Valerie. *The Patchwork Quilt*. Illus. by Jerry Pinkney.
    Dial, 1995.
Manushkin, Fran. *The Matzah that Papa Brought Home*.
    Illus. by Ned Bittinger. Scholastic, 1995.
Paulsen, Gary. *The Tortilla Factory*. Illus. by Ruth Wright Paulsen,
    Harcourt Brace, 1995.
Riggio, Anita. *A Moon in My Teacup*. Boyds Mills, 1993.

SESSIONS: 2
ELEMENTS: line, form/shape, color, space
PRINCIPLES: proportion, informal balance, variety, harmony
MATERIALS:
◆ pencil, charcoal, colored pencils, markers, and/or pastels
◆ newsprint
◆ white drawing paper

DIRECTIONS:

Day One
◆ Collect a variety of bottles, baskets, bread, draping cloths, fruits, and vegetables.
◆ Set up two or three still life arrangements on tables around the room for small groups of students.

- Discuss how the objects look from their individual perspectives. It is important that neither the still life arrangement nor the students move until the first discussion is done. Students should be able to discuss within their groups the shape of the arrangement from any perspective, light and shadow, as well as how to use the nine lines of drawing with this project.
- Give students time to practice sketching the objects on newsprint. Their drawings may be as detailed as time allows. If students do not have time to complete the activity, direct them to be as detailed as possible on at least one area of their renderings.

Day Two
- Set up new still life arrangements, using at least three objects and a drape in this grouping.
- Before drawing, instruct students to discuss the objects within their group as before.
- Distribute white drawing paper and direct students to draw the still life arrangements.
- Color the pencil drawings with pastels, colored pencils, crayons, or markers. Charcoal drawings may be left in black and white.

Giles Laroche ◆ Wend
mmelman ◆ Tom Feelin
Tord ◆ Leslie Sills ◆ H
◆ Leonard Everett Fish
Novak ◆ Giles Laroch
◆ John Himmelman
Bijou Le Tord ◆ Lesl
Pinkney ◆ Leonard Ev
otto ◆ Matt Novak ◆ G
n Halperin ◆ John Himi
◆ Linda Shute ◆ Bijou
ilhelm ◆ Brian Pinkney
Peter Catalanotto ◆ Ma
◆ Wendy Anderson Ha
mmelma ◆ Tom Feel
Tord ◆ Leslie Sills ◆

ILLUSTRATORS

◆ Leonar Everett is
Novak ◆ iles Laroch
◆ John immelman
Bijou Le ord ◆ eslie
Pinkney ◆ Leonard Eve
otto ◆ Matt Novak ◆ Gi
n Halperin ◆ John Him
◆ Linda Shute ◆ Bijou
ilhelm ◆ Brian Pinkne
Peter Catalanotto ◆ 1
◆ Wendy Anderson H

SPEAK

man ◆ Tom Feelings ◆
Leslie Sills ◆ Hans Wilh
Everett Fisher ◆ Peter C
Giles Laroche ◆ Wendy
mmelman ◆ Tom Feelin
Tord ◆ Leslie Sills ◆ H
◆ Leonard Everett Fish
Novak ◆ Giles Laroch
◆ John Himmelman
Bijou Le Tord ◆ Lesl
Pinkney ◆ Leonard Ev
otto ◆ Matt Novak ◆ G
n Halperin ◆ John Himi
◆ Linda Shute ◆ Bijou
ilhelm ◆ Brian Pinkney
elings ◆ Linda Shute ◆ 1

ART: A HUMAN EXPERIENCE

by Leonard Everett Fisher

There is in my temperament a love of form, shape, line, and their arrangements as seen rhythmically, with or without color, under a light. Everything I look at or imagine is translated in these terms and stored in my memory bank. These are the elements to which I as an artist respond. These, the cells that structure an artistic soul, are the unmeasurable passage to my artistic nirvana. While form, rhythm, color, and light—words, too—serve my artistic passion, the immediate focus of my work in books for young readers is on who we are, where we originated, and what we have done for and to each other. I want my books to be avenues of knowledge, grace, and civility literally conceived and artistically expressed. I try to convey the humanizing aspects of art beyond the illustrative match of picture and word. My artistic compulsion welded as it is to varied interests, and having been transposed—in large part—to the book, has resulted, more or less, in the communication of my internal visions of the observable world, the dynamics of which I try to graphically and verbally express. I work mightily in language and pictures to deliver from the depths of my soul an indelible sense of the human experience as a work of art, and art as human experience.

Abstracted from Leonard Everett Fisher's Arbuthnot Honor Lecture
delivered at the University of Wisconsin, Milwaukee, May 5, 1995. Used by permission.

ARTISTIC DISCOVERY: EXTENDING THE STORY

by Peter Catalanotto

When I illustrate a picture book I'm always looking to extend the story with my paintings. Attractive pictures are not enough. The art must speak and add new dimensions to the story. I work in watercolor because I like the versatility. I can use it in thin layers to achieve a transparent look to show the passage of time as in *Cecil's Story*, or I can use many layers of paint to create a more solid, grittier look as I did in *An Angel for Solomon Singer*.

I also enjoy playing with the format of a book. I often put the title page after the story has started as in *Who Came Down That Road?* and *The Painter* (see p. 109). I love in movies where the story starts, then you see the title and credits, then the story continues. So I do it in my books. In *The Painter* I put the title on the back cover. I thought since the name of the book is *The Painter* it should only have a painting on the front.

I'm always surprised when people say they recognize my style of painting when they see a new book of mine. I never really thought about having a style. I believe an artist's style should be the artist's natural approach to painting. I'm never quite sure what a painting is going to look like when I start. I'll figure out the composition in advance, but the colors and what I'll render and what I'll leave muted and faded is figured out as I go along. The discovery as I paint is the most fun for me. An artist needs to be constantly using the mind as well as the hand.

CARTOONING

by Matt Novak

Cartooning is definitely an important aspect of my work. To many it may seem a frivolous and easy way to make a living, but I take art and humor very seriously. An acute knowledge of drawing humans and animals realistically is important before the artist can hope to draw simplified cartoons that really spring to life. Also, it is helpful to study body language and facial expressions. The way someone stands or the way they scrunch up their face can sometimes be funnier than anything they might say. Anyone who has a pet knows that animals can be very funny without uttering a sound. Combine that with the idea of talking animals and a whole new world of humor opens to the artist.

Above all the cartoon artist must be able to make people laugh with just a few strokes of a pencil, pen, or brush. It is all about simplifying and exaggerating those elements that will really bring out the most humor. Is someone's face long? Then make it really long! Is someone's nose big? Then make it really big! Duck feet, tiny heads, fat cats, or skinny dogs. Millions of things can be found in every day life to create humorous art, and that's what it's all about, taking the average everyday occurrence and turning it into something that will bring joy to millions. If not millions, at least maybe your mother will like it.

Cut-Paper Collage

by Giles Laroche

In the five children's picture books I have illustrated, the medium I have used is cut-paper collage or paper relief. Since my art school days I have experimented with various forms of collage in abstract works as well as more representational works and illustration.

The process of collage is what I find so appealing: the cutting out of shapes, the arrangement and overlapping of shapes, and finally gluing them into position according to a plan or by intuition. Add to the process the introduction of drawing and color media and we have the recipe for my interpretation of collage. For dramatic effect, at times, I will add spacers between selected collage elements and the support to create a sense of dimension. Since my collages must be photographed in order to be printed, they are carefully lit and of course shadows occur from the collage elements which protrude from the support. These shadows are intentional and help to enhance the dimensional quality of each illustration.

I have always enjoyed studying collages by Picasso, Braque, Schwitters, Ernst, Matisse, and in children's books, especially those of Leo Lionni. In my workshops with children in cut-paper relief we examine the various collage styles, and I encourage the children to pursue their own personal style. We begin with simple materials: white glue, scissors, and paper. Then we set a theme: a rainforest, coral reef, self-portraits and allow intuition and experimentation to lead us to completion of our individual projects or group mural.

DRAWING WITH CHILDREN

by Wendy Anderson Halperin

I love children's art. One of my dreams is to create a children's art museum. I would like to suggest the following drawing activities with children:

1) The Drawing Game: One student at a time draws something she/he likes to draw on the blackboard. The rest of the students copy it. Through this exercise students increase their drawing (visual) vocabulary. Later they can color the drawings. *Copying* is a magical way to learn to draw.

2) When children are beginning to learn to use crayons, I suggest that you offer them *small* pictures, not large areas for them to color! Encourage the children to color small pictures well. I find most coloring books and assignments overwhelming.

3) Memorization Game: To increase children's awareness of sight memory, hold up a picture, a cereal box, or simple design you have drawn. Have them look at the object for one minute and then take it away and ask them questions about it. If it is a simple design, have the children draw it.

4) People Drawing: It is never too early to expose children to the human skeleton. Learning to draw the skeleton is the beginning to learning how to draw people. Have children sketch the skeleton and then draw clothes on it, then hair, etc. Try drawing the skeleton in different positions. Allow children to discover their own bones. For example, the length from the top of the head to the bottom of the pelvis is approximately one-half of the body length. Notice how long the arms are, how the eyes are in the center of the head, and so forth.

A natural point of departure from studying and drawing the human skeleton is the amazing comparison of the human skeleton with an animal's. Drawing animal skeletons makes drawing animals easier and understandable.

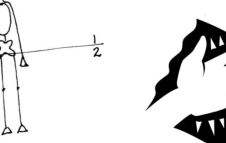

The Element of Surprise

by John Himmelman

The funny thing about my illustrations is that they rarely come out as they were originally perceived in my head. The mood is there, as is the theme and other necessary elements, but the visual representation is always slightly altered.

The concept starts as pictures in my brain, but that image has a long way to travel before it gets to paper. It goes from my head, down through my arm, into my hand, then through two fingers and a thumb, where finally it emerges at the tip of a pen or brush. Somewhere along that path is where the "distortion" takes place. I suspect it is in the cold, inanimate pen and brush. If I close my eyes and draw in the air with my finger I feel that I am drawing exactly what I am picturing. But the problem with that technique is that no one *else* can see it.

Over the years I have learned to compensate for this. I no longer see this as a bad thing. What ends up happening is I become surprised at the outcome, and that is what keeps my job interesting! You need surprises. You need challenges. In the case of challenging illustrations, where I have a difficult time conceiving how I will tackle it, something takes over and the picture makes its way to paper, seemingly without me, originating from somewhere I do not know.

Confidence plays a big part. I know from experience that the picture will come if I just sit down and start drawing.

ILLUSTRATING WITH SCRATCHBOARD

by Brian Pinkney

The way I make my pictures is with scratchboard. Do you know what scratchboard is? Well, if you do not know I will tell you. First, I buy my scratchboard from an art supply store. Scratchboard is a white board with black ink covering it. Then, I "scratch" my drawing into the black surface with a sharp tool called a "scratchboard nib." Now I have a very nice black and white drawing, but I am missing something. Color! So, I add colors with oil paint or gouache. I add the paint by rubbing it into the scratched lines. This is why my pictures look as if the color was added first.

When I was in elementary school we did scratchboard drawings by covering pieces of paper with colored crayons. Then, we covered the color crayon drawings with black crayons or ink. Finally, we scratched off part of the black crayon or inked surface with a toothpick or nail to make a colorful drawing. Maybe you can try it!

ILLUSTRATION FROM AN AFRICAN-AMERICAN PERSPECTIVE

by Tom Feelings

The talent that we possess does not belong to us. It was passed down to us from our ancestors, and they who can best express what our ancestors gave us have the most responsibility to pass this message on to the living and the unborn, so that it can live forever.

When I am asked what kind of work I do, my answer is that I am a storyteller, in picture form, who tries to reflect and interpret the lives and experiences of the people that gave me life. When I am asked who I am, I say, I am an African who was born in America. Both answers connect me specifically with my past and present . . . therefore I bring to my art a quality which is rooted in the culture of Africa . . . and expanded by the experience of being black in America. I use the vehicle of "fine art" and "illustration" as a viable expression of form, yet striving always to do this from an African perspective and African world view and above all to tell the African story—this is my content. The struggle to create artwork, as well as to live creatively under any conditions and survive (like my ancestors), embodies my particular heritage in America.

ILLUSTRATION FROM AN ASIAN PERSPECTIVE

by Linda Shute

Momotaro, the Peach Boy was my son-in-law's favorite story when he was growing up in Japan. With his and other advice, I retold the folktale. Making the pictures was harder. What clothes did the characters wear? When and where did they live?

Japanese art held the answers. In library books and museums I discovered *emaki*, the storytelling picture scrolls painted during Japan's medieval period (tenth to sixteenth centuries). Since Western fairy tales are set in Europe's Middle Ages, the time period of the *emaki* scrolls seemed perfect for *Momotaro*.

When I studied the old pictures, I found the characters of Momotaro's story. My monkey frolicked with rabbits in a twelfth century scroll and *oni* monsters prowled through other scenes. Scrolls held the wardrobes of costumes, too: Grandfather's straw boots and rain cape, Momotaro's armor, the tiger skin loincloths of the *oni*, even the patterns on the grandparents' kimonos.

The Japanese paintings often viewed scenes from above, the way I showed Momotaro leaving home and storming the *oni* gate. They let me peep into houses and yards to find tools and furnishings for my illustrations, such as the kimono "clothesline."

In these ancient scrolls, I discovered a prince weeping to leave his flowering plum tree, robed animals celebrating, ghosts and goblins marauding, neighbors tricking each other. I could not imitate the Japanese painters' style in my book, but I tried to honor qualities I found in their work: love of nature, emotion, imagination, and humor—art from the human perspective.

PICTURE BOOK DESIGN TIPS

by Robert Quackenbush

① ALWAYS KEEP PLENTY OF SPACE AROUND TEXT (AT LEAST 3/4" FROM TOP, BOTTOM, AND SIDES).

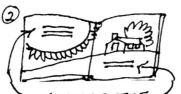

② IF TEXT IS PART OF THE PICTURE, CONTAIN IT IN A SHAPE, ON A SOLID COLOR WITH NOTHING TO INTERFERE WITH THE WORDS.

③ KEEP DIAGONALS OUT OF THE CENTER OF A SPREAD OR THEY WILL BECOME CROOKED WHEN THE BOOK IS BOUND.

④ LARGE HORIZONTAL SHAPES (AND LINES, TOO) CAN BE PLACED ACROSS THE CENTER OF A SPREAD, PROVIDING THERE ARE NO IMPORTANT DETAILS IN THE CENTER THAT MIGHT GET LOST IN THE BINDING.

⑤ LARGE VERTICAL SHAPES CAN BE PLACED AT THE CENTER OF A SPREAD, PROVIDING THERE ARE NO IMPORTANT DETAILS THAT MIGHT GET LOST DIRECTLY IN THE CENTER.

⑥ FOR OTHER VARIATIONS OF DESIGN, THE TEXT CAN BE PLACED IN BETWEEN VIGNETTE DRAWINGS WHERE ILLUSTRATIVE EXAMPLES ARE NEEDED FOR PHRASES.

From "Creating a Picture Book from Start to Finish," published by Robert Quackenbush Studios.
© copyright 1994. Used by permission.

RESEARCH: AN ADVENTURE

by Bijou Le Tord

Research is many things in my work: it is an adventure, a tool to help me be more authentic, a way to learn, a means of collecting and seeing things. Reading is the greatest part of this adventure. Everything I read and see is carefully recorded within me. This valuable information comes back to me at the precise moment I need it—when I create, when watercolor becomes sky, trees, a bird's feather. When words say what I want them to say, then I take from my collection of thoughts, emotions, and images.

Reading is one way for me to constantly add to my collection, to continue the adventure. I read more poetry than anything else because of the pictures in poems. I like to paint with words, as poets often do. Reading poetry makes me feel at peace with the world. It gives me warmth, like when you first meet someone you really like. At times it makes me feel like taking a pencil and immediately sitting down to work.

It happened that way when I read May Sarton's poem "Seascape" (1984). In her poem there is a sentence that refers to the gentle singing of the sea. I had found a friend, someone who felt the same way I did. I thought, "She expressed a feeling I have and want to talk about." It moved me, and I too needed to talk about the sea, whales, birds in the air. But, I also wanted to say something about God creating all living creatures and the earth and its natural order. I had recently researched the Book of Genesis. Inspired by May Sarton's poem and by my research, I found that words flew onto the page, and the story sparkled. May Sarton's sea was singing. My book, *The Deep Blue Sea,* was born.

At times I need a structure upon which to build. While writing *Joseph and Nellie,* a book about a family of fishermen, it was important for me to know how to draw a real fishing boat. How big was it? Where, exactly, in the hull would the lower cabin be? Would the motor run on diesel fuel or gas? Was the vision I had of Joseph's and Nellie's life at sea a realistic one? Did it represent a typical lifestyle for a family, a husband and wife who worked side by side on a trawler in the middle of the ocean? I had many questions, few answers.

Although I had spent a great deal of time on board many different kinds of boats, I needed reassurance. By chance, I have a friend who is a sea captain and a naval architect. From his house on the Chesapeake Bay, we drew the plans for Joseph's and Nellie's new fishing trawler. We carefully designed every inch of their boat. It would be a forty-footer, big enough for our fishermen to make a good living but small enough for two people to operate it safely and efficiently. I learned how to fold ropes neatly. I learned the meaning of starboard and port lights while steering in and out of the harbor. This new knowledge gave me the confidence I needed to go ahead and finish the illustrations with accuracy. From the beginning, my concern was whether Joseph's and Nellie's boat would float. And it did: it is still sailing across the sea.

If someone were to ask what makes research so important to the way I work, I would answer without hesitation, "Research adds dimension to my craft. It forces me to pay attention. It simplifies my work. It is probably the best tool a writer/artist has. There is no such thing as having too much information. Actually, one never has enough." Now, think of the adventure.

excerpt © 1992 by Bijou Le Tord. Used by permission.
Article first appeared in *Beyond Words; Picture Books for Older Readers and Writers.*
Heinemann, 1992.

SCULPTURE

by Leslie Sills

Although I am the author of *Inspirations: Stories About Women Artists* and *Visions: Stories About Women Artists*, I am also an artist. When I am not writing or teaching, I create sculptures out of clay, wood, papier-mâché, fabric, paint, and any unusual material I think my sculpture needs.

My most recent sculptures are bird women. First I model a woman's head out of clay. Sometimes I look at a photograph or examine myself in the mirror or just make up a face based on my feelings. Then I build the body with wire mesh by cutting out shapes and "sewing" them together with wire. Afterwards, I have to think about how it will stand and hold up the clay head which is fired in a kiln. I usually put a dowel inside that extends from the hollow head into the tail. Then I attach carved wooden feet to the dowel through openings in the wire mesh. But before I put the head on permanently, I cover the body with papier-mâché and fill it with plaster for balance. The most fun comes when deciding how to paint her face and dress her feathers.

The face of Hen (see photograph) is pink, green, and yellow with lilac eyes! The body is covered with flowered magenta velvet fabric. I also painted on the fabric with silver and bronze oils which makes it feel like an angel, in addition to being a bird.

All my pieces are different but they all reflect my feelings about being female and connected to nature.

THE VERSATILITY OF WATERCOLORS

by Hans Wilhelm

My favorite medium is watercolor. I like it because you never know in advance how the pictures will come out. Watercolor seems to have a life of its own. It is full of surprises.

When the wet colors run into each other they may create the most astonishing effects—but they can also ruin the entire picture. Then I have to do it all over again. And again—if necessary—until I am happy with the picture. Some of the drawings in my books were redone as many as six times before I finally got it right. So, do not give up when it does not work out the first time.

When the picture is dry I often add colored pencil or another medium. I may also sprinkle some water—or even bleach—on the dry painting to create some startling effects. This often works well on pictures of trees and bushes. They come alive when I sprinkle some water on them and let the water soak into the paint for a few moments before drying the painting with a paper towel.

Never be shy when you use watercolor paints. The more you play with them the more surprising pictures you will create. Have fun! Hopefully it will be as much fun as I have when I make my books for you!

APPENDICES

The Ten Commandments
of Teaching Art to Children

1. Thou shalt allow budding artists to have more than one sheet of paper.

2. Thou shalt not compare the artwork of young artists to each other or the work of the masters.

3. Thou shalt not criticize the efforts of young artists.

4. Thou shalt allow young artists to trace, mimic, or reproduce the work of other artists.

5. Thou shalt display all artwork created by young artists on every available bulletin board, wall, storage cabinet, shelf, filing cabinet, teacher's desk, and any other free classroom surface before sending them on to the refrigerator galleries at home.

6. Thou shalt ignore all desktop disaster areas supporting the creative process (until clean-up time, of course).

7. Thou shalt not allow the words "I can't draw!" to be spoken in your classroom.

8. Thou shalt say, "Tell me about your picture" no matter how abstract it may be.

9. Thou shalt exalt the insecure, magnify the minute, praise the artistically challenged, and applaud all efforts.

10. Thou shalt have fun!

Art Curriculum Basics K-6

Perhaps you are wondering how to teach the elements of art and make them relevant to the students in your classroom. Will you need to create a whole new set of situations to teach art? How can you use what your students already know? Students in grades K–6 are capable of understanding the content and exploring the activities suggested below. These suggestions are not exhaustive, but relate specifically to the art projects in this book.

KINDERGARTEN
The following are ideas and feelings appropriate for this grade level when teaching art to children:
◆ personal experiences with family, friends, pets, toys, common plants, animals, birds, vehicles, buildings, seasons of the year, kinds of weather, and familiar places—being aware of how they look, move, sound and feel
◆ imaginative experiences including dreams, dramatic play, and pretend
◆ stories, poems, movies, TV, videos, computer, photographs, music, and reproductions of works of art

The art elements kindergarten children can readily learn are:
◆ recognition and use of color: red, yellow, blue, orange, green, violet, black, white, brown
◆ recognition and use of line: long, short, thick, thin, curved, straight, looped, zigzagged, dotted
◆ recognition and use of form/shape: circle, square, rectangle, triangle
◆ understanding similarities and differences in texture: thick/thin, rough/smooth, coarse/slick, warm/cold, soft/hard
◆ recognition and use of two-dimensional space:
   • manipulate large, thick crayons using point, side, and end
   • experiment with tempera paint and large brush
   • paint directly on large paper to express ideas and feelings
   • draw with chalk or crayon on a variety of colored papers
   • finger paint with one color and develop patterns
   • cut paper freely with scissors
   • tear or cut paper of different hues and textures into free forms and arrange and fasten on a background
   • lace or sew with yarn on open-mesh material
   • assemble precut pieces of cloth using large needle and coarse thread
   • use expression in a class book, video, greeting card, curtains or wallpaper for a playhouse, costume accessories, holiday decoration, puppets (stick, finger, or one-string), or large group picture from assembled cutouts
   • make rubbings or splatter prints
   • make original cuttings or tearings
◆ recognition and use of three-dimensional space:
   • fold, cut, and build with strips of paper
   • roll, pinch, press, mold with clay or dough
   • cut and assemble pieces of soft wood
   • relationships: near/far, above/below, high/low

GRADES ONE AND TWO
The following are ideas and feelings appropriate for these grade levels when teaching art to children:
◆ personal experiences with family, friends, other people, seasons of the year, travel and transportation, plants and animals, sensory experiences with seeing, touching, listening, tasting, and smelling, exploring materials and processes
◆ imaginative experiences including pretending to be other people or things, using objects and natural forms to create a fantasy world, and dreams
◆ stories, poems, music, movies, TV, videos, computer, slides, photographs, and reproductions of works of art

The art elements first and second grade children can readily learn in addition to previously mentioned grade level concepts are:

- ◆ recognition and use of color:
  - • primary and secondary hues
  - • warm and cool hues
  - • shaded and tinted hues
  - • dark and light hues
- ◆ recognition and use of line: the nine drawing lines
- ◆ recognition and use of form/shape: basic geometric shapes
- ◆ understanding similarities and differences in texture: same as above
- ◆ recognition and use of two-dimensional space:
  - • essential characteristics of places and things
  - • likenesses and differences in shape and size of objects in the environment
  - • use crayon, paint, and chalk on various papers in an exploratory and manipulative way
  - • combine crayon and paint in a resist process
  - • make rubbings or prints from nature, found objects, string, or original forms
  - • stitch a design on coarse cloth
  - • fasten cut-out material to background with thread or yarn
  - • use expression in illustrations for individual or group book, mural, greeting cards, charts, holiday decorations
- ◆ recognition and use of three-dimensional space:
  - • fold, cut, bend, curl, fringe, paste, staple, and slot paper of different shapes, sizes, and weight
  - • build with strips of paper over a form
  - • use simple tools in wood construction
  - • make objects and structures for room displays, items in a unit of study, illustrate a story or song, create holiday decorations and gifts, or build a diorama

GRADES THREE AND FOUR

The following are ideas and feelings appropriate for these grade levels when teaching art to children:

- ◆ personal experience with people doing things: playing, working, traveling
- ◆ personal experience with different places: inside and outside
- ◆ personal experiences with nature: plants, animals, weather, water
- ◆ faraway places and ties as well as the immediate environment as experienced in stories, poems, music, TV, movies, videos, slides, photographs, and reproductions of works of art.

The art elements third and fourth grade children can readily learn in addition to previously mentioned grade level concepts are:

- ◆ recognition and use of color: primary, secondary, and tertiary hues, neutral hues, analogous and complementary hues, light and dark value, dull and bright intensity, warm and cool qualities
- ◆ recognition and use of line: the nine drawing lines, broken, horizontal, vertical, diagonal
- ◆ recognition and use of form/shape: geometric, representational, and natural
- ◆ understanding similarities and differences in texture: variation in surface quality, regular and irregular pattern, large and small scale, understanding relationships
- ◆ recognition and use of two-dimensional space:
  - • scratch through layers of crayon
  - • use several hues of chalk with point or side on wet or dry surfaces
  - • paint with tempera using a variety of brushes, sponges, or pieces of cardboard
  - • paint with watercolors on wet and dry surfaces
  - • print with various objects including kitchen gadgets, rubber cutouts, vegetables, and stencils
  - • cut, tear, and arrange a variety of paper into free, geometrical, or representational shapes

- stitch original designs with a variety of yarns
- appliqué original cut pieces of material
- use expression to illustrate books, charts, videos, murals, wall hangings, greeting cards, maps, and dictionaries
◆ recognition and use of three-dimensional space:
  - build forms with clay by pinch, slab, and coil methods
  - use a variety of surface treatments for clay objects
  - cut, assemble, and finish forms of woods
  - construct forms from paper by cutting on several folds, bending, slotting, fringing, curling, pasting, and stapling

GRADES FIVE AND SIX

The following are ideas and feelings appropriate for these grade levels when teaching art to children:

◆ personal experiences in direct observation of changing conditions in nature, how people appear as they move or change positions, people engaging in a variety of activities, animals at rest and at play, buildings and vehicles from many points of view, sensory reactions to people, objects, and nature
◆ imaginative experiences including daydreams and projection into the future
◆ research experiences in books, music, movies, videos, computer, TV, photographs, scientific experiments, and reproductions of works of art

The art elements fifth and sixth grade children can readily learn in addition to previously mentioned grade level concepts are:

◆ recognition and use of color: primary, secondary, and tertiary hues and how to change them in value or intensity, monochromatic hues
◆ recognition and use of line: different kinds, qualities, and direction
◆ recognition and use of form/shape: geometric, representational, and organic
◆ understanding similarities and differences in texture: qualities of surface, regular and irregular pattern
◆ recognition and use of two-dimensional space:
  - draw with pencil, crayon, and felt tip pens in contour and gesture
  - use crayon and charcoal in many ways on a variety of surfaces
  - use watercolors for color fusion, flat and graded washes, free brush drawing, bleeding and shading on wet and dry surfaces
  - combine several drawing and painting media
  - select, cut, and arrange various materials as a collage
  - use stitchery and appliqué with a variety of materials
  - use expression in books, murals, wall hangings, greeting cards, maps, charts, and time lines
◆ recognition and use of three-dimensional space:
  - carve soap, soft wood, wax, or plaster
  - use pliable wire and thin metal for construction

The Elements of Art

There are five basic elements of art: color, form/shape, line, space, texture. The elements are governed by the principles of art.

COLOR

color • red, orange, yellow, green, blue, indigo, violet
hue • a color's name or its position in the spectrum
primary hues • yellow, red, blue
secondary hues • orange, purple, green
tertiary hues • yellow-green, yellow-orange, red-orange, red-purple, blue-purple, blue-green; intermediate hues
neutral hues • white, black, gray
analogous hues • adjacent hues on the color wheel
complementary hues • opposite colors on the color wheel
intensity • brightness or dullness of a hue
monochromatic hues • different values of a single color
value • lightness or darkness of a hue
shade • any hue blended with black
tint • any hue blended with white
warm hues • tints of red, yellow, and orange
cool hues • shades of green, blue, and purple

FORM/SHAPE

form/shape • the outline or external contour of an object
organic • forms or shapes that occur in nature
geometric • forms or shapes characterized by points, lines, angles, planes, and measure

LINE

line • a continuous mark or stroke: long, short, thick, thin, straight, zigzagged, curved, looped, dotted

SPACE

space • the area occupied by an object
two-dimensional space • objects reflecting height and width
three-dimensional space • objects reflecting height, width, and depth; positional perspective (overlapping) and horizontal/vertical perspective (vanishing point)

TEXTURE

texture • the surface characteristics of an object: soft, hard, smooth, rough, even, uneven

The Color Wheel

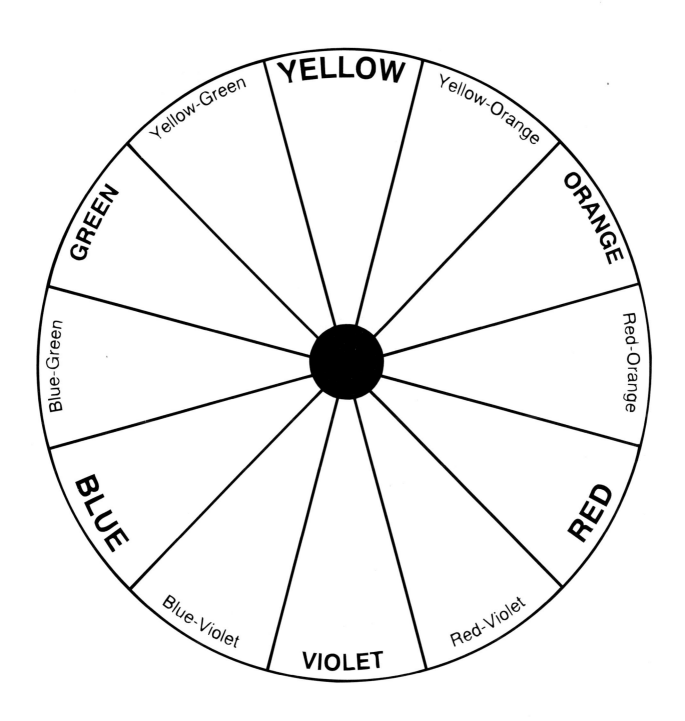

The Principles of Art

The principles of art are balance, variety, harmony, emphasis, proportion, movement, rhythm, and unity. They are guidelines that govern the way the elements of art work together.

The first principle of art—balance—works independently of the other principles, ensuring that the elements of art are arranged in a pleasing manner so that certain parts of a work do not seem heavier than other areas.

BALANCE • the arrangement of elements in a work of art so that no single part overpowers another part
    formal balance • when one half of a work of art is symmetrical or mirrors the opposite half
    informal balance • when asymmetrical elements through the use of hues, values, intensities, and shapes appear to be equally arranged
    radial balance • when objects are positioned equally around a focal point

Variety, harmony, emphasis, and proportion are principles of art that work together to ensure that a work of art is interesting and pleasing to the eye.

VARIETY • the combined use of distinct elements of art in a work to create visual excitement; the opposite of harmony
HARMONY • the blended use of distinct elements of art in a work to create visual repose; the opposite of variety
EMPHASIS • the use of an element of art in a work to draw immediate attention to a certain part of the whole
PROPORTION • the way the elements of art cause individual parts of a work to connect with one another and to the whole

The principles of movement and rhythm help the elements of art to make a work of art come alive.

MOVEMENT • the way the elements of art cause the observer to sense motion in a work; the principle that invites the observer to become involved with a work
RHYTHM • the repetition of elements in a work of art that make it appear active

Unity

Unity integrates the elements and principles of art in a work, giving it an intangible quality that holds it together. An observer is able to discern both when unity is present and when it is missing from a work of art.

UNITY • the combined use of the elements and principles of art to create a sense of wholeness

Picture Books to Take Your Breath Away

Howard: Hey Martha, while we've got these picture books spread all over the floor we ought to pick out our favorites and compile a bibliography so we won't forget what they are.

Martha: Okay, but just a few because I'm not going to be here typing all night.

Howard: We could publish the list in *Art Projects Plus*, but why would anyone value our opinions?

Martha: Oh, come on Howard, we've only spent thousands of dollars on picture books, hitting every distributor's warehouse, publisher's outlet, Barnes & Noble, used bookstore, and sale table between Miami and Manhattan.

Howard: Well, we've read picture books to our students for years, and we know what kids like. . . . so what will the selection criteria be?

Martha: How about the same criteria that the Caldecott committees use?

Howard: You know how often we accurately predict the Caldecott winners!

Martha: You're right, Howard. Though we love them dearly, somehow the Caldecott committees always fail to select our favorites, even as Honor titles.

Howard: Well, I think we should just teach the American Library Association a thing or two. Who cares if P. J. Lynch is British?

Martha: Howard, you know how you always say, "Ooh!" when you first open a pretty book. Why don't we just list books that have taken our breath away?

Howard: That's a great idea, but we will not be influenced at all by the picture books that make us squall.

Martha: Oh, okay, I would *never* let a moving story affect my perceptions of the illustrations in a picture book like you did when you read *Pink and Say* to me on the way home from Haslam's or when you read to Carla *My Great-Aunt Arizona* on the way to Gloria's house.

Howard: Are you making fun of me, Ms. Cry-At-Commercials?

Martha: I would never do that! (Sniff! Sniff!) I think we should pick only picture books that we *both* think are exceptional.

Howard: And you know how often we agree . . . on anything.

Martha: Okay, let's pick out the ones we both like and then some personal favorites.

Howard: Okay, but we have to have the same number, and only one Thomas Locker each!

Disclaimer: We don't claim to have considered or have even seen every lovely picture book ever published, and we don't deny the beauty of thousands of books not listed, possibly some of your personal favorites. These are just some titles that are guaranteed to take your breath away. Some we paid through the nose for and other treasures were found on sale tables, but we didn't allow ourselves to be prejudiced at all by the dollar sign. Some of the titles feature well-known and popular artists, and others are illustrated by relatively unknown names or newcomers with a certain future. Though we love many books by our favorite artists, we have limited our mutual selections to the single titles we believe to be superior for each illustrator. The titles are listed alphabetically by the authors' last names to simplify acquisition, however we have highlighted the illustrators' names in boldface to give honor where honor is due.

MUTUAL FAVORITES

Alexander, Lloyd. *The Fortune-Tellers*. Illus. by **Trina Schart Hyman**. Dutton, 1992.
Baillie, Allan. *Drac and the Gremlin*. Illus. by **Jane Tanner**. Dial, 1989.
Base, Graeme. *Animalia*. Abram, 1987.
Conrad, Pam. *The Lost Sailor*. Illus. by **Richard Egielski**. HarperCollins, 1992.
Feelings, Tom. *The Middle Passage*. Dial, 1995.
Foreman, Michael. *War Game*. Arcade, 1993.
Graham, Ruth Bell. *One Wintry Night*. Illus. by **Richard Jesse Watson**. Baker, 1994.

Harris, Robie H. *Happy Birth Day!* Illus. by **Michael Emberley**. Candlewick Press, 1996.

Heller, Ruth. *Merry-Go-Round: A Book About Nouns.* Grosset & Dunlap, 1990.

Houston, Gloria. *Littlejim's Gift: An Appalachian Christmas Story.* Illus. by **Thomas B. Allen**, Philomel, 1994.

Houston, Gloria. *My Great-Aunt Arizona.* Illus. by **Susan Condie Lamb**. HarperCollins, 1992.

————. *The Year of the Perfect Christmas Tree.* Illus. by **Barbara Cooney**. Dial, 1988.

Jewell, Nancy. *Christmas Lullaby.* Illus. by **Stefano Vitale**. Clarion, 1994.

Johnson, James Weldon. *The Creation.* Illus. by **James E. Ransome**. Holiday House, 1994.

Kalman, Esther. *Tchaikovsky Discovers America.* Illus. by **Laura Fernandez** and **Rick Jacobson**. Orchard, 1994.

Kismaric, Carole. *The Rumor of Pavel and Paali: A Ukrainian Folktale.* Illus. by **Charles Mikolaycak**. Harper & Row, 1988.

Lester, Julius. *John Henry.* Illus. by **Jerry Pinkney**. Dial, 1994.

Lucado, Max. *Tell Me the Story: A Story for Eternity.* Illus. by **Ron DiCianni**. Crossway, 1992.

Macaulay, David. *Cathedral: The Story of Its Construction.* Houghton Mifflin, 1973.

MacLachlan, Patricia. *All the Places to Love.* Illus. by **Mike Wimmer**. HarperCollins, 1994.

McKissack, Patricia C. and Fredrick L. *Christmas in the Big House, Christmas in the Quarters.* Illus. by **John Thompson**. Scholastic, 1994.

McMillan, Bruce. *Grandfather's Trolley.* Candlewick Press, 1995.

Melville, Herman. *Catskill Eagle.* Illus. by **Thomas Locker**. Philomel, 1991.

Myers, Walter Dean. *Brown Angels: An Album of Pictures and Verse.* HarperCollins, 1993.

Novak, Matt. *Claude and Sun.* Bradbury, 1987.

Pinkney, Andrea Davis. *Dear Benjamin Banneker.* Illus. by **Brian Pinkney**. Gulliver/Harcourt Brace, 1994.

Polacco, Patricia. *Pink and Say.* Philomel, 1994.

Reid, Barbara. *Two by Two.* Scholastic, 1992.

Rohmann, Eric. *Time Flies.* Crown, 1994.

Rosenberg, Liz. *The Carousel.* Illus. by **Jim LaMarche**. Harcourt Brace, 1995.

Rylant, Cynthia. *The Dreamer.* Illus. by **Barry Moser**. Blue Sky/Scholastic, 1993.

Sabuda, Robert. *Arthur and the Sword.* Atheneum, 1995.

Scieszka, Jon. *The Stinky Cheese Man and Other Fairly Stupid Tales.* Illus. by **Lane Smith**. Viking, 1992.

Shannon, David. *The Amazing Christmas Extravaganza.* Blue Sky/Scholastic, 1995.

Shelby, Anne. *Homeplace.* Illus. by **Wendy Anderson Halperin**. Orchard, 1995.

Tazewell, Charles. *The Littlest Angel.* Illus. by **Paul Micich**. Ideals, 1991.

Van Allsburg, Chris. *The Polar Express.* Houghton Mifflin, 1985.

Whatley, Bruce and Rosie Smith. *Whatley's Quest.* Illus. by **Bruce Whatley**. HarperCollins, 1994.

Wiesner, David. *Tuesday.* Clarion, 1991.

Wisniewski, David. *Sundiata: Lion King of Mali.* Clarion, 1992.

Wojciechowski, Susan. *The Christmas Miracle of Jonathan Toomey.* Illus. by **P. J. Lynch**. Candlewick Press, 1995.

Wood, Audrey. *King Bidgood's in the Bathtub.* Illus. by **Don Wood**. Harcourt Brace, 1985.

Yolen, Jane. *Water Music.* Photographs by **Jason Stemple**. Wordsong/Boyds Mills, 1995.

HOWARD'S FAVORITES

Armstrong, Jennifer. *King Crow.* Illus. by **Eric Rohmann**. Crown, 1995.

Birchman, David F. *The Raggly Scraggly No-Soap No-Scrub Girl.* Illus. by **Guy Porfirio**. Lothrop, 1995.

Brett, Jan. *The First Dog.* Harcourt Brace, 1988.

Froehlich, Margaret Walden. *That Kookoory!* Illus. by **Marla Frazee**. Browndeer/Harcourt Brace, 1995.

Dewan, Ted. *3 Billy Goats Gruff.* Scholastic, 1994.

Locker, Thomas. *Anna and the Bagpiper.* Philomel, 1994.

Polacco, Patricia. *Just Plain Fancy.* Bantam, 1990.

Spier, Peter. *Peter Spier's Rain.* Doubleday, 1982.

Rylant, Cynthia. *The Relatives Came.* Illus. by **Stephen Gammell**. Macmillan, 1985.

MARTHA'S FAVORITES

Brett, Jan. *The Wild Christmas Reindeer.* Putnam, 1990.
Day, Alexandra. *Carl's Masquerade.* Farrar, Straus & Giroux, 1992.
Frank, Josette (ed.). *Snow Toward Evening: A Year in a River Valley.* Illus. by **Thomas Locker**. Dial, 1990.
Hodges, Margaret. *St. George and the Dragon.* Illus. by **Trina Schart Hyman**. Little, Brown, 1984.
Melmed, Laura Krauss. *The Rainbabies.* Illus. by **Jim LaMarche**. Lothrop, 1992.
Polacco, Patricia. *Babushka Baba Yaga.* Philomel, 1993.
Shepard, Aaron. *The Baker's Dozen: A Saint Nicholas Tale.* Illus. by **Wendy Edelson**. Atheneum, 1995.
Van Allsburg, Chris. *Jumanji.* Houghton Mifflin, 1981.
Yolen, Jane. *Owl Moon.* Illus. by **John Schoenherr**. Philomel, 1987.

Resources

ART-RELATED PICTURE BOOKS

Baker, Alan. *White Rabbit's Color Book.* Kingfisher, 1994.
Capek, Michael. *Artistic Trickery: The Tradition of Trompe L'Oeil Art.* Lerner, 1995.
Catalanotto, Peter. *The Painter.* Orchard, 1995.
Christelow, Eileen. *What Do Authors Do?* Clarion, 1995.
dePaola, Tomie. *The Art Lesson.* Putnam, 1989.
Kramer, Stephen. *Theodoric's Rainbow.* Illus. by Daniel Mark Duffy. Freeman, 1995.
Pellowski, Michael Morgan. *The Art of Making Comic Books.* Illus. by Howard Bender. Lerner, 1995.
Locker, Thomas. *The Young Artist.* Dial, 1989.
Rosen, Michael J. (ed.). *Purr . . . Children's Book Illustrators Brag about Their Cats.* Harcourt Brace, 1996.
———. *SPEAK! Children's Book Illustrators Brag about Their Dogs.* Harcourt Brace, 1993.
Stevens, Janet. *From Pictures to Words: A Book about Making a Book.* Holiday House, 1995.
Swain, Gwenyth. *Bookworks: Making Books by Hand.* Carolrhoda, 1995.

PROFESSIONAL REFERENCE BOOKS

Amoss, Berthe and Eric Suben. *Writing and Illustrating Children's Books for Publication: Two Perspectives.* Writer's Digest Books, 1995.
Benedict, Susan and Lenore Carlisle. *Beyond Words: Picture Books for Older Readers and Writers.* Heinemann, 1992.
Bennett, Peter. *The Illustrated Child.* Putnam, 1979.
Children's Book Council. *75 Years of Children's Book Week Posters: Celebrating Great Illustrators of American Children's Books.* Knopf, 1994.
Fleischman, Paul. *Copier Creations: Using Copy Machines to Make Decals, Silhouettes, Flip Books, Films, and Much More!* Illus. by David Cain. HarperCollins, 1993.
Hopkins, Lee Bennett. *Pauses: Autobiographical Reflections of 101 Creators of Children's Books.* HarperCollins, 1995.
Marantz, Sylvia S. *Picture Books for Looking and Learning: Awakening Visual Perceptions through the Art of Children's Books.* Oryx, 1992.
Melton, David. *Written & Illustrated by . . . .* Landmark, 1985.
Pinsent, Lynsy. *Art for Children: Face Painting.* Chartwell, 1995.
Ritter, Darlene. *Literature-Based Art Activities (Grades K–3).* Illus. by Gary Hoover. Creative Teaching Press.
———. *Literature-Based Art Activities (Grades 4–6).* Illus. by Gary Hoover. Creative Teaching Press.
Roberts, Ellen. *The Children's Picture Book: How to Write It • How to Sell It.* Writer's Digest Books, 1981.
Zwerger, Lisbeth. *The Art of Lisbeth Zwerger.* Neugebauer, 1993.

Sources

BOOKS

Butterfield, Moira. *Art for Children: How to Draw and Paint the Outdoors*. Chartwell, 1995.

Craig, Diana. *Art for Children: How to Draw and Paint Pets*. Chartwell, 1995.

Cummings, Pat (ed.). *Talking with Artists*. Bradbury, 1992.

———. *Talking with Artists Volume Two*. Simon & Schuster, 1995.

Englebaugh, Debi. *Art through Children's Literature: Creative Art Lessons for Caldecott Books*. Teacher Ideas Press, 1994.

Gair, Angela. *Art for Children: How to Draw and Paint People*. Chartwell, 1995.

Hodge, Anthony. *Hands On Arts and Crafts: Collage*. Gloucester, 1992.

Jackson, Paul and Angela A'Court. *The Ultimate Papercraft and Origami Book*. Smithmark, 1992.

Kehoe, Michael. *A Book Takes Root: The Making of a Picture Book*. Carolrhoda, 1993.

Kent, Jean and Candace Shelton. *The Romance Writers' Phrase Book*. Perigee, 1984.

Milord, Susan. *Adventures in Art: Art & Craft Experiences for 7- to 14-Year-Olds*. Williamson, 1990.

Romberg, Jenean and Miriam Rutz. *Art Today and Every Day: Classroom Activities for the Elementary School Year*. Parker, 1972.

Society of Illustrators. *The Very Best of Children's Book Illustrations*. North Light Books, 1993.

Temko, Florence. *Made With Paper*. Dragon's World, 1991.

PERIODICALS

Elleman, Barbara. "Illustration as Art: Perspective." *Book Links*, July 1996.

———. "Illustration as Art: Shape." *Book Links*, March 1996.

———. "Illustration as Art: Techniques." *Book Links*, May 1994.

Illustration and Photograph Credits

BOOK JACKET ART FROM ANDREWS AND MCMEEL

From MRS. NOAH'S PATCHWORK QUILT by Janet Bolton. Illustration copyright ©1994 by Janet Bolton. Reproduced by permission of Andrews and McMeel.

BOOK JACKET ART FROM CAROLRHODA BOOKS, INC

From A BOOK TAKES ROOT: THE MAKING OF A PICTURE BOOK by Michael Kehoe. Illustration copyright ©1993 by Michael Kehoe. Reproduced by permission of Carolrhoda Books, Inc.

From GRANDFATHER'S LAIKA written by Mats Wahl, illustrated by Tord Nygren. Illustration copyright ©1990 by Tord Nygren. Reproduced by permission of Carolrhoda Books, Inc.

From GREEN BEANS written by Elizabeth Thomas, illustrated by Vicki Jo Redenbaugh. Illustration copyright ©1992 by Vicki Jo Redenbaugh. Reproduced by permission of Carolrhoda Books, Inc.

From THE LONG RED SCARF by Nette Hilton, illustrated by Margaret Power. Illustration copyright ©1990 by Margaret Power. Reproduced by permission of Carolrhoda Books, Inc.

BOOK JACKET ART FROM CLARION BOOKS/HOUGHTON MIFFLIN COMPANY

From ADD IT, DIP IT, FIX IT: A BOOK OF VERBS written and illustrated by R. M. Schneider. Illustration copyright ©1995 by R. M. Schneider. Reproduced by permission of Houghton Mifflin Company.

From BAD DAY AT RIVERBEND written and illustrated by Chris Van Allsburg. Illustration copyright © 1995 by Chris Van Allsburg. Reproduced by permission of Houghton Mifflin Company.

From BLACK AND WHITE written and illustrated by David Macaulay. Illustration copyright ©1990 by David Macaulay. Reproduced by permission of Houghton Mifflin Company.

From CATHEDRAL written and illustrated by David Macaulay. Illustration copyright ©1973 by David Macaulay. Reproduced by permission of Houghton Mifflin Company.

From CHRISTMAS LULLABY written by Nancy Jewell, illustrated by Stefano Vitale. Illustration copyright ©1994 by Stefano Vitale. Reproduced by permission of Clarion Books/Houghton Mifflin Company.

From GRANDFATHER'S JOURNEY written and illustrated by Allen Say. Illustration copyright © 1993 by Allen Say. Reproduced by permission of Houghton Mifflin Company.

From JUMANJI written and illustrated by Chris Van Allsburg. Illustration copyright © 1981 by Chris Van Allsburg. Reproduced by permission of Houghton Mifflin Company.

From THE POLAR EXPRESS written and illustrated by Chris Van Allsburg. Illustration copyright ©1985 by Chris Van Allsburg. Reproduced by permission of Houghton Mifflin Company.

From SUNDIATA written and illustrated by David Wisniewski. Illustration copyright © 1992 by David Wisniewski. Reproduced by permission of Clarion Books/Houghton Mifflin Company.

From TWIST WITH A BURGER, JITTER WITH A BUG written by Linda Lowery, illustrated by Pat Dypold. Illustration copyright ©1995 by Pat Dypold. Reproduced by permission of Houghton Mifflin Company.

From THE WALL written by Eve Bunting, illustrated by Ronald Himler. Illustration copyright ©1990 by Ronald Himler. Reproduced by permission of Clarion Books/Houghton Mifflin Company.

BOOK JACKET ART FROM HARCOURT BRACE

From BETWEEN EARTH & SKY by Joseph Bruchac, illustrated by Thomas Locker. Illustration copyright ©1996 by Thomas Locker. Reproduced by permission of Harcourt Brace & Company.

From DEAR BENJAMIN BANNEKER by Andrea Davis Pinkey, illustrated by Brian Pinkney. Illustration copyright ©1994 by Brian Pinkney. Reproduced by permission of Harcourt Brace & Company.

From THE HIGHWAYMAN by Alfred Noyes, illustrated by Neil Waldman. Illustration copyright ©1990 by Neil Waldman. Reproduced by permission of Harcourt Brace & Company.

From RED LEAF, YELLOW LEAF written and illustrated by Lois Ehlert. Illustration copyright ©1991 by Lois Ehlert. Reproduced by permission of Harcourt Brace & Company.

From THE SEASONS SEWN: A YEAR IN PATCHWORK by Ann Whitford Paul, illustrated by Michael McCurdy. Illustration copyright © 1996 by Michael McCurdy. Reproduced by permission of Harcourt Brace & Company.

From SMOKY NIGHT by Eve Bunting, illustrated by David Diaz. Illustration copyright ©1994 by David Diaz. Reproduced by permission of Harcourt Brace & Company.

From THE TORTILLA FACTORY written by Gary Paulsen, illustrated by Ruth Wright Paulsen. Illustration copyright ©1995 by Ruth Wright Paulsen. Reproduced by permission of Harcourt Brace & Company.

BOOK JACKETS FROM HARPERCOLLINS PUBLISHERS

From BROWN ANGELS: AN ALBUM OF PICTURES AND VERSE by Walter Dean Myers. Jacket art copyright ©1993 by HarperCollins Publishers. Reproduced by permission of HarperCollins Publishers.

From GLORIOUS ANGELS by Walter Dean Myers. Jacket art copyright ©1995 by HarperCollins Publishers. Reproduced by permission of HarperCollins Publishers.

From PETER'S CHAIR written and illustrated by Ezra Jack Keats. Illustration copyright ©1976 by Ezra Jack Keats. Reproduced by permission of HarperCollins Publishers.

From SKY TREE: SEEING SCIENCE THROUGH ART written and illustrated by Thomas Locker. Illustration copyright ©1995 by Thomas Locker. Reproduced by permission of HarperCollins Publishers.

From WHAT YOU KNOW FIRST by Patricia MacLachlan, illustrated by Barry Moser. Illustration copyright ©1995 by Barry Moser. Reproduced by permission of HarperCollins Publishers.

BOOK JACKET ART FROM HOLIDAY HOUSE

From THE CREATION written by James Weldon Johnson, illustrated by James E. Ransome. Illustration copyright ©1994 by James E. Ransome. Reproduced by permission of Holiday House.

BOOK JACKET ART FROM ORCHARD BOOKS

From A B CEDAR: AN ALPHABET OF TREES by Geogre Ella Lyon, illustrated by Tom Parker. Illustration copyright ©1989 by Tom Parker. Reproduced by permission of Orchard Books, New York.

From THE CATSPRING SOMERSAULT FLYING ONE-HANDED FLIP FLOP by SuAnn Kiser, illustrated by Peter Catalanotto. Illustration copyright ©1993 by Peter Catalanotto. Reproduced by permission of Orchard Books, New York.

From HOMEPLACE written and illustrated by Wendy Anderson Halperin. Illustration copyright ©1995 by Wendy Anderson Halperin. Reproduced by permission of Orchard Books, New York.

From HUNTING THE WHITE COW by Tres Seymore, illustrated by Wendy Anderson Halperin. Illustration copyright © 1993 by Wendy Anderson Halperin. Reproduced by permission of Orchard Books, New York.

From THE PAINTER written and illustrated by Peter Catalanotto. Illustration copyright ©1995 by Peter Catalanotto. Reproduced by permission of Orchard Books, New York.

From 'TWAS THE NIGHT BEFORE THANKSGIVING written and illustrated by Dav Pilkey. Illustration copyright ©1990 by Dav Pilkey. Reproduced by permission of Orchard Books, New York.

From THE VOYAGER'S STONE by Robert Kraske, illustrated by Brian Floca. Illustration copyright ©1995 by Brian Floca. Reproduced by permission of Orchard Books, New York.

BOOK JACKET ART FROM PUTNAM & GROSSET GROUP

From LITTLEJIM'S GIFT written by Gloria Houston, illustrated by Thomas B. Allen. Illustration copyright ©1994 by Thomas B. Allen. Reproduced by permission of Philomel Books a division of the Putnam & Grosset Group.

BOOK JACKET ART FROM RICHARD JESSE WATSON

From ONE WINTRY NIGHT written by Ruth Bell Graham, illustrated by Richard Jesse Watson. Illustration copyright ©1995 by Richard Jesse Watson. Reproduced by permission of Richard Jesse Watson.

BOOK JACKET ART FROM SCHOLASTIC CANADA LTD

From GIFTS written by Jo Ellen Bogart, illustrated by Barbara Reid. Illustration copyright ©1994 by Barbara Reid. Reproduced by permission of Scholastic Canada LTD.

PHOTOGRAPH CREDITS
CATALANOTTO, PETER - courtesy of artist
FEELINGS, TOM - courtesy of artist
FISHER, LEONARD EVERETT - courtesy of artist
HALPERIN, WENDY ANDERSON - courtesy of artist
HEN - photographed by Thomas Lang
HIMMELMAN, JOHN - photographed by Betsy Himmelman
LAROCHE, GILES - courtesy of artist
LE TORD, BIJOU - photographed by Lynda Sylvester
NOVAK, MATT - courtesy of artist
PINKNEY, BRIAN - courtesy of artist
QUACKENBUSH, ROBERT - courtesy of artist
SHUTE, LINDA - courtesy of artist
SILLS, LESLIE - photographed by Thomas Lang
WILHELM, HANS - photographed by Anne Weber Mannheim

Acknowledgments

Our eternal thanks to:
- Thomas B. Allen—for words as lovely as his art

- The illustrators: Tom Feelings, John Himmelman, Robert Quackenbush, Linda Shute, Wendy Anderson Halperin, Leonard Everett Fisher, Hans Wilhelm, Peter Catalanotto, Bijou Le Tord, Leslie Sills, Giles Laroche, Matt Novak, Brian Pinkney—for their insightful contributions

- Gloria Houston—a source of endless inspiration who makes us proud to be "members of the most influential profession in the world"

- Walt Shaffner—for accommodating our writers' retreat

- Carol Lane—an executive research specialist and jewelry consultant to the stars

- Susan Williamson—who wanted to write a book with us and did

- Vicki Callicutt—for reading inspirational stories from *Chicken Soup* and making us cry

- Tracy Funk—for reading picture book bibliographies and telling us all about "Hoooughton Mifflin"

- Carol Field—our resident literary authority, game show host, and fellow lover of art

- Sandra Swoope—who sacrificed her likeness for the sake of creativity and a unique makeover of sorts

- Brad Streetman—your pictures painted a thousand words

Requests were submitted to all publishers of the focus titles to duplicate book jackets. We gratefully acknowledge Richard Jesse Watson and the following houses who granted gratis permission:
- Andrews and McMeel
- BridgeWater/Troll
- Carolrhoda
- Clarion
- Harcourt Brace
- HarperCollins
- Holiday House
- Houghton Mifflin
- Orchard
- Putnam
- Scholastic Canada Ltd.
- Whitman

About the Authors

R. Howard Blount, Jr. has been a teacher in Hillsborough County, Florida, since 1980. He earned a B.A. in Elementary Education from Southeastern College and an M.Ed. in Educational Leadership from the University of South Florida. Mr. Blount also works as an educational consultant, freelance writer, proofreader, and reviewer of children's books. He is the author of several professional resource books for teachers. His work-in-progress is the life story of children's author Gloria Houston.

Martha Venning Webb holds a B.A. in Elementary Education. She was born in Virginia, but now lives in Plant City, Florida, with her son Nathan and Bodger their yellow lab. Everyone who knows her understands her unusual affinity for bread. Before she became a teacher she co-owned a health club, designed and sold houses, and worked at Disney World. She introduced Howard to Gloria Houston.

Howard and Martha met in 1989 when she was an intern in his sixth-grade classroom. They have taught together ever since. Martha has critiqued Howard's writing for years, and she was a contributing writer for *Implementing Literature-Based Instruction and Authentic Assessment.*

We'd Like to Hear from You . . .

If you have found this resource to be useful and you have a success story to share, we would love to hear from you. And, of course, feedback of any kind is always welcomed. Remember to send all correspondence with a SASE.

We are available for speaking engagements at schools, libraries, workshops, and conferences on the topics of corresponding with authors, literature-based instruction, authentic assessment, literature-based art, and how educators can get their ideas published. Please write or call us for more information.

R. Howard Blount, Jr.
603 W. Dixie St.
Plant City, FL 33566
(813) 752-4131

Martha Venning Webb
1303 E. Oakdale Ave.
Plant City, FL 33566
(813) 754-3275

Also by R. Howard Blount, Jr.

The Address Book of Children's Authors and Illustrators
The Address Book on Disc (electronic version for Mac and Windows)
Implementing Literature-Based Instruction and Authentic Assessment
Instructional Fair • TS Denison

'Round the world cooking library

Eastern Mediterranean Cooking

Exotic delicacies from Greece, Turkey, Israel, Lebanon and Iran

Recipe contributions by Roger Debasque
author of 'The Art of Mediterranean Cooking'

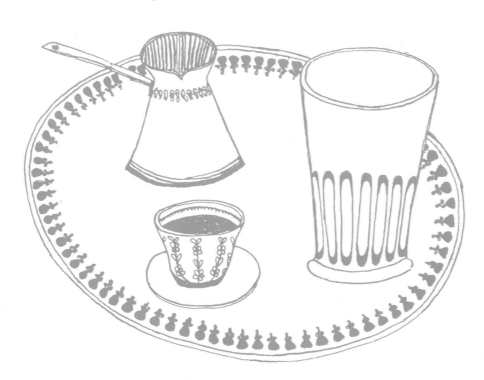

GALAHAD BOOKS • NEW YORK

Contents

Recipe contributions	Roger Debasque, Israel, author of 'The Art of Mediterranean Cooking'
American editor	Irena Kirshman, graduate Cordon Bleu Cooking School, lecturer on international cuisines, food consultant
Associate American editor	Susan Wright
Editorial staff for 'Round the world cooking library:	
Project editor	Wina Born, Dame de la Chaîne des Rôtisseurs and member of the board of the Fédération Internationale de la Presse Gastronomique
Executive editor	Ton van Es
Text editor U.S.A.	Martin Self B.A., J.D.
Cover photo	Henk van der Heijden, Amsterdam
Text photos	Han Born, Amsterdam
Recipe photos	Edrei Sharon Publications, Tel Aviv, Israel, Conny van Kasteel, Milan, Italy and Ed Suister, Amsterdam
Design and drawings	Rosemarijn van Limburg Stirum
Created by	Meijer Pers B.V., Amsterdam, The Netherlands
Typeset by	Service Type Inc., Lancaster, Pennsylvania and Internationaal Zetcentrum B.V., Wormerveer, The Netherlands
Printed by	Drukkerij Meijer B.V., Wormerveer, The Netherlands
Bound by	Proost & Brandt N.V., Amsterdam, The Netherlands
Publisher	Drake Publishers Inc., New York, N.Y.
Distributor	Galahad Books, New York, N.Y.

Copyright © 1973, 1974 by Meijer Pers B.V., Amsterdam, The Netherlands

Cup measures in this book are based on an eight ounce cup.

From Greece to Israel, the cuisines of the countries along the Eastern Mediterranean have much in common. The smell of glowing charcoal and roasting mutton pervades the air in all of these countries. Stuffed eggplants, tomatoes, vine leaves, zucchini and peppers are popular everywhere, and sweet cakes and pastry floating in rosewater syrup and jet black coffee are common favorites. Wherever you go, you can see that people calmly take their time and enjoy a meal. The art of cooking in the Middle East largely ignores national boundaries and differing languages, politics and religion. It is original, extremely old and exquisitely refined. The culinary art forms a bridge between these many different peoples.

The basis for Middle Eastern cooking comes from Persia (present-day Iran), where wine and cheese probably originated and where people discovered how to capture the flavor of roses and jasmin by distilling them more than a thousand years ago. Persia is also a land where people were making ice cream and sherbet centuries ago (in fact, the word sherbet is of Persian origin). And the Persians were already well versed in refined and imaginative combinations of fruit, herbs and tropical spices centuries before Europe could even speak of a culinary art. When the Turkish horsemen of Central Asia swept westward and conquered the whole Middle East in the 13th century, they were careful enough not to destroy this age-old culinary culture. Instead, they merged it with their unsurpassed art of roasting meat on spits and skewers. The Turks were first of all soldiers and spent most of their day on horseback. At night, they pitched tent and built a huge campfire on which they roasted their meat. In the course of centuries, the Turks perfected the old soldiers' art of roasting meat, and wherever the Turkish flag once flew, this art has become one of the specialties of that place's culinary traditions.

And yet, in spite of the great similarities among all the countries of the Eastern Mediterranean, striking contrasts have arisen over the years as well. In Greece, the Italian influence can be tasted in spaghetti and cheese sauces, which are reminders of the centuries that Venice ruled many of the Greek islands. In Lebanon, there are definite Arabic influences, and the Lebanese drink quite different coffee from the Turks. There is also an Arab heritage in Israel, but this new nation also has European and North African influences working as well.

Let us now travel from west to east, along the eastern coast of the Mediterranean, tasting the food and drink that these countries have to offer.

Greece

We begin our journey in Greece, a European country of course, but one whose cuisine stems from Middle Eastern traditions. The Greeks are not enormous eaters; they are a people of unpretentious tastes who satisfy themselves with the simple things this very beautiful, but not very rich, land yields. Greek breakfast often consists of a cup of warm milk and a piece of dry bread. A hot meal is served both in the afternoon and very late in the evening. Just as in all Mediterranean countries, the beginning of the evening is the pleasantest part of the day. Work is done, and it is not yet time to eat.

With the heat of the day over, the Greeks sit down to relax. Children and babies are dressed in their Sunday best, mother dresses up and father puts on his neat, dark suit. Then the whole family goes for its evening walk. They stroll back and forth along the wide streets of towns and villages, or along the waterfront in the port cities. Young girls walk arm-in-arm and young boys group together. (Young people are still very strictly brought up, and boys and girls can never be seen together in public until they are officially engaged, and then only in the company of a chaperone). The men gather in their own favorite cafe or club to participate in the favorite Greek pastime, talking. They talk and talk incessantly. If you pass one of these men's

A very typical sight in all the countries of the Middle East: small, shaded outdoor restaurants in picturesque spots where you take your time to enjoy the meal.

Greece grows delicious olives which are shipped all over the world either preserved in brine or after being pressed into valuable olive oil.

cafes, the sound of the breaking tide fills one ear; and the continuous and even louder noise of arguing voices floods into the other. At this pleasant hour terraces and sidewalk cafes fill up, and it is time to drink an aperitif and eat 'mezedhes', small tasty appetizers. The better the cafe, the more varied the collection of mezedhes they serve. White sheep's cheese, garlic sausage, roast mutton, salted pistachio nuts, olives, slices of hardboiled eggs, and shrimp, are only a rough sample of the abundance. In the small fishing harbors of remote islands, the mezedhes are much simpler. They are prepared from the large collections of dried squid hanging over the doors of small cafes. The squid is first beaten against rocks to soften it and then left for a day in the sun to dry out. Small charcoal fires are built along the sidewalks and the long tentacles of the squid are roasted. A strong love of Greece may be necessary at first to appreciate these tough, charcoal-flavored pieces of squid. But the Greeks eat squid with raw string beans or raw artichokes and consider it a very satisfying treat.

The best eating places in Greece are 'tavernas', small restaurants where you often sit outdoors in a small garden. These are usually extremely simple, with stone floors, no tablecloths, a large refrigerator in the middle of the room and very dim lights.

Turkey

But the Greeks bring a pleasant atmosphere with them when they come in, with the whole family from grandmother down to the smallest baby. Families eat and chat for hours. There is no menu at a taverna. You walk right through the kitchen so that you can see what is simmering and sizzling in the pans and what is being roasted over the charcoal fire. You point to the salad you want, or to the piece of meat or chicken. And in Greece, you do not have to observe strict rules concerning the order dishes in which are served. You eat what you want when you want it. And if you still feel like having a cup of coffee and dessert after the meat, you go to the 'pastelleria', the pastry shop, for a cup of black Turkish coffee and one of a large assortment of sweet puddings and cakes in the showcase window.

Anyone who wants to taste the best of Greek specialties must spend Easter in Greece, and best of all in a small island village. The prize lamb that is to be roasted is chosen weeks in advance. The Greeks still observe Lent very strictly and eat little more than beans during those weeks, or very rarely, a small fish. Early Easter morning, a large fire is built on an open spot of ground somewhere in the village, and while the church service is still in process, the delicious aroma of roasting meat begins to fill the village square. Thyme, oregano and rosemary are generously sprinkled on the fire so that the flavor can penetrate the meat even better. The traditional opening course of an Easter meal is the 'avgolemono', a golden chicken broth, thickened with a beaten egg and made slightly sour with lemon juice. If a stranger comes to a village on Easter morning, he is always greeted with the words 'Christos anesti', Christ has risen, and is offered a flaming red Easter egg and a piece of fresh bread and roasted lamb. When Greece still had a king, it was traditional for the monarch to be the guest of his bodyguards (the soldiers in white kilts) and for him to eat the Easter lamb that had been roasted in front of the barracks.

Although Ankara, in the middle of the barren Anatolian Plateau, is the capital of Turkey, the country's most beautiful and most famous city is Istanbul, on the Bosporus. It is an ancient city, at least three thousand years old, and a beautiful one, with mosques, fairy-tale castles and eastern bazaars. It is also a city with some of the most delicious food in the world. A visitor can eat very well and very cheaply in one of the small restaurants in the old part of the city. There is usually an open kitchen right on the street with a charcoal grill and oven so that you can see what there is to eat as soon as you enter the door. A shish-kebab of succulent lamb and veal, roast veal or sheep liver, even roast lamb kidneys (a very refined delicacy) or mutton meatballs, are the day's delights. There are pans in which white and green beans simmer in a herb sauce with a penetrating aroma of garlic. In the oven, there is a tray filled with stuffed eggplants, tomatoes or zucchinis covered with a delicious yoghurt sauce. And in all probability, you can also get a 'döner kebab', the greatest dish Turkey can offer the connoisseur. It consists of a vertical grill on which meat rotates in front of a vertically arranged charcoal fire. On the grill is arranged an endless number of thinly sliced pieces of lamb, seasoned with herbs such as garlic, oregano and thyme. Rotating the meat allows the outsides to become crisp, brown and well flavored. This hard crust is cut off with an enormous knife and the meal is served with salad, cucumber, onion rings and slices of tomatoes. By the time the first serving is finished, a new hard crust has roasted and you can get a second serving. But you had better not go to the restaurant too late in the afternoon, because there is unlikely to be any 'döner kebab' left. On warm summer evenings, you can eat in the outdoor restaurants on the Bosporus. The boat leaving from near the Galata bridge goes on to the outer, European section of Istanbul, where the terraces of restaurants are built right out over the water. From far away, the lights of boats seem garlands from their reflection in the water. The whole evening must be taken to enjoy your meal in Istanbul, because it is always a special occasion. The waiter first comes with 'mezeler', the appetizers we are already familiar with from Greece, but in Turkey they are even more impressive. The choice is enormous and if you can't make up your mind the first time around, the waiter will be glad to come again. There is every possible kind of roasted meat, lamb's kidneys, lamb or chicken liver, and small roast fish, the delicious large Bosporus shrimp, stuffed mussels, salty red caviar, 'pastirma' (thin slices of meat dried in the wind and wrapped around flaming red peppers), beans in piquant sauce, small stuffed tomatoes, eggplants, different kinds of goat and sheep cheeses, and a limitless variety of salted nuts. All the time in the world seems available, and there is always plenty of raki (anise liqueur). Anyone still hungry after this course can then order a main dish: perhaps an exquisite lobster from the caves along the small islands of the Bosporus, or a broiled fish, or roast chicken in cucumber and yoghurt sauce, or rice pilaf prepared with lamb and seasoned with saffron and cinnamon. And as dessert, there are those delicious Turkish cakes and pastries made from the finest puff pastry dough and filled with chopped nuts and honey, or with rose jelly. It is a feast of 'a thousand-and-one-nights'!

Cyprus

When there is a feast in a Turkish village, the women prepare large copper pots of soup outdoors over an open fire.

Turkish winegrowers in Anatolia must work this barren land very hard. (photo top left)

Fetching water at the well is still a daily task for the Turkish village women. (photo top)

'Döner Kebab': a cone made of thin pieces of tender meat which has been roasted over a charcoal fire. (photo left)

On Cyprus, the freshly caught fish is cleaned on the beach before it is sold to the restaurants. (photo right)

Near that corner of Asia Minor, where the Mediterranean coastline bends sharply to the south, is Cyprus, an island nation inhabited by Greeks and Turks. The Cypriots are known for their hospitality. If a stranger comes to the island, he is welcomed with the friendly word 'Kopiaste', which is something like 'please sit down', or 'make yourself at home'. And the Cypriots do know how to make you feel at home. In any cafe the customer will get five stools: one to sit on, one for his right elbow, one for his left elbow, one to rest his feet on, and one for the coffee. Even to pay for coffee is out of the question. The only thing asked in return for this hospitality is to talk: about your country, your family, children, work and travels. All the small harbor towns have outdoor restaurants sheltered under straw roofs. Here you can eat delicious fish, roasted or cold, with mayonnaise. And the spring is the time for lamb prepared as

only Cypriots know how, in brick farm ovens. First they build a strong fire in the oven. When the bricks become glowing hot, the fire is put out, the meat placed in the oven and cooked on the hot bricks. By the time the bricks have cooled the meat is meltingly tender and ready.

Anyone with a sweet tooth will find Cyprus a paradise! Nowhere else in the world but Nicosia can you find such good 'loukoum' (Turkish delight), and such fine, sweet 'halava', made with sesame seed oil and sugar. They literally do melt in your mouth.

Lebanon

*Windmills along the coast of
Lebanon pump the seawater into
salt pots. The pots are then set
in the hot sun so that the water
evaporates and leaves the salt
behind.*

The real connoisseur's paradise
of the Middle East is without
doubt the small country wedged
in between the snow-covered
Lebanese mountains and the
blue Mediterranean Sea.
Nowhere else (except France,
perhaps) are people as critical
about what they eat. In Lebanon
the visitor can taste Eastern
cooking in all its refinement, as
a perfect harmony of Turkish,
Persian, and Arab cuisines.
Nowhere else in the world is it
possible to eat in such grand
fashion: Beirut, the capital, has
more than 300 restaurants
alone, and in one of the cool
mountain valleys, along a
rushing stream, there can be
dozens of outdoor restaurants.

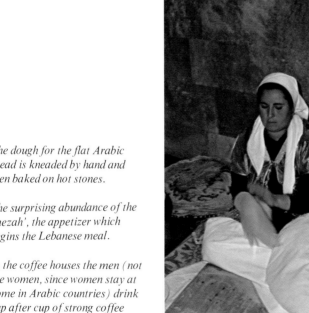

*The dough for the flat Arabic
bread is kneaded by hand and
then baked on hot stones.*

*The surprising abundance of the
'mezah', the appetizer which
begins the Lebanese meal.*

*In the coffee houses the men (not
the women, since women stay at
home in Arabic countries) drink
cup after cup of strong coffee
and smoke their water pipes.*

Israel

Anyone walking through a Lebanese village will find two things immediately strike his attention: the baking of bread and the mincing of 'kibbe'. The flat Arab bread of Lebanon is made from dough pressed out to a thin sheet by hand and then stretched around hot stones for a few minutes to bake. The flat layer is served folded up on the plate. You break off a piece, roll it up and use it as a spoon. 'Kibbe' is the national dish of Syria and Lebanon. It is made from raw lamb which is ground in a stone mortar together with cracked wheat to make a thick, creamy mixture. It is eaten raw, often accompanied by chopped onions, garlic and basil, or it is fried together with pine nuts and then seasoned with fresh mint. The small appetizers that left us in a daze in Turkey, here make us wonder if we will ever make it to the main dish! Hors d'œuvres reach their absolute perfection in Lebanon. In any good Lebanese restaurant, when appetizers are ordered with the aperitif, at least fifty different concoctions are brought to the table. They consist of the most refined snacks: small dough shells filled with vegetables, meat or fish; crumbled sharp cheeses in oil, fried cheese morsels, snails, squid, shrimp, vegetables in an assortment of sharp sauces, small marinated roasted fish, chickpea puree in sesame oil, lamb's liver and kidneys, chicken livers, shellfish,

roasted eggplant or onion puree, pistachio nuts, almonds... the list is virtually endless. And it is all so artful that no matter how much you promised to be careful, all your good intentions melt like snow.

But then comes the main course: braised lamb, so tender that you can 'cut' it with a spoon, roast meat and chicken, or the classical Lebanese 'moghrabié', a dish of Arab origin made of coarsely ground wheat with butter and chicken, seasoned with saffron. And to please the host there must still be room for dessert, 'khatayf', made with honey and rose syrup and filled with candied orange blossoms, or 'osmallich', a pie made with thin slices of dough, filled with cottage cheese and covered with honey. Before the dinner is finished, the coffee waiter will appear, holding a large pot with a double bottom in one hand, and several clinking porcelain cups in the other. The pot contains jet black Yemeni coffee, with glowing charcoal in the double bottom to keep it hot. Instead of an after-dinner cigarette there is the nargileh, or water-pipe, brought right to the table. The secret is to put a pinch of tobacco on top, place a glowing coal on the tobacco, and then draw on the mouthpiece, sucking the cool, fragrant smoke through the reservoir filled with water (or even more pleasantly, rose water)

Israel is still creating itself into a nation, and this is true even in cooking. The thousands of immigrants have brought with them their own cuisines from all parts of the world: Russian 'borsht' is as common in Israel as Yemeni coffee, and North

African 'couscous' as familiar as Yiddish 'gefillte fish', Polish carp or Hungarian goulash. And all this is in addition to the indigenous Turkish-Arabic art of cooking and the Jewish dietary laws. Israel is anxious to create a distinctive culinary tradition of its own, characteristic of the country and of the products that the land brings forth. The government has even sponsored cooking contests to discover new recipes really typical of Israel, dishes which use the produce Israel is known for, such as citrus fruit, avocados, figs, lamb, and fish. In the future, Israel will probably have a unique cuisine integrating very many differing traditions. But at present the national dish is 'falafel', a spicy snack that is eaten everywhere. It consists of a flat Arab bread ('pitta') stuffed with balls of a fried, sharply seasoned chick-pea mixture, and it is always accompanied by a very flavorful salad. Falafel is sold along the streets by men wheeling small carts. The meal that brings out the rich variety of Israel's fruit crop is breakfast, considered by most tourists as the most delicious meal of the day, with oranges, grapefruits, good fresh bread, and unique salads made of tomatoes, pimentos, radishes, and cucumbers. And breakfast tastes best, of course, in the cool of the morning on a hotel terrace overlooking the Mediterranean.

Beverages

The Middle East has been the land of the grape vine since time immemorial. According to the Bible, Noah planted the first grape vines when he descended from the ark on Mount Arrarat in eastern Turkey. And in one very old legend, it was a Persian prince who, by accident, first tasted fermented grape juice and dicovered that it made him happy. The eastern edge of the Mediterranean Sea is the ancient home of wine. King Solomon drank wine from Cyprus, the prophet Hosea drank it from Lebanon, and the Greek wine god, Dionysus, introduced grape vines into Greece from Asia Minor. But when the teachings of Mohammed spread throughout the Middle East, it was the end of wine making and drinking, for it was prohibited by the Koran. And wherever Turks or Arabs ruled, the vineyards were allowed to sink into decay. Only Greece to this day has remained a major wine producing country. The everyday drink in Greece is a very light wine to which resin has been added to help preserve it in this hot climate. The resin gives it a rather strong, almost turpentine taste, and it is sometimes difficult for a non-Greek to get used to the taste. But in the Greek climate, and together with Greek food, it is a delicious table wine. Greece also produces very strong, sweet dessert wines such as the yellow gold Samos,

Water is very expensive in Turkey and in many places you can see the 'waterman' carrying a copper water can on his back. He fills the glasses with a motion that must be an age-old gesture.

'Rozaki' is a juicy, pinkish-blue Greek grape that is good both for eating and winemaking.

named after the island from which it comes, and the dark red Mavrodaphne. Turkey became a secular, westernized nation through the reforms of Kemal Atatürk earlier in this century, and it too now produces wine from its abundance of grapes. The wine is far from poor in quality, but the Turks are only slowly getting used to the idea. Very good wines also come from Cyprus. One is Commandatia, the wine of the Knights of the Cross, which was already drunk in Europe in the Middle Ages and became a favorite wine of Queen Elizabeth I of England. In Lebanon it was the French priests who first planted grape vines in the fertile area of Bekaa. These have produced exceptional wines which can hold their own with many French wines, and go superbly with refined Lebanese cooking. These are wines so pure and strong they can be exported to tropical countries without harm. In all these lands of hot summers, people look for refreshing drinks. This is why water has always had an almost sacred significance. The Greeks drink wine, but they appreciate water. Standing in front of the village cafes in Greece, they talk about water just as Frenchmen talk about wine. They compare the qualities of the different wells in the area, and the greatest compliment a mayor can be given is to tell him how good 'his' water tastes. In

Turkey, a bottle of water is automatically placed on the table in any restaurant. It is called 'kapalesu', or water from a 'capsule', the assurance that the water is sanitary. You can also buy freshly squeezed fruit juices on almost every street corner in Turkey. There are usually piles of whatever fresh fruit the season has to offer, to be squeezed on the spot. And for those who doubt the hygiene of street vendors, there are many large fruit juice bars.

The aperitif of the Middle East, from Greece to Lebanon, is raki, a very strong drink distilled from grapes and flavored with anise oil. It is never drunk straight, but always with ice or ice water. When water is added it turns a cloudy blue. The taste of raki becomes even more remarkable when combined with the salt air of the sea. It should be drunk on the small terraces of Greek port cities, or on the Bosporus at Istanbul, or on the luxury terraces of Beirut on the Mediterranean. And with raki there should always be an accompanying appetizer, but we've already talked about those, havent't we ?

Entrees

Where the discovery of stuffing all kinds of vegetables with delectable fillings was first made is unknown, but it is at least likely that the idea came from Persia. Whatever their origin, stuffed vegetables are a very important part of Middle Eastern cooking, especially as hors d'œuvres. Any kind of vegetable that can be scooped out, such as tomatoes, eggplants or onions, can be used, as well as leaves, which can be wrapped around fillings. Soft, flexible vine leaves are preferred, and they can be bought in neat packets at any market in Greece, Turkey or Lebanon. In winter, when vine leaves cannot be obtained, cooks use cabbage leaves, and in spring, spinach leaves. Even the large yellow flowers of pumpkin plants are used to wrap around fillings. The stuffing or filling must be tasty and surprising, and to top it all there is often a slightly sour yoghurt sauce poured over the dish. On hot summer days nothing is more delicious than these fresh, tasty, lightly stuffed green snacks.

In Turkey, the passion for stuffing and filling does not stop with vegetables. The Turks even stuff eggs and the large mussels from the Bosporus, with their beautiful dark-blue shells. In fact, hors d'œuvres are the highlight of a Turkish or Lebanese dinner. In private homes, this part of the meal is served on large copper trays which are placed on low, folding wooden tables. The whole family sits on low couches or cushions around the tables, possibly drinking raki (a strong anise liqueur taken with ice-water), but always eating and talking endlessly.

When the tray is emptied, it is taken away and replaced by a full one, because the joy and pleasure of drinking, talking and eating hors s'œuvres goes on as long as possible.

Tirakia tiganita

Cheese puffs

4 servings

- 2 egg whites
- 1 cup grated Parmesan cheese (or Greek Kefalotiri if available)
- Freshly ground black pepper
- Oil for deep frying

Beat the egg whites until stiff peaks are formed. Fold in the Parmesan cheese and pepper. (The egg whites will deflate.) Form the mixture into small smooth balls with your fingers. Fry the balls in deep hot fat for about 3 minutes until they rise to the surface of the fat and are golden brown. Drain on paper towels and serve immediately.

Poca

Cheese in pastry

8 to 10 servings

Pastry:
- 1 egg
- 1 cup yogurt
- 2 tablespoons olive oil
- 1 cup butter, melted
- 4 cups flour
- 1 teaspoon salt
- 1½ teaspoons baking powder

Filling:
- 6 ounces farmer cheese, or other soft white cheese
- ⅛ teaspoon salt
- Freshly ground black pepper
- 3 tablespoons chopped chives
- 1½ tablespoons chopped parsley
- 4 tablespoons milk

Combine the egg, yogurt, olive oil and butter and beat with a whisk until well blended. Add the flour, salt and baking powder and stir to form a smooth dough. Cover and refrigerate for 15 minutes. In another bowl, combine the cheese, salt, pepper, chives and parsley. Roll a piece of dough the size of a walnut into a smooth ball. Hollow out the middle and fill with ½ teaspoon of cheese mixture. Seal the dough around the filling and form into a ball again. Continue until all the dough is used. Butter a cookie sheet and place the cheese balls on the sheet. Brush each with milk. Bake in a preheated 400° oven for 20 to 25 minutes. Serve hot.

Tamara keftedes

Omeleta me rizi

Dolmadakia

Fried tamara rissoles

4 servings

½ pound smoked cod's roe
1 onion, coarsely chopped
2 cloves garlic, crushed
1 slice day old bread, without
crust, crumbled
¼ teaspoon cinnamon
Freshly ground black pepper
1 tablespoon chopped fresh
mint or
1 teaspoon dried mint
2 tablespoons chopped parsley
1 egg
1 tablespoon water
¼ cup flour
Oil for deep frying

Combine all the ingredients
except the flour and oil. Put
through a mincer or chop
finely. Set aside in a cool place
for 3 hours. Form into small
patties, coat with flour and
deep fry in preheated 375° oil
until nicely browned.

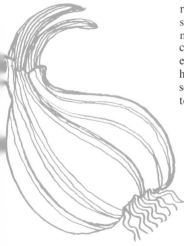

Rice omelet

4 servings

3 medium sized tomatoes
1 teaspoon salt
Freshly ground black pepper
½ teaspoon sugar
½ cup dried breadcrumbs
¼ cup flour
4 tablespoons butter
1 onion, thinly sliced
5 eggs
½ cup cooked rice

Peel the tomatoes and cut into
thick slices. Season with ½
teaspoon salt, pepper and sugar.
Mix the breadcrumbs and flour
together and coat the tomato
slices. Heat 2 tablespoons of the
butter in a large skillet, add the
tomatoes and fry for about 3
minutes on each side until nicely
browned. Remove from the pan
and keep warm. Add the
remaining butter and fry the
onion until soft and golden
brown. Beat the eggs, add the
remaining salt and pepper and
stir in the cooked rice. Add this
mixture to the frying pan and
cook over medium heat until the
eggs are set. Fold the omelet in
half and transfer to a warm
serving dish. Place the fried
tomatoes on top and serve hot.

Stuffed vine leaves

4 servings

1 (16 ounce) jar vine leaves
6 small onions, finely chopped
¾ pound ground veal
⅔ cup rice, soaked for 5
minutes in boiling water and
drained
1 teaspoon crushed dried mint
leaves
2 teaspoons finely chopped
parsley or dill weed
Pinch of cinnamon
1 teaspoon salt
Freshly ground black pepper
2 tablespoons olive oil
Chicken broth or water
Juice of 1 lemon

Carefully unfold the vine leaves
and rinse under cold, running
water. In a bowl, combine the
onions, veal, rice, mint, parsley,
cinnamon, salt, pepper and olive
oil. Form about 1 tablespoon of
the mixture into an oval shape,
place on a vine leaf and roll up
as illustrated on page 19.
Continue until all the stuffing is
used. Arrange a layer of leftover
leaves on the bottom of a small
casserole just large enough to
hold all the stuffed leaves. Place
a layer of stuffed leaves very
close together over the layer of
leftover leaves. Make another
layer of leftover leaves and
continue layering until all the
stuffed leaves are tightly packed
into the casserole. Pour over
enough broth or water to barely
cover the vine leaves and
sprinkle with lemon juice.
Weight the stuffed leaves with a
plate. Cover the casserole and

bring to a boil over moderate
heat. Reduce the heat and
simmer slowly 1 hour. Let the
leaves cool in the broth. Drain
and serve cold. The vine leaves
may also be served hot and the
broth enriched with the egg and
lemon mixture used in Soupa
Avgolemono on page 25.
Served cold, the vine leaves are
an excellent cocktail snack.

Finely ground fish roe and stuffed vine leaves (recipe page 15, 3rd column) are among the best loved Greek appetizers and are never absent in any restaurant.

Taramasalata

Fish roe paté

4 servings

¼ pound smoked cod's roe
 3 slices day old bread,
    without crusts, crumbled
 4 tablespoons olive oil
 2 tablespoons lemon juice
 1 teaspoon water
 1 teaspoon grated onion
    (optional)
 1 teaspoon chopped parsley
    Black pitted olives

Mash the fish roe, add the breadcrumbs and gradually stir in the oil and lemon juice, beating until smooth. Beat in the water to make it light and fluffy. Add the onion and parsley. Transfer to a serving bowl and garnish with olives.

Stuffed eggplant (recipe page 18, 1st column) is the national vegetable of all the countries along the east coast of the Mediterranean and one of the cheapest vegetables in the marketplace.

Imam bayıldı

Stuffed eggplant

4 servings

2 small eggplants
2 tablespoons oil
2 tablespoons butter
2 small onions, chopped
3 medium sized tomatoes,
  peeled, seeded and sliced
2 cloves garlic, crushed
1 bay leaf
1 cinnamon stick
¼ cup chopped parsley
½ teaspoon salt
  Freshly ground black pepper
8 black olives
8 anchovy fillets

Remove the stems from the
eggplants. Heat the oil and fry
the eggplants on all sides for 5
minutes. Remove from the pan,
peel, cut in half lengthwise and
scoop out some of the pulp.
Heat the butter and cook the
onions 5 minutes until soft and
golden. Add the tomatoes and
simmer for 10 minutes over low
heat. Add garlic, bay leaf,
cinnamon stick, parsley, salt and
pepper and simmer for another
10 minutes. Remove the bay leaf
and cinnamon stick and stuff the
eggplants with the mixture.
Place the stuffed eggplants in a
buttered ovenproof dish and
bake in a preheated 350° oven
for 30 minutes. Garnish with
olives and anchovy fillets and
serve warm.

Melitzanes salata

Eggplant salad

4 servings

2 medium sized eggplants
2 tablespoons lemon juice
2 tablespoons finely chopped
  onion
2 tomatoes, peeled, seeded
  and chopped
½ teaspoon salt
  Freshly ground black pepper
½ teaspoon oregano
1 tablespoon wine vinegar
3 tablespoons olive oil

Place the eggplants on a wire
rack and bake in a preheated
350° oven for 1 hour until the
skins have wrinkled and the
eggplants feel soft to the touch.
Remove from the oven and
let cool. Remove the stalks and
peel off the skins. Cut each
eggplant in half lengthwise
and discard the seeds. Chop
eggplants into small pieces
and sprinkle with lemon juice.
Place in a bowl and add onion,
tomatoes, salt, pepper, oregano,
wine vinegar and olive oil.
Cover and chill. Serve the
salad cold.

Borani bademjan

Eggplant and yogurt salad

4 servings

2 eggplants
1 tablespoon oil
2 small tomatoes, peeled,
  seeded and chopped
¼ teaspoon salt
  Freshly ground black pepper
2 cups yogurt
1 clove garlic, crushed
2 tablespoons chopped walnuts

Bake the eggplants as described
in the previous recipe
Melitzanes salata. Peel, place in
a bowl and mash the flesh.
Add all the ingredients except
¼ cup chopped tomatoes and
the walnuts and combine
thoroughly. Chill 2 hours.
Place on a serving dish and
garnish with the remaining
tomatoes and walnuts
before serving.

Kukye bademjan

Eggplant and eggs

4 servings

1 small eggplant
2 tomatoes, peeled, seeded
  and chopped
1 small onion, finely chopped
1 tablespoon parsley
1 teaspoon salt
  Freshly ground black pepper
½ cup oil
8 eggs
¼ teaspoon saffron soaked in
  1 teaspoon water

Spear the eggplant on a fork
and sear evenly over a flame.
Peel with a knife and dice.
Combine eggplant with the
tomatoes, onion, parsley,
½ teaspoon salt and pepper
and fry in ½ the oil until tender.
Mash with a fork until smooth
and keep warm. Beat the eggs
with the remaining salt, pepper
and saffron until well combined.
Heat the remaining oil in an
omelette pan. Pour in the eggs
and cook over medium heat
until set. Turn over and cook
for another ½ minute. Transfer
to a serving dish, spoon the
eggplant mixture onto one half
and fold the other half over.
Serve immediately.

Mastva khiar

Cucumber and yogurt salad

servings

- *1 large or 2 small cucumbers, peeled and grated*
- *1 medium sized onion, finely chopped*
- *1 cup yogurt*
- *½ cup white Sultana raisins, soaked overnight in water*
- *½ teaspoon salt*
  Freshly ground black pepper
- *3 tablespoons freshly chopped mint or*
- *½ teaspoon dried mint*
- *1 tablespoon freshly chopped basil or*
- *½ teaspoon dried basil*

Place the cucumber and onion in a bowl. Add the yogurt, raisins, salt and pepper and mix well. Sprinkle with mint and basil and serve chilled.

Yalanci dolma

Rice stuffed vine leaves

6 servings

- *1 (16 ounce) jar vine leaves*
- *1½ tablespoons olive oil*
- *1 medium sized onion, finely chopped*
- *⅔ cup rice*
- *1⅓ cups water*
- *½ cup white raisins, soaked overnight in cold water and chopped*
- *½ cup pine nuts*
- *1 tablespoon finely chopped parsley*
- *½ teaspoon salt*
  Freshly ground black pepper
  Pinch of cinnamon
- *2 small tomatoes, peeled, seeded and chopped*
  Water
  Juice of 1 lemon

Carefully unfold the vine leaves and rinse under cold, running water. Heat the olive oil in a saucepan and sauté the onion until golden brown. Add the rice and sauté 3 minutes, stirring constantly. Add the water, raisins and pine nuts. Stir once with a fork, cover and simmer slowly for 25 minutes or until the water has been absorbed. Remove from the heat and stir in the parsley, salt, pepper, cinnamon and tomatoes. Place about 1 tablespoon of the rice mixture on a vine leaf and roll up as illustrated right. Repeat until all the rice is used. Line a casserole just large enough to hold the stuffed leaves with leftover vine leaves. Place a tightly packed layer of stuffed leaves on top. Repeat the layers until all the stuffed leaves are used. Add water to the casserole to barely cover the stuffed leaves and sprinkle with lemon juice. Weight the vine leaves with a plate and cover the casserole. Bring to a boil, lower the heat and simmer 1 hour. Let the stuffed leaves cool in the casserole. Drain, place on a serving plate and serve cold.

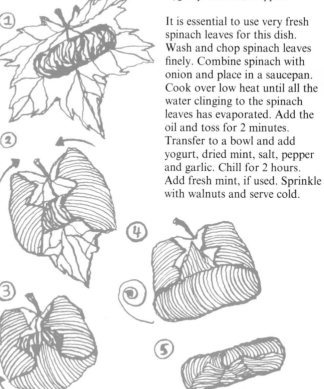

Borani Esfanaj

Spinach and nut salad

4 servings

- *1½ pounds fresh, young spinach*
- *1 small onion, finely chopped*
- *2 teaspoons olive oil*
- *1 cup yogurt*
- *½ teaspoon dried mint or 1 tablespoon finely chopped fresh mint*
- *¼ teaspoon salt*
  Freshly ground black pepper
- *1 clove garlic, crushed*
- *½ cup walnuts, chopped*

It is essential to use very fresh spinach leaves for this dish. Wash and chop spinach leaves finely. Combine spinach with onion and place in a saucepan. Cook over low heat until all the water clinging to the spinach leaves has evaporated. Add the oil and toss for 2 minutes. Transfer to a bowl and add yogurt, dried mint, salt, pepper and garlic. Chill for 2 hours. Add fresh mint, if used. Sprinkle with walnuts and serve cold.

By making full use of modern irrigation techniques, Israel grows wonderful avocados and delicious citrus fruits. Through cooking competitions, the producers try to discover new ways to prepare these priceless fruits.

The eastern coast of the Mediterranean is a rich fishing ground whose catch eventually finds its way to delicious fish cocktails. (recipe page 21, 1st column)

Avocado Hadar

Avocado with citrus fruit

6 servings

> 3 *medium sized avocados*
>   *Juice of 1 lemon*
> 2 *oranges*
> 2 *grapefruit*
> 12 *pitted cherries*

Slice each avocado lengthwise into 2 halves. Rub the exposed surfaces of the avocados with lemon juice to prevent discoloring. Peel the oranges and grapefruit. Cut into segments and remove the thin membrane around each segment. Arrange the orange and grapefruit sections in each avocado half and let stand 30 minutes. Decorate each half with 2 cherries and arrange on individual serving plates.

Kocktail Yafo

Fish cocktail

5 servings

- 1 onion, sliced
- 2 carrots, sliced
- ½ teaspoon salt
  Freshly ground black pepper
- 2 cups water
- ¾ pound white fish (bass,
  haddock, etc.), filleted
- 2 pickled cucumbers, diced
- 1 tablespoon capers

Dressing:

- ½ cup mayonnaise
- 3 tablespoons brandy
- 2 tablespoons lemon juice
- ½ cup catsup
- 1 lemon, sliced

Simmer the onion, carrots, salt
and pepper in the water for 5
minutes. Add the fish and
simmer gently for 15 minutes.
Remove the fish and allow it to
cool. Cut fish into ½ inch
squares or flake it with a fork.
Add the cucumbers and capers
to the fish and arrange on
individual serving plates. To
prepare the dressing, combine
the mayonnaise, brandy, lemon
juice and catsup and stir until
smooth. Spoon the dressing
over each serving. Garnish with
catsup and a lemon slice.

Avocado Haifa

Stuffed avocado

4 servings

- 4 avocados
- 1 tablespoon lemon juice
- 4 tablespoons olive oil
- 2 tablespoons brandy
- 1 tablespoon wine vinegar
- ½ teaspoon salt
- 1 teaspoon sugar
  Freshly ground black pepper
- ½ cup cubed cucumber
- 2 small sour apples, peeled and
  cubed
- 1 cup small shrimp, boiled
  Few sprigs fresh dill weed

Cut the avocados in half
lengthwise. Remove the seeds
and scoop out some of the pulp.
Brush the avocado halves with
lemon juice. Combine the oil,
brandy, vinegar, salt, sugar and
pepper. Add the cucumber,
apples and shrimp, toss well and
marinate in a cool place for
30 minutes. Spoon the mixture
into the halved avocados and
garnish with a sprig of fresh dill
or parsley.

Avocado Sinai

Avocado with tuna fish

6 servings

- *3 medium sized ripe avocados*
- *1 (7 ounce) can tuna fish*
- *2 cloves garlic, crushed*
- *1 small onion, finely minced*
- *2 teaspoons capers or*
  1 pickled cucumber, cut
  in ¼ inch cubes
- *¼ teaspoon salt*
  Freshly ground black pepper
- *1 small onion, peeled and*
  thinly sliced
- *6 stuffed olives*
  Lettuce leaves
  6 black olives, pitted

Peel the avocados. Cut in half lengthwise and remove the seeds. Flake ¾ of the tuna fish. Add the garlic, onion, capers or pickled cucumber, salt and pepper. Mix until well combined. Fill the avocado halves with the mixture and decorate with sliced onions and stuffed olives. Place on a bed of lettuce leaves and garnish with pitted olives.

Prasa yahnisi

Stewed leeks

4 servings

- *2 pounds leeks*
- *3 tablespoons olive oil*
- *3 medium sized onions, thinly*
  sliced
- *3 tomatoes, peeled, seeded and*
  chopped
- *½ teaspoon salt*
  Freshly ground black pepper
- *1 cup chicken broth*
- *2 tablespoons chopped fresh*
  dill or
  1 tablespoon dried dill weed

Remove the outer leaves of the leeks and cut off the root end. Wash thoroughly and cut in half crosswise. Heat the olive oil in a large saucepan and sauté the onions slowly until lightly browned. Add the leeks and sauté a few minutes, turning them carefully so they remain intact. Add tomatoes, salt, pepper and broth and bring to a boil. Reduce the heat and simmer 30 minutes. Remove from the heat and let the leeks cool completely. Sprinkle with dill and serve.

Pilpel memuleh wusach Tiveria

Peppers stuffed with rice

6 servings

- *6 green peppers*
- *½ pound ground beef*
- *2 tablespoons water*
- *1 (4 ounce) can tomato purée*
- *¼ cup chopped parsley*
- *½ cup raw rice*
- *1½ teaspoons salt*
  Freshly ground black pepper
- *3 tablespoons oil*
- *1 medium sized onion, sliced*
- *½ teaspoon sugar*
- *1 egg, beaten*
- *1 teaspoon paprika*

Cut a slice from the top of each pepper. Remove membranes and seeds. Rinse and dry them thoroughly. Combine the beef, water, ¼ of the tomato purée, parsley, rice, 1 teaspoon salt and pepper. Stuff the peppers with the mixture. Add the oil to a skillet and arrange the peppers snugly in the pan, cut side up. Place a slice of onion on each pepper. Dilute the remaining tomato purée with water and pour over the peppers so they are almost covered. Add ½ teaspoon salt and sugar. Simmer for 1 hour in the tightly covered pan. Add water if necessary to maintain the liquid level in the skillet. Place the egg in a medium sized bowl and gradually stir in the sauce in which the peppers were cooked. Add the paprika and return the sauce to the pan. Simmer gently for 10 minutes. Serve the peppers with the sauce.

Kukye sabzi

Eggs and greens

4 servings

- *8 eggs*
- *1 tablespoon flour*
- *1 onion, finely chopped*
- *12 scallions, finely chopped*
- *1 Bibb lettuce, chopped*
- *½ pound spinach leaves,*
  chopped
- *3 tablespoons chopped chives*
- *2 tablespoons finely chopped*
  parsley
- *1 tablespoon finely chopped*
  coriander leaves (optional)
- *1 tablespoon chopped fresh*
  dill or
  ½ teaspoon dried dill weed
- *⅛ teaspoon saffron soaked*
  5 minutes in
  1 teaspoon hot water
- *½ teaspoon salt*
  Freshly ground black pepper
- *4 tablespoons olive oil*

Beat the eggs lightly. Add all the remaining ingredients except the oil. Stir until well combined. Heat the oil in a large skillet. Pour in the egg mixture and cook over moderate heat until the eggs are set. Turn and cook 3 to 5 minutes on the second side over low heat until browned. Serve immediately.

Kabab müjveri

Shezifim memulaim

Salat Hasharon

Zucchini balls

4 to 6 servings

1 *large zucchini (about*
   1 pound)
1 *pound ground lamb*
1 *onion, finely chopped*
4 *tablespoons cream cheese*
2 *eggs, lightly beaten*
1 *tablespoon finely chopped*
   fresh dill or parsley
1 *tablespoon olive oil*
3 *teaspoons salt*
   Freshly ground black pepper
¾ *cup flour*
½ *cup flour for dredging*
   Oil for deep frying

Peel the zucchini, remove the
seeds and chop into small pieces.
Place in a bowl and add the
lamb, onion, cream cheese, eggs,
chopped dill (or parsley), olive
oil, salt and pepper. Mix well.
Add ¾ cup flour and shape into
small balls. Dredge balls in
remaining flour. Deep fry in oil
preheated to 375° for 5 minutes
until crisp and brown. Drain and
serve hot.

Stuffed prunes with veal

8 servings

1 *onion, chopped*
2 *tablespoons butter*
¾ *pound ground veal*
1 *cup walnuts, finely chopped*
¼ *cup raisins*
2 *teaspoons salt*
   Freshly ground black pepper
30 *ready-to-eat pitted prunes*
4 *tablespoons tomato sauce*
1½ *cups water*
   Juice of 1 lemon
⅓ *cup sugar*

Fry the onion for 5 minutes in
the butter. Stir together the veal,
walnuts, raisins, 1 teaspoon salt
and pepper to form a smooth
mixture. Fill the cavity of each
prune with a 1 inch ball of meat
stuffing. Place in a baking dish.
Combine the tomato sauce,
water, lemon juice, sugar,
1 teaspoon salt and pepper and
pour over the prunes. Cover the
dish and bake in a preheated
350° oven for 45 minutes.

Celery salad with egg slices

6 servings

6 *celery stalks*
⅓ *cup olive oil or vegetable oil*
2 *hard boiled eggs, sliced*
6 *pitted black olives, sliced*
1½ *teaspoons mild mustard*
2 *tablespoons vinegar*
¼ *teaspoon salt*
   Freshly ground black pepper

Cut the celery stalks into thin
slices. Place in a shallow dish,
add the oil and marinate for
1 hour. Add the sliced eggs
and olives. Combine the
mustard, vinegar, salt and
pepper and stir into the oil.
Chill and serve.

Soups

Egg-and-lemon soup is traditional fare for the Greek Easter dinner. It is the most refined soup that the Greek kitchen has to offer and somewhat tricky to prepare.

In Eastern Europe and the Middle East, slightly sour soups are preferred. To get the sour flavor they add yogurt. These soups are very refreshing on hot summer days.

Soupa Avgolemono

Egg and lemon soup

8 servings

   8 cups rich chicken broth
   ½ to ¾ cup rice, vermicelli or
      other small pasta
   3 eggs
      Juice of 2 small lemons
   ½ teaspoon salt
      Freshly ground black pepper

Bring the chicken broth to a boil. Add the rice or vermicelli and simmer 15 minutes. Meanwhile, beat the eggs until frothy. Slowly add the lemon juice to the eggs, beating constantly. Add 1½ to 2 cups of the broth, 1 tablespoon at a time, beating constantly. Remove the remaining broth from the heat and beat in the egg mixture. Season with salt and pepper and serve immediately.

Tavuk tshorbası yogurtlu

Chicken soup with yogurt

6 servings

   6 cups chicken broth
   ¼ cup raw rice
   1 teaspoon salt
      Freshly ground black pepper
   1 cup yogurt
   2 egg yolks, lightly beaten
   ½ tablespoon freshly chopped
      mint or
      ½ teaspoon dried mint
   2 tablespoons chopped parsley

Bring the chicken broth to boiling point. Add the rice, salt and pepper, cover and simmer for about 20 minutes until the rice is tender. Stir the yogurt into the egg yolks. Add 4 tablespoons of the hot broth and beat until smooth. Add the egg yolk mixture to the hot rice and broth. Stir well but do not let it boil again. Garnish with mint and parsley and serve hot.

Kakavia

Balik tshorbasi

In Genesis the symbolic story is told of how Esau came home one day tired and hungry from hunting, and smelled what was probably lentil soup which his brother Jacob had cooked. Esau was so hungry he sold his birthright for some of the soup. Lentil soup is still a part of the daily diet throughout the Middle East, and it is probably the oldest dish in the world. Usually the soup is made with mutton or chicken, and the lentils are the small orange-red variety that can be bought at any Eastern market. With these lentils the soup becomes a beautiful vermilion-red color, much more attractive than the dull brown of the soup we know.

Certainly the most classic Greek soup is 'avgolemono', made from chicken broth, very slightly soured by lemon and thickened with a lightly beaten egg. It is a very fine gold-yellow soup, tasty and light and a necessary part of the Easter dinner.

And throughout the East when the summer comes, yoghurt soup is a refreshing dish. Yoghurt is one of the most ancient ingredients in the cooking of the entire Middle East. The soup is thinned with water or chicken broth.

Greek bouillabaisse

8 servings

2½ to 3 pounds assorted fish
    fillets
  1 teaspoon salt
     Juice of 1 lemon
     Heads, tails and bones of
     filleted fish
 10 to 12 cups water
  4 tablespoons olive oil
  2 onions, thinly sliced
  1 potato, peeled and thinly
     sliced
  6 to 8 medium sized tomatoes,
     peeled, seeded and chopped
  2 tablespoons finely chopped
     celery leaves
  2 cloves garlic, crushed
  ¼ cup dry white wine
  1 bay leaf
     Freshly ground black pepper
  2 tablespoons finely chopped
     parsley

Wash the fish fillets, dry them and cut into small serving pieces. Sprinkle the fish with the salt and juice of ½ a lemon and set aside. Place the fish trimmings and the water in a large pan and bring to a boil. Lower the heat and simmer 20 minutes. (If fish trimmings are not available, use half clam juice and half water.) Strain and reserve the broth. Heat the olive oil in a large heavy pan. Add the onions, potato, tomatoes, celery leaves and garlic and sauté slowly 5 minutes. Add the reserved broth, wine and bay leaf and bring to a boil. Lower the heat, cover and simmer 40 minutes. Strain the broth, pressing down on the vegetables to extract all the juices. Return the broth to the pan. There should be at least 10 cups. If not, add water to measure 10 cups. Bring the broth to a rolling boil and add the pepper, parsley and the firmest of the fish fillets. Cook 5 minutes and add the more delicate fish. Cook over moderate heat 10 minutes more. Just before serving, add the remaining juice of ½ a lemon and taste for seasoning.

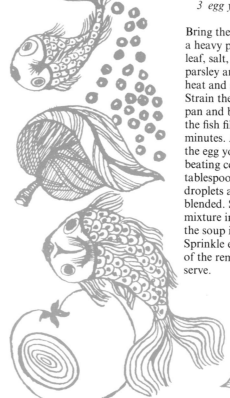

Fish soup

6 servings

  6 cups fish broth or half clam
     juice and half water
  1 bay leaf
  ¼ teaspoon salt
     Freshly ground black pepper
  3 tablespoons finely chopped
     parsley
     Pinch of saffron
  1 pound haddock fillets or
     fillets of other firm fleshed
     fish
     Juice of 1 lemon
  3 egg yolks, lightly beaten

Bring the fish broth to a boil in a heavy pan and add the bay leaf, salt, pepper, 2 tablespoons parsley and saffron. Reduce the heat and simmer 25 minutes. Strain the broth, return to the pan and bring to a simmer. Add the fish fillets and poach 15 minutes. Add the lemon juice to the egg yolks by droplets, beating constantly. Then add 4 tablespoons of the fish broth by droplets and beat until well blended. Stir the egg yolk mixture into the soup and ladle the soup into individual bowls. Sprinkle each serving with some of the remaining parsley and serve.

Psarosoupa

Fish soup

6 servings

- 6 cups fish broth or half clam juice and half water
- 4 medium sized tomatoes, peeled, seeded and chopped
- ½ teaspoon sugar
- ¼ teaspoon salt
  Freshly ground black pepper
- 1½ tablespoons olive oil
- ½ cup rice
- 1 tablespoon lemon juice
- 2 tablespoons finely chopped parsley

Place the fish broth, tomatoes, sugar, salt, pepper and olive oil in a heavy saucepan. Bring to a boil and cook 5 minutes over high heat. Reduce the heat and simmer 30 minutes. Bring to a boil, add the rice and cook over high heat 15 minutes. Stir in the lemon juice and parsley and serve immediately.

Sayadieh

Rice in fish broth

6 servings

- 2 pounds haddock, sea bass or cod fillets
- 1¼ teaspoons salt
- 4 tablespoons olive oil
- 2 small onions, chopped
  Head bones and other trimmings from filleted fish
- 4 cups water
  Freshly ground black pepper
- 1½ cups rice
- ½ cup combined almonds and pine nuts
- 1 tablespoon lemon juice

Sprinkle the fish fillets on both sides with 1 teaspoon salt and refrigerate for 2½ hours. Meanwhile, heat 1 tablespoon olive oil in a saucepan and sauté the onions until golden brown. Add the fish trimmings, water and pepper and bring to a boil. Reduce the heat and simmer 30 minutes. (If fish trimmings are not available, use half clam juice and half water.) Strain and reserve the broth. Soak the rice in water to cover for 30 minutes and drain. Bring 3 cups of the reserved fish broth to a boil, add the rice and stir once with a fork. Lower the heat, cover the pan and simmer until the rice has absorbed all the liquid (about 25 minutes). While the rice is cooking, heat the remaining olive oil in a skillet and sauté the fish fillets about 4 minutes on each side or until the flesh flakes easily with a fork. Remove from the pan and keep warm. Oil a shallow pan or ring mold and arrange the almonds and pine nuts on the bottom in a decorative pattern. Carefully place the cooked rice on the nuts and press down firmly with a wooden spoon or spatula. Unmold the rice on a serving dish and surround with the fish fillets. Bring the remaining fish broth to a boil and stir in the lemon juice and remaining salt. Pour into a sauce dish and serve with the fish and rice.

Kuzu ciger tshorbasi

Liver soup

6 servings

- 4 tablespoons butter
- ½ pound lamb's liver
- 16 scallions, coarsely chopped
- 4 large ripe tomatoes, peeled, seeded and coarsely chopped
- 6 cups beef broth
- 2 cloves garlic, crushed
- ¼ teaspoon dried marjoram, crumbled
- 1 teaspoon salt
  Freshly ground black pepper

Heat 2 tablespoons of butter, add the liver and fry for 1½ minutes each side. Remove from the pan and cut into ¼ inch cubes or chop coarsely. Heat the remaining butter in a large pan and fry the scallions for 1½ minutes, stirring frequently. Add the tomatoes, beef broth, garlic, marjoram, salt and pepper. Bring to a boil and add the liver. Reduce the heat and simmer for 40 minutes. Serve hot.

*Weddings are still the occasion
for festive and abundant eating.
The many dishes set on the table
are a traditional assurance that
the marriage will prove fertile.*

Düğün tshorbası

Wedding soup

6 servings

- 6 cups chicken broth
- 3 tablespoons butter
- 1 pound lean lamb, coarsley ground
- 2 tablespoons flour
- 1 onion, halved
- 1 teaspoon salt
  Freshly ground black pepper
- 2 teaspoons paprika
- 4 egg yolks, lightly beaten
  Juice of 1 lemon
- ¼ teaspoon cinnamon

Heat the chicken broth to boiling point. Melt the butter in a large skillet. Add the lamb and fry, stirring constantly until well browned. Stir in the flour and cook for 2 minutes. Add lamb, onion, salt, pepper and paprika to the hot broth. Bring to boiling point, reduce the heat and simmer for 1½ hours. Remove the onion. Beat the egg yolks and lemon juice together in a small bowl. Add egg yolk mixture to the soup, stirring constantly. Stir until hot but do not allow the soup to boil. Sprinkle with cinnamon and serve immediately.

Tchorba Toptsita

Traditional meatball soup

6 servings

- 2 pounds soup bones
- 6 cups water
- ½ cup ground beef
- ½ teaspoon salt
  Freshly ground black pepper
- 3 tablespoons finely chopped parsley
- 2 tablespoons olive oil
- 1 teaspoon paprika
- ½ cup rice
- 2 cloves garlic, crushed
- ¼ cup vinegar

Place the bones in a large saucepan. Add the water, cover and simmer for 3 hours. Skim off the foam which rises to the surface. Strain the broth and discard the bones. Add more water if necessary to make up the 6 cup quantity. Return the broth to a clean saucepan and bring to simmering point. Combine the beef with salt, pepper and 2 tablespoons chopped parsley. Form into small balls 1 inch in diameter. Add meat balls to broth and simmer for 15 minutes. Heat the oil in a small saucepan and stir in paprika. Cook the paprika in oil for 2 minutes and add to the soup. Add the rice. Cover the saucepan and simmer for 20 minutes. Stir in the remaining 1 tablespoon of parsley, the garlic and vinegar. Serve immediately.

Since the time of the Old Testament, soup has been loudly 'sipped' along the eastern Mediterranean coast. It is served cold in summer and hot in winter.

Meatball soup (recipe page 28, 4th column)

Aashe Mast

Yogurt soup

6 servings

     6 *cups water*
    ¾ *pound ground lamb*
     2 *onions, finely chopped*
    ½ *cup yellow split peas*
    ½ *pound spinach, chopped*
    10 *scallions, chopped*
     1 *teaspoon salt*
        Freshly ground black pepper
     1 *cup raw rice*
     2 *cups yogurt*
     1 *tablespoons olive oil*
     2 *tablespoons fresh dill*

Place the water, lamb, onions, split peas, spinach, scallions, salt and pepper in a saucepan. Bring to a boil, cover and simmer for 40 minutes. Stir in the rice and cook over moderate heat for about 25 minutes, stirring occasionally. Add the yogurt. Stir 1 minute without boiling and remove from the heat. Heat the oil in a frying pan, add the dill and stir for 1 minute. Add to the soup and serve.

Soupa lakhana

Cabbage soup

8 servings

  2 pounds white cabbage
  2 small onions, chopped
1½ tablespoons olive oil
  4 medium sized ripe tomatoes,
     peeled, seeded and chopped
 ½ teaspoon salt
     Freshly ground black pepper
 10 cups beef broth
  1 cup croutons

Shred the cabbage finely, wash and drain. Fry the onions in the oil until golden brown and transfer to a large sauce pan. Add the cabbage, tomatoes, salt and pepper and cook for 1 minute. Add the beef broth and bring to a boil. Reduce the heat, partially cover and simmer for 30 minutes or until the cabbage is tender. Serve in individual bowls and garnish with croutons just before serving

Fasolada

Bean soup

8 servings

  1 pound dried white beans
 10 cups water
  3 medium sized onions,
     chopped
  1 carrot, finely chopped
1½ tablespoons chopped parsley
  2 tablespoons chopped celery
     leaves
  2 tablespoons tomato purée
1½ tablespoons olive oil
 ½ teaspoon salt
     Freshly ground black pepper

Soak the beans overnight. Wash, drain and place them in a large saucepan. Add the water and boil for 2 minutes. Pour off all the water and add the same quantity of fresh water. Bring to a boil, add the onions, carrot, 1 tablespoon parsley, celery leaves, tomato purée, oil, salt and pepper. Simmer for about 1 hour or until the beans are soft and tender. Season to taste, sprinkle on the remaining parsley and serve hot.

Makhluta

Lentil soup with chick peas

8 servings

  1 cup chick peas
 ½ cup black beans
  1 cup lentils
  8 cups water
  1 cup rice
  2 tablespoons olive oil
 ½ cup chopped onion
1½ teaspoons salt
 ½ teaspoon crushed caraway
     seeds

Soak the chick peas and black beans together overnight in water to cover. Drain and place in a large, heavy pan with the lentils and water. Bring to a boil, lower the heat and simmer 1½ hours or until beans and peas are tender. Add the rice and simmer 20 minutes more. Meanwhile heat the olive oil in a small skillet and sauté the onions until golden brown. Drain off all the oil and add the onion to the bean soup. Stir in the salt and caraway seeds and simmer 5 minutes.

Fakki

Lentil soup

8 to 10 servings

  1 pound yellow or brown lentils
 10 cups water
  2 onions, chopped
  1 carrot, grated
  2 cloves garlic, crushed
  1 stalk celery, chopped
  1 tablespoon olive oil
  2 bay leaves
2½ teaspoons salt
     Freshly ground black pepper
  2 tablespoons vinegar

Wash and drain the lentils. Place the lentils and water in a large saucepan. Add the onions, carrot, garlic, celery, oil, bay leaves, salt and pepper. Bring to a boil and simmer for 45 to 50 minutes until the lentils are tender. Remove the bay leaves. Purée the soup in the blender or force it through a strainer. Stir in the vinegar, reheat and serve.

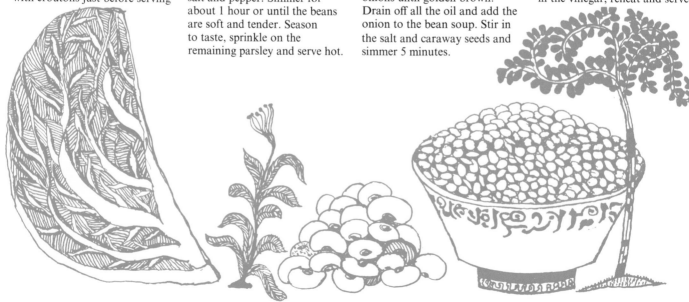

Patsas

Lamb soup

6 servings

6 to 8 cups water
2 to 3 pounds lamb shanks
2 small onions, peeled
1 teaspoon salt
    Freshly ground black pepper
    Few springs parsley
3 eggs
    Juice of 2 lemons

Bring the water to a boil and add the lamb shanks. Bring to a boil again and skim the broth. Reduce the heat, add the onions, salt and pepper and simmer 1½ hours. Remove the lamb shanks, strip the meat from the bones and return the meat to the broth. Simmer ½ hour more. Remove and discard the onions. Prepare the egg and lemon juice mixture as described in the recipe for Avgolemono soup on page 25 and add it to the soup. Serve immediately.

Shorabat Kharoof

Lamb's soup with zucchini

6 servings

1 pound lamb with marrow
    bone
6 cups water
1 teaspoon salt
    Freshly ground black pepper
6 tablespoons raw rice
½ pound zucchini, peeled and
    chopped
¼ teaspoon cinnamon

Place the lamb in a medium-sized saucepan. Add the water, salt and pepper. Cover and simmer for 1½ hours. Discard the bone and cut the lamb into 1 inch cubes. Return the lamb to the saucepan with the cooking liquid. Add the rice and zucchini. Cover and simmer 20 minutes. Sprinkle with cinnamon just before serving.

Mayeritsa

Greek Easter soup

6 servings

3 tablespoons butter
1 pound lean lamb, cut into
    ¼ inch cubes
10 scallions, finely chopped
1 bunch fresh dill, finely
    chopped or
    1 tablespoon dried dill weed
2 tablespoons finely chopped
    parsley
1 tablespoon finely chopped
    fresh mint or
    1 teaspoon dried mint
6 cups water
½ teaspoon salt
    Freshly ground black pepper
6 tablespoons rice
3 eggs
    Juice of 2 lemons

Heat the butter in a large saucepan. Add the lamb, scallions, dill, parsley and mint and sauté 3 minutes. Add the water, salt and pepper and bring to a boil. Lower the heat, cover the pan and simmer 1 hour. Add rice and simmer 15 minutes more. Beat the eggs and add the lemon juice slowly, beating constantly. Stir a few tablespoons of the soup into the egg mixture and return to the soup. Do not allow it to boil or the eggs will curdle. Remove from the heat and serve immediately.

Koyun et suyu

Lamb's broth

8 servings

3 tablespoons butter
2 pounds boneless neck or
    shoulder of lamb, cubed
8 cups water
2 large onions, coarsley
    chopped
3 carrots, coarsley chopped
1 leek, coarsley chopped
2 tablespoons chopped celery
    leaves
4 scallions, coarsley chopped
1 bay leaf
1 teaspoon salt
    Freshly ground black pepper
¼ cup yogurt
1 teaspoon finely chopped
    parsley

Heat the butter in a large saucepan and sauté the lamb until lightly browned. Add the water, bring to a boil and skim the broth. Add all the remaining ingredients except the yogurt and parsley. Bring to a boil again, reduce the heat and simmer 1½ hours. Combine the yogurt with 2 tablespoons broth. Stir the yogurt mixture into the soup, sprinkle with parsley and serve.

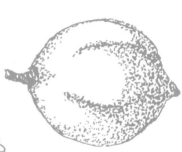

'Bortsh' is the common name for the slightly sour soups with cream which can be found everywhere in Eastern Europe. The exact origin is unknown, but it probably came from the Caucasus Mountain region, from which it made its way to neighboring Turkey.

Bortsh

Turkish borsch soup

6 servings

- 4 tablespoons butter
- 2 medium sized onions, diced
- 1 green pepper, seeded and diced
- 2 cloves garlic, crushed
- 1 small head cabbage, cut into chunks
- 6 cups beef broth
- 2 large beets, sliced
- 3 potatoes, diced
- 3 tomatoes, peeled, seeded and quartered
- 1 tablespoon lemon juice
- 2 bay leaves
- ⅛ teaspoon dill seeds, crushed
- ⅛ teaspoon cumin seeds, crushed
- 1 chili pepper, seeded and mashed
- 2 tablespoons coarsely chopped celery leaves
- 1 cup sour cream
- 2 tablespoons chopped parsley

Heat the butter in a large saucepan. Add the onions and green pepper and sauté about 2 minutes. Add garlic and cabbage and sauté 2 more minutes, stirring constantly. Add all the remaining ingredients except the sour cream and parsley. Bring to a boil, reduce the heat and simmer 45 to 60 minutes. Taste for seasoning and add salt and pepper if necessary. Serve in individual bowls and garnish with a liberal spoonful of sour cream and a little chopped parsley.

Al-fallah

Peasant soup

6 servings

- 3 tablespoons butter
- 1 medium sized onion, finely chopped
- 6 cups water
- ¾ cup rice
- 2 medium sized tomatoes, peeled, seeded and chopped
- 1 tablespoon salt
- Pinch of cinnamon

Heat the butter in a large, heavy saucepan and sauté the onion over moderate heat until lightly browned. Add all the remaining ingredients except the cinnamon and bring to a boil over high heat. Reduce the heat and simmer slowly for 1½ hours. Serve in individual soup bowls and sprinkle each serving with a little cinnamon.

Hortosoupa kalokariano

Summer vegetable soup

6 servings

- 4 tablespoons butter
- 1 medium sized onion, finely chopped
- 2 small zucchini, chopped
- ½ cucumber, peeled and chopped
- ½ head Boston lettuce, chopped
- 6 tablespoons fresh peas
- 2 tomatoes, peeled, seeded and chopped
- 12 scallions, sliced
- 2 tablespoons finely chopped parsley
- ½ tablespoon finely chopped fresh mint leaves or ½ teaspoon crushed dried mint leaves
- ½ tablespoon finely chopped fresh basil leaves or ½ teaspoon crushed dried basil
- 8 cups boiling chicken broth
- ½ teaspoon sugar
- ½ teaspoon salt
- Freshly ground black pepper

Heat the butter in a large saucepan and sauté the onion over low heat until softened. Add the zucchini, cucumber, lettuce, peas, tomatoes and scallions and toss in the hot butter for 1 minute. Add all the remaining ingredients and bring to a boil. Reduce the heat and simmer 10 minutes.

Aashe Sak

Spinach soup

4 servings

- 1½ cups red lentils, soaked overnight and drained
- 1 onion, finely chopped
- 5 cups water
- 1 pound ground lean lamb
- ¾ teaspoon salt
- Freshly ground black pepper
- 1½ pounds fresh spinach
- ½ teaspoon turmeric
- 2 tablespoons lemon juice
- 3 eggs, beaten
- 1 tablespoon finely chopped dill or parsley

Place the lentils, onion and water in a large saucepan and bring to a boil. Lower the heat, cover and simmer 20 minutes. Meanwhile, combine the lamb with ¼ teaspoon salt and pepper and form into small balls. Add the meatballs, spinach, turmeric and remaining salt and pepper to the soup and continue simmering 40 minutes. Stir in the lemon juice and simmer 10 minutes more. Remove from the heat and stir in the beaten eggs. Sprinkle with dill or parsley and serve.

Bezelye tshorbası

Revydia

Mercimek tshorbası

Split pea soup

8 servings

¾ pound split peas, soaked
   overnight
8 cups chicken broth
½ teaspoon salt
   Freshly ground black pepper
2 tablespoons butter
1 medium sized onion, sliced
1 tablespoon finely chopped
   carrot
2 tablespoons finely chopped
   celery leaves
¼ pound spinach
1 tablespoon chopped fresh
   mint or
1½ teaspoons crushed dried
   mint
2 tablespoons finely chopped
   parsley

Drain the split peas and place
in a large pan with the broth,
salt and pepper. Bring to a boil,
reduce the heat and simmer
1 hour or until peas are tender.
Meanwhile, heat the butter in a
skillet and sauté the onion 2
minutes. Add the carrot and
celery and sauté 2 minutes more.
Add the spinach and sauté
1 minute. Add the sautéed
vegetables to the soup and
continue cooking 30 minutes.
Purée the soup in a blender and
force through a sieve. Taste for
seasoning, bring to a boil and
stir in the mint and parsley.
Serve immediately.

Chick pea soup

6 servings

6 cups chicken broth
1 (16 ounce) can chick peas
   (garbanzos) drained
2 medium sized onions, thinly
   sliced
½ teaspoon salt
   Freshly ground black pepper
¼ cup olive oil
1 tablespoon lemon juice
1 tablespoon finely chopped
   parsley

Heat the broth and add the
chick peas, onions, salt, pepper
and olive oil. Bring to a boil,
reduce the heat and simmer 20
minutes. Stir in the lemon juice
and taste for seasoning. Sprinkle
with parsley and serve
immediately.

Red lentil soup

6 servings

2 tablespoons butter
3 small onions, finely chopped
1 clove garlic, crushed
1 cup red lentils, soaked
   overnight and drained
1 teaspoon paprika
2 bay leaves
   Pinch of basil
½ teaspoon salt
   Freshly ground black pepper
8 cups chicken or beef broth
2 tablespoons finely chopped
   parsley

Heat the butter in a large
saucepan and sauté the onions
and garlic over medium heat for
2 minutes. Add the lentils,
paprika, bay leaves, basil, salt,
pepper and broth and bring to a
boil. Lower the heat, cover and
simmer 1½ hours. Purée the
soup in a blender and force
through a sieve. Reheat the soup
until steaming, sprinkle with
parsley and serve.

Abgushte adas

Lentil soup

4 servings

- *1 pound lamb, cut into ¼ inch cubes*
- *1 cup red lentils, soaked overnight and drained*
- *1 onion, chopped*
  Peel of 2 limes or lemons
  Juice of 1 lime or lemon
  Pinch of saffron
- *3 cups beef broth or water*
- *¼ teaspoon salt*
  Freshly ground black pepper
- *1 cup chopped cabbage*

Place the lamb, lentils, onion, lime or lemon peel and juice, saffron and beef broth in a large saucepan. Bring to a boil and skim the broth. Add salt and pepper, reduce the heat, cover and simmer 1 hour. Add cabbage and simmer 45 minutes more. Remove lime or lemon peel and serve.

Yayla tshorbası

Anatolian soup

4 servings

- *2 tablespoons butter*
- *1 onion, chopped*
- *4 cups chicken broth*
- *¼ cup barley, soaked in water overnight*
- *1 teaspoon salt*
  Freshly ground black pepper
- *1 cup yogurt*
- *2 tablespoons chopped parsley*
- *1 tablespoon chopped fresh mint or*
  1 teaspoon dried mint

Melt the butter in a saucepan, add the onion and fry for 5 minutes until soft and golden. Add the chicken broth and bring to boiling point. Add the barley, salt and pepper and simmer for 45 minutes or until the barley is tender. Add a few tablespoons of hot broth to the yogurt, beat until well blended and add to the soup. Reheat the soup but do not boil. Sprinkle with parsley and mint and serve.

Shorabat Sabanekh

Abgushte Beh

Spinach soup

6 servings

1½ *pounds rack of lamb*
 6 *cups water*
 6 *tablespoons raw rice*
½ *teaspoon salt*
 2 *tablespoons butter*
 1 *onion, finely chopped*
 2 *cloves garlic, crushed*
 2 *tablespoons finely chopped parsley*
 1 *pound fresh spinach, finely chopped*

Simmer the lamb in the water for 1½ hours until tender. Remove the lamb and cut the meat into 1 inch cubes. Return to the pan and bring to the boil. Add the rice and salt and continue cooking for 5 minutes. Melt the butter in a skillet. Add the onion and garlic and cook 3 minutes until soft and golden. Add the parsley and fry for 2 more minutes. Add this mixture to the soup and simmer for 15 minutes. Add the chopped spinach and cook for 10 minutes until the spinach is tender.

Quince soup

4 servings

¾ *pound lean lamb, in 1 piece*
 2 *onions, finely chopped*
¼ *cup split peas, soaked overnight and drained*
 3 *cups water*
¼ *teaspoon salt*
  Freshly ground black pepper
½ *teaspoon turmeric*
  Pinch of cinnamon
 2 *tablespoons oil*
 2 *quinces, peeled, seeded and chopped*
 2 *tablespoons lemon juice*
  Pinch of sugar
 1 *tablespoon finely chopped parsley*

Place the lamb, onions, split peas, water, salt, pepper, turmeric and cinnamon in a large saucepan and bring to a boil. Lower the heat, cover and simmer 1½ hours. Meanwhile, heat the oil and sauté the quinces over low heat until soft. Stir in the lemon juice and sugar. Add the quince mixture to the soup and simmer 40 minutes more. Remove the lamb and cut it into small pieces. Sprinkle the soup with parsley and serve the meat and soup separately accompanied by crusty bread and a green salad.

Abgushte Sib

Apple and sour cherry soup

6 servings

- ¾ *pound lean lamb, in 1 piece*
- 1 *onion, finely chopped*
- ½ *cup yellow split peas, soaked overnight and drained*
- 6 *cups water*
- ½ *teaspoon salt*
  Freshly ground black pepper
- ½ *teaspoon turmeric*
  Pinch of cinnamon
- 2 *tablespoons butter*
- 4 *small cooking apples, peeled, cored and chopped*
- ¾ *pound sour cherries, pitted or substitute canned cherries*
- 1 *tablespoon chopped fresh mint or*
- 1 *teaspoon dried mint*

Place the lamb, onion, split peas, water, salt, pepper, turmeric and cinnamon in a large saucepan and bring to a boil. Lower the heat, cover and simmer 1½ hours. Heat the butter in a skillet and sauté the apples and cherries over medium heat 4 minutes. Add the fruits to the soup and continue simmering 40 minutes. Remove the lamb, chop into small pieces and return to the soup. Sprinkle with mint and serve.

Abgushte Miveh

Dried fruit soup

4 servings

- ¾ *pound lamb*
- ½ *cup yellow split peas*
- 1 *onion, chopped*
- 3 *cups water*
- 1 *teaspoon salt*
  Freshly ground black pepper
- ½ *teaspoon ground cumin*
- ¼ *teaspoon ground coriander*
  Pinch of powdered saffron
- 1 *teaspoon turmeric*
- ½ *cup dried apricots and prunes, chopped*
- 1 *tablespoon lemon juice*

Place the lamb, peas and onion in a saucepan with the water, salt and spices. Bring to a boil, cover and simmer for 1 hour. Add the apricots and prunes and simmer for another ½ hour. Remove the lamb, cut into small pieces and return it to the saucepan. Add the lemon juice. Reheat the soup and serve hot.

Shorabat Karéi

Pumpkin soup

6 servings

- 1 *pound lamb stew meat with bones*
- 1 *pound pumpkin, cut into cubes*
- 1 *tablespoon salt*
  Freshly ground black pepper
- 6 *cups water*
- 3 *tablespoons butter*
- 4 *tablespoons flour*

Place the lamb, pumpkin, salt, pepper and water in a large, heavy saucepan. Bring to a boil over high heat and skim the broth. Reduce the heat, cover and simmer 1 hour. Heat the butter in a separate pan. Stir in the flour and cook 2 minutes. Add 1 to 1½ cups of the simmering broth, stirring constantly until a very thick sauce is formed. Remove the lamb from the pan, strip the meat from the bones and return the meat to the broth. Add the sauce to the simmering broth, stirring constantly. Cover and simmer 45 minutes. Serve immediately.

Fish dishes

The fish market in Istanbul is where the Bosporus meets the Golden Horn. There is a wide wharf (actually a square facing the water), and small fishing boats bring their catch there from the Bosporus, the Sea of Marmora and the Black Sea. Fresh fish, mussels, large shrimp, and even lobsters are brought in by hundreds of small boats, all flying the red Turkish flag with its white crescent in the center. On the wharf itself there are stalls where freshly-fried fish can be bought. There is no better place to eat cheaply in Istanbul. Wooden tables and benches, partitioned off by sails, form these improvised restaurants, with their large frying pans set over oil burners. The crisp fried fish is served with the simplest of accompaniments – bread, and perhaps a cucumber salad. Further on, at the point where the Galata bridge across the Golden Horn joins old and new Istanbul, there are more elaborate seafood restaurants. Under the bridge are a line of small places where the visitor can dine on lobster and large shrimp, stuffed mussels and that delectable fish, the John Dory, grilled over a charcoal fire.

Barbounia sto harti

Red mullet in foil

4 servings

- 4 small red mullet
- 6 tablespoons olive oil
- 2 tablespoons lemon juice
- ½ teaspoon marjoram
- 4 tablespoons finely chopped parsley
- ½ teaspoon salt
  Freshly ground black pepper
- 8 thin slices lemon

Rub the mullet inside and out with a little of the oil. In a small bowl, combine 5 tablespoons olive oil, lemon juice, marjoram, parsley, salt and pepper. Cut 4 pieces of aluminum foil large enough to wrap each fish securely. Brush the pieces of foil with a little oil. Place each fish on its piece of foil and arrange 2 lemon slices on top of each fish. Spoon some of the oil-lemon juice mixture over each fish. Wrap the foil around each mullet making sure the packages are securely closed. Place in an ovenproof dish and bake in a 350° oven for 30 minutes. Serve the mullet wrapped in their foil packages.

Psari fournou spetsiotiko

Baked fish Spetsos style

4 servings

2 pounds haddock, sea bass
  or other firm white fish
½ teaspoon salt
  Juice of ½ lemon
4 tablespoons olive oil
3 ripe tomatoes, peeled,
  seeded and chopped
1 tablespoon tomato paste
3 tablespoons chopped parsley
2 cloves garlic, crushed
  Freshly ground black pepper
4 tablespoons dried
  breadcrumbs

Clean the fish and rub with salt
and lemon juice. Oil a baking
dish with 1 tablespoon of the
oil and place the fish in the
dish. Combine the remaining
oil with the tomatoes, tomato
paste, parsley, garlic and pepper
until well mixed. Spread
⅔ of the sauce over the fish.
Combine the remaining sauce
with the breadcrumbs and
spread over the top. Bake in a
preheated 350° oven for about
35 minutes until the fish is
tender. Sprinkle with lemon
juice and serve hot.

Psari plaki

Baked fish with tomatoes

6 servings

1 (3 pound) bass or other
  whole fish
1 teaspoon salt
  Freshly ground black pepper
½ teaspoon oregano
1 tablespoon lemon juice
3 onions, sliced
6 tablespoons olive oil
4 ripe tomatoes, peeled and
  sliced
2 tablespoons chopped parsley
  Lemon slices

Clean the fish and make a few
incisions in the sides. Combine
the salt, pepper, oregano and
lemon juice. Rub this mixture
into the slits and over the sides
of the fish. Fry the onions in
½ of the oil until soft and
golden. Place ½ the onions in
a buttered casserole, add ½ the
tomatoes and parsley and cover
with the fish. Add the rest of
the onions, tomatoes and parsley
and pour the remaining oil over
the fish. Bake in a preheated
400° oven for 35 to 40 minutes
or until the fish is tender.
Garnish with lemon slices.
Serve hot.

Psari fournou me krassi

Baked fish in wine sauce

6 servings

1 (3 pound) red snapper or
  blue fish
1 teaspoon salt
  Freshly ground black pepper
1½ cups dry white wine
1 cup water
3 teaspoons mild mustard
1½ tablespoons butter, melted

Sprinkle the fish inside and out
with salt and pepper and place
in an oiled baking dish. Combine
the wine, water and mustard and
pour over the fish. Bake in a
preheated 350° oven for 40
minutes, basting occasionally
with the liquid. Pour melted
butter over the fish and serve
hot.

Uskumru papaz yahnisi

Cold mackerel

6 servings

1 (2 to 3 pound) mackerel
4 tablespoons olive oil
3 medium sized onions, thinly
  sliced
2 carrots, peeled and sliced
1 green pepper, seeded and cut
  into thin strips
2 cloves garlic, crushed
3 medium sized tomatoes,
  peeled, seeded and chopped
4 tablespoons finely chopped
  parsley
½ teaspoon salt
  Freshly ground black pepper
½ cup water
8 pitted black olives, cut in half
12 lemon wedges

Score the mackerel on both
sides. Heat the oil in a large
skillet and sauté the mackerel
quickly on both sides until
nicely browned. Carefully
remove the fish from the skillet
and set aside. Add the onions to
the skillet and sauté until lightly
browned. Add the carrots and
green pepper and sauté 3
minutes. Add the garlic,
tomatoes, parsley, salt, pepper
and water and bring to a boil.
Reduce the heat and simmer 15
minutes. Return the mackerel to
the pan, spoon some of the sauce
over the fish and simmer 10
minutes more. Transfer the
mackerel and the sauce to a
serving dish and let cool
completely. Garnish with the
olives and lemon wedges before
serving.

Balık köftesi

Fish balls

4 to 6 servings

1½ *pounds haddock or cod fillets*
  2 *slices stale bread, crusts*
    removed
  1 *onion, finely chopped*
  1 *egg, beaten*
  2 *tablespoons finely chopped*
    parsley
½ *teaspoon salt*
    Freshly ground black pepper
½ *teaspoon cumin*
    Pinch of saffron soaked in
    1 teaspoon water
    Cornstarch
    Oil for deep frying

Remove skin and bones from
the fish and blend to a paste in
an electric blender. You will
have to do this in 2 or 3 batches.
Place the fish in a mixing bowl
and add all the remaining
ingredients except the cornstarch
and oil. Mix until thoroughly
combined. Shape into small
balls and roll in cornstarch.
Heat the oil for deep frying and
fry the balls for 4 to 5 minutes
until golden brown. Drain
on paper towels and
serve immediately.

Psari me kolokitia

Fish with zucchini

6 servings

  1 *(3 to 4 pound) whole*
    striped bass
  1 *teaspoon salt*
    Freshly ground black pepper
  2 *tablespoons olive oil*
  2 *onions, sliced*
  2 *cloves garlic, minced*
  2 *tablespoons chopped parsley*
  1 *tablespoon chopped fresh*
    mint or
    ½ *teaspoon dried mint*
  3 *medium sized tomatoes,*
    peeled, seeded and chopped
½ *teaspoon sugar*
⅛ *teaspoon cinnamon*
¾ *cup water*
  6 *small zucchini, cut into 1 inch*
    pieces
    Juice of ½ lemon

Wash and dry the fish and
sprinkle inside and out with ½
teaspoon salt and pepper. Heat
the oil in a large skillet and fry
the onions until light golden and
soft. Add the garlic, parsley,
mint, tomatoes, remaining salt
and pepper, sugar and
cinnamon. Fry for 1 minute.
Add water, cover and simmer
for 30 minutes. Add the zucchini
and the whole fish. Cover and
cook in a preheated 350° oven
for 20 to 25 minutes until the
fish is tender. Sprinkle with
lemon juice and serve hot.

Barbounia sti-skara

Grilled mullet

4 servings

  4 *small red mullet*
½ *teaspoon salt*
    Freshly ground black pepper
  4 *tablespoons olive oil*
  1 *tablespoon lemon juice*
  1 *tablespoon finely chopped*
    parsley

Have the mullet cleaned but
leave them whole. Sprinkle on
both sides with salt and pepper
and set aside 10 minutes.
Combine the olive oil and
lemon juice. Preheat the broiler
and oil the broiler rack. Place
the mullet on the rack, brush
with the oil mixture and broil
about 5 minutes on each side or
until nicely browned. Brush
frequently with the oil mixture.
Place the fish on a serving plate,
sprinkle with parsley and serve
with a tomato sauce.

Psari me rigani

Grilled fish with oregano

4 servings

  1 *(2 pound) striped bass or*
    other salt water fish
  1 *teaspoon salt*
    Freshly ground black pepper
½ *teaspoon oregano*
  4 *teaspoons lemon juice*
3½ *tablespoons olive oil*
  1 *small onion, sliced into thin*
    rings
  2 *teaspoons chopped parsley*

Wash and dry the fish. Combine
the salt, pepper and oregano and
rub the fish with this mixture
inside and out. Mix 2 teaspoons
lemon juice with 3 tablespoons
olive oil and brush over the fish.
Place on an oiled rack and broil
for 15 minutes, turning once
during the cooking. Baste with
the lemon-oil mixture several
times. Sprinkle the onion rings
with the remaining 2 teaspoons
lemon juice and ½ tablespoon of
oil. Remove the fish and place
on a heated serving dish.
Garnish with the marinated
onion rings and chopped parsley
and serve.

The best way to prepare really fresh fish is to roast it over a glowing-hot charcoal fire that has been sprinkled with fine dried herbs from the hills. Grilled mullet (recipe page 40, 3rd column)

Grilled fish with oregano (recipe page 40, 4th column).

Uskumru dolmasi

Stuffed mackerel

6 servings

- 6 *small mackerel*
- 8 *tablespoons olive oil*
- 3 *onions, finely chopped*
- ⅓ *cup ground walnuts*
- ¼ *cup ground filberts*
- 2 *tablespoons pine nuts*
- ⅓ *cup golden raisins*
- ½ *teaspoon salt*
  Freshly ground black pepper
  Pinch of cinnamon
- 3 *tablespoons finely chopped parsley*
- 1½ *tablespoons chopped fresh dill or*
  2 teaspoons dried dill weed
- 2 *eggs, beaten*
- ½ *cup fine dry breadcrumbs*
- 3 *lemons, thinly sliced*

Wash and clean the mackerel. Dry thoroughly inside and out. Heat 2 tablespoons oil in a skillet and sauté the onions until lightly browned. Add the nuts and sauté 1 minute. Add raisins, salt, pepper, cinnamon, parsley and dill and cook 5 minutes more. Remove from the heat and let cool. Stuff the mackerel with the prepared mixture and secure with skewers or toothpicks. Heat the remaining oil in a large skillet. Dip each fish first in beaten egg, then in breadcrumbs and fry over moderate heat until nicely browned (about 4 minutes on each side). Transfer to a serving plate and garnish with lemon slices.

Levrek firin

Stuffed bass

4 servings

- 1 *(2 to 3 pound) bass*
- 1 *teaspoon salt*
- 2 *tablespoons lemon juice*
- 2 *tablespoons butter*

Stuffing:
- 2 *tablespoons olive oil*
- 1 *small onion, finely chopped*
- 4 *tablespoons chopped celery leaves*
- 2 *tablespoons chopped parsley*
- 1 *cup dry breadcrumbs*
- ½ *teaspoon salt*
  Freshly ground black pepper
- 1 *tablespoon lemon juice*

Sauce:
- 1½ *tablespoons olive oil*
- 1 *medium sized onion, finely chopped*
- 1 *green pepper, seeded and thinly sliced*
- 4 *tomatoes, peeled, seeded and chopped*
- ¼ *teaspoon salt*
  Pinch of cayenne pepper
  Pinch of basil
  Pinch of sugar
- 1 *tablespoon lemon juice*
- 2 *tablespoons water*
- 2 *tablespoons chopped parsley*

Have the fishman clean the bass and remove the bones. Sprinkle the fish inside and out with salt and lemon juice and set aside while preparing the stuffing. Heat the olive oil in a skillet and sauté the onion 2 minutes. Add the celery leaves and parsley and sauté 2 minutes more. Add the breadcrumbs, salt, pepper and lemon juice and blend well.

Remove from the heat and let the mixture cool. Stuff the fish and secure the opening with skewers or toothpicks. Butter a baking dish large enough to hold the fish. Place pats of butter on top of the bass and bake in a 350° oven for 30 minutes or until the flesh flakes easily with a fork. Do not overcook. Meanwhile, heat the olive oil for the sauce and sauté the onion 2 minutes. Add the green pepper and tomatoes and sauté 3 minutes more. Add salt, cayenne, basil, sugar, lemon juice and water and bring to a boil. Boil a few minutes until the sauce is thick. Stir in the parsley, pour the sauce over the fish and serve.

Firinda mezit

Baked haddock

4 servings

* 4 haddock fillets (2 pounds)
* 1 teaspoon salt
  Freshly ground black pepper
* 2 cups cooked rice
* 4 hard boiled eggs, chopped
* 6 tablespoons chopped parsley
* 3 tablespoons butter
* 2 tablespoons dried
  breadcrumbs
* ½ teaspoon paprika
* 8 slices lemon

Wash the haddock fillets, dry and sprinkle with salt and pepper to taste. Mix together the rice, eggs and 4 tablespoons parsley. Place the mixture in an oiled baking dish. Dot with 2 tablespoons of butter. Lay the haddock fillets on top, sprinkle with breadcrumbs and paprika and dot with the remaining butter. Bake in a preheated 350° oven for 30 to 40 minutes. Sprinkle with the remaining 2 tablespoons parsley, garnish with lemon slices and serve.

Samak bi tahini

Fish in sesame sauce

4 servings

* 2 pounds haddock fillets
* 1 teaspoon salt
* 3 tablespoons olive oil
* 2 medium sized onions,
  finely chopped
* 1½ cups sesame oil
* ¾ cup lemon juice

Sprinkle the fish on both sides with salt and refrigerate for 2 hours. Bring the fish to room temperature and place in an oiled shallow baking dish. Brush with ½ the olive oil and broil under a hot oven broiler 2 to 3 minutes on each side. In the remaining olive oil, sauté the onions until golden brown. Beat the sesame oil and lemon juice together until creamy. Add the onions and pour the mixture over the fish. Return to the broiler for 2 minutes or until sauce is bubbling. Let the fish cool in the sauce to room temperature before serving.

Sebzeli levrek

Bass with vegetables

4 servings

* 1 (2½ to 3 pound) bass
* 1 teaspoon salt
  Freshly ground black pepper
* 1 onion, cut into rings
* 2 potatoes, peeled and cubed
* 3 carrots, peeled and cut in
  ¾ inch pieces
* 1 green pepper, seeded and cut
  into strips
* 2 cloves garlic, chopped
  Juice of ½ lemon
* 2 tablespoons chopped parsley

Cut the fish crosswise into 1 inch thick pieces. Sprinkle with ½ teaspoon salt and pepper. Place all the vegetables and the garlic in a large skillet with enough water to cover. Add remaining salt, bring to boiling point and simmer for 15 minutes. Place the fish on top of the vegetables. Cover and simmer for about 30 minutes or until the fish is tender. Transfer the fish to a serving dish and surround with the vegetables. Sprinkle fish with lemon juice and garnish with parsley.

44

Loukhoz

Bass with vegetables

6 servings

2½ *pounds bass or other firm white fish*
1½ *teaspoons salt*
  2 *medium sized potatoes, peeled and sliced ¼ inch thick*
  4 *medium sized carrots, peeled and sliced ¾ to 1 inch thick*
  1 *medium sized zucchini, cut in thick strips lengthwise*
  3 *tablespoons butter*
  8 *small white onions, sliced Freshly ground black pepper*
  4 *medium sized tomatoes, peeled and sliced*
  1 *cup water*

Clean the fish and sprinkle with salt. Partially cook potatoes, carrots and zucchini in boiling salted water (about 10 minutes for potatoes and carrots and 7 minutes for zucchini). Drain. Heat the butter in a pan and fry the onions until lightly browned. Remove from the pan and keep warm. Add the partially cooked vegetables and fry for 10 minutes, turning occasionally. Place the fish in a fireproof casserole, add the vegetables, sprinkle with salt and pepper and top with the tomato slices. Add 1 cup hot water, cover and simmer gently for 1 hour.

The East is the land of perfumes: perfumed fountains in the palaces of former sultans and emirs, and dishes on the table perfumed with herbs.

Fish with rice (recipe page 46, 1st column)

Samak Makli

Fish with herbs

4 servings

1½ *pounds firm white fish*
   6 *tablespoons salt*
 ½ *cup oil*
   2 *onions, finely chopped*
   3 *tablespoons finely chopped coriander leaves or parsley*
   1 *clove garlic, crushed*
   1 *cup clam juice*
   1 *cup water*
 ½ *teaspoon powdered cumin*
   3 *tablespoons lemon juice*
      Cayenne pepper to taste

Wash the fish, dry, sprinkle with salt and set aside for ¹/₂ hour. Wipe all excess salt from the fish. Heat the oil in a pan, add the fish and fry 7 minutes or until golden brown on both sides. Remove from the pan. Add the onions, coriander leaves (or parsley) and garlic and fry slowly for about 5 minutes over moderate heat. Drain and place in a casserole dish. Place the fish on the onion mixture. Add the clam juice, water and cumin and poach in a preheated 350° oven for 15 minutes. Add the lemon juice, sprinkle with cayenne, garnish with lemon slices and parsley cool completely before serving.

Mahi Polou

Fish with rice

4 servings

- 3 tablespoons butter
- 1 tablespoon cumin seeds
  Pinch of saffron
- ½ cup raisins, soaked in hot water and drained
- 2 cups cooked rice
- ¾ pound cooked firm white fish
- 1 tablespoon finely chopped parsley
- ½ teaspoon salt
  Freshly ground black pepper
- 2 tablespoons water

Heat the butter, add the cumin seeds, saffron and raisins and fry gently for 3 minutes. Add the rice and stir until each grain is shiny with butter. Add the fish, parsley, salt, pepper and 2 tablespoons water. Cover and bake in a preheated 300° oven for 1 hour.

Kibbet Samak

Mashed fish

8 servings

- 1 pound bass, filleted
- 1½ cups bulgar or cracked wheat
- 3 cups hot water
- 2 teaspoons salt
- 2 small onions, finely chopped
  Freshly ground black pepper
  Thin peel of ½ an orange, finely chopped
- 1 teaspoon ground coriander
- 4 tablespoons olive oil
- 3 small onions, sliced
  Few threads saffron

Chop the fish into small pieces. Soak the bulgar in the hot water with 1 teaspoon salt for ½ hour. Drain. Place onions, pepper, orange peel and coriander in a bowl. Add fish and bulgar and mix thoroughly. Heat 2½ tablespoons oil in a heatproof casserole. Add the sliced onions, remaining salt, pepper and saffron. Cook for 5 to 10 minutes until the onion is soft. Spread the fish mixture over the onions. Brush with the remaining oil and bake in a preheated 400° oven for 30 minutes. Let cool. Cut into serving pieces and serve with Yakni Samak. (Recipe page 47.)

Kababe Mahi

Stuffed baked fish

4 to 6 servings

- 1 (4 pound) striped bass or other firm fleshed white fish
- 4 tablespoons butter, melted
- ¼ cup dried apricots, soaked, drained and chopped
- ¼ cup raisins, soaked and drained
- 3 tablespoons chopped walnuts
- 2 tablespoons chopped pistachios
- ¼ teaspoon salt
  Freshly ground black pepper
- ½ teaspoon ground cloves
  Pinch of saffron
- ¼ teaspoon ground cardamom
  Pinch of cinnamon
  Grated peel of 1 orange
- 1 tablespoon lemon juice
- 1 tablespoon finely chopped parsley

Clean the fish, leaving head and tail intact. Heat 2 tablespoons butter in a skillet, add all the remaining ingredients except the lemon juice and parsley and sauté over low heat 4 minutes. Stuff the fish with this mixture and secure the opening with skewers. Place the fish in a buttered baking pan and brush with the remaining butter and lemon juice. Cover the pan with aluminum foil and bake in a 375° oven for 25 minutes. Uncover and bake 10 minutes more. Carefully transfer to a serving platter, sprinkle with parsley and serve.

Yakhni Samak

Fish stew

4 servings

> 2 pounds filleted sea bass,
>   haddock or cod
> 2 teaspoons salt
> 4 tablespoons olive oil
> 1 cup sliced onions
>   Pinch of saffron
> ¼ cup lemon juice
>   Water

Sprinkle the fish fillets on both sides with 1 teaspoon salt and refrigerate for 2½ hours. Wipe off the excess salt. Heat the olive oil in a large skillet and sauté the fish over medium heat until golden brown on both sides. Transfer to a flameproof casserole. In the same oil, sauté the onions until golden brown. Remove the onions from the skillet with a slotted spoon and combine with the remaining 1 teaspoon salt, saffron and lemon juice. Pour the mixture over the fish and add water to barely cover. Bring to a boil, reduce the heat and simmer 10 minutes. Remove any bones from the fish and place on a serving dish. Boil the cooking liquid over high heat for 3 minutes and pour over the fish. Let cool to room temperature before serving.

Kukye Mahi

Baked fish with eggs

4 servings

> 2½ tablespoons butter
> 1 onion, finely chopped
> 1 pound red snapper, or other
>   white fish fillets
> ⅛ teaspoon cloves
> ½ teaspoon salt
>   Freshly ground black pepper
> 1 tablespoon chopped parsley
> 6 eggs
> 1 tablespoon flour
> 4 tablespoons butter

Heat the butter in a frying pan. Add the onion and cook until golden brown. Remove and reserve the onion. Fry the fish in the same butter until lightly browned and tender. Flake the fish with a fork. Combine the fish with the onion, cloves, salt, pepper and parsley and allow to cool. Beat the eggs with the flour and stir in the fish mixture. Heat 4 tablespoons butter in a large frying pan and pour in the egg mixture. Cover and bake in a preheated 350° oven for 20 minutes until the eggs are set. Cut into wedges and serve either hot or cold.

Maglubet Samak

Fish with rice

6 servings

> 2 pounds bass or other firm
>   salt water fish
> 1 cup clam juice
> 1 cup water
> 1 onion, sliced
> 6 peppercorns, crushed
> ¼ teaspoon paprika
> 1 tablespoon lemon juice
> 2 onions, chopped
> 2 tablespoons olive oil
> ½ teaspoon salt
> ½ cup raw rice
> 1 cup water
> 1 teaspoon ground coriander
>   Few threads saffron
> 1 cup yogurt
> 4 tablespoons chopped parsley

Cut the fish in 1½ inch slices and marinate overnight in combined clam juice, water, onion, peppercorns, paprika and lemon juice. Pour off the marinade and reserve. Discard sliced onion. Fry the chopped onions for 5 minutes in 1½ tablespoons of the oil. Add the salt, rice, 1 cup of water and 1 cup of the marinade. Simmer for 10 minutes and drain. Brush a casserole with the remaining oil and cover the bottom with half of the rice. Lay the fish on top and cover with the remaining rice. Heat the remaining marinade with the coriander and saffron and pour over the rice. Cover and bake in a preheated 350° oven for 30 minutes. Remove from oven. Cover with yogurt and sprinkle with chopped parsley.

Yakhnit Samak Harrak

Fish stew with paprika

4 servings

> 1½ to 2 pounds haddock, sea
>   bass or cod, cut into 1½ inch
>   thick fillets
> ½ teaspoon salt
>   Head, tail and bones of the
>   filleted fish
> 2 cups water
> 4 tablespoons olive oil
> 1 cup chopped onions
> 4 cloves garlic, crushed
> 1 teaspoon paprika
> ½ teaspoon coriander
> ¼ teaspoon crushed caraway
>   seeds
> ¼ cup lemon juice

Sprinkle the fish fillets on both sides with salt and set aside in the refrigerator for 2½ hours. Meanwhile, place the head, tail and fish bones in a pan with the water and bring to a boil. Lower the heat and simmer 20 minutes. Strain the broth. (If fish trimmings are not available, substitute half clam juice and half water for the fish broth.) Heat the olive oil in a large pan and sauté the fish fillets over high heat until nicely browned on both sides. Remove the fish from the pan. Add the onions and garlic and sauté until nicely browned. Pour off all the oil and add the fish broth, fish fillets, paprika, coriander and caraway seeds. Bring to a boil, lower the heat and simmer 15 minutes. Stir in the lemon juice and remove the pan from the heat. Taste for seasoning and add salt and pepper if necessary. Let cool to room temperature before serving.

Photo below: fish stew with paprika (recipe page 47, 4th column).

Unfortunately, fine prawn are becoming more and more rare in the Mediterranean Sea. They can still be found, however, in the waters around Egypt and in the Bosporus near Istanbul.

Wherever they come from, they taste quite delicious in a wine sauce.

Garides me saltsa

Shrimp in wine sauce

4 servings

  6 *tablespoons butter*
  2 *small onions, chopped*
  4 *medium sized ripe tomatoes, peeled, seeded and chopped*
  ¾ *cup dry white wine*
  2 *tablespoons chopped parsley*
  ¼ *teaspoon oregano*
  1 *teaspoon salt*
     Freshly ground black pepper
1½ *pounds jumbo shrimp*

Heat the butter in a skillet. Add the onions and fry 3 minutes until golden brown and soft. Add the tomatoes and fry for 2 minutes. Add the wine, parsley, oregano, salt and pepper and simmer over low heat for 10 minutes. Shell the shrimp but leave the tail intact. Remove the black vein. Add the shrimp to the sauce and cook slowly over low to moderate heat for 6 minutes.

Midye pilavı

Mussels with rice

4 servings

  4 *tablespoons oil*
  2 *onions, chopped*
  2 *cups mussels, cleaned or substitute canned mussels*
  4 *cups cooked rice*
  ¼ *cup raisins*
  1 *cup beef broth*
  ½ *teaspoon salt*
     Freshly ground black pepper
  1 *tablespoon preserved ginger, finely chopped*

Heat the oil in a heavy pan. Add the onions and cook for 5 minutes until soft and lightly browned. Add the mussels and heat for 2 minutes. Add rice, raisins, and beef broth, mix well and simmer over a low heat, covered, for 15 minutes. Season with salt, pepper and ginger before serving.

Every morning, delicious large mussels from the Bosporus make their way to the fish market in Istanbul. And Turkish cooks know how to make something very special out of them.

Mussels with rice (recipe page 48, 4th column)

Karidesli pilav

Midye pilakisi

Pilaf with shrimp

4 servings

- 4 tablespoons butter
- 1 pound large shrimp, shelled and deveined
- ¼ teaspoon salt
- 2 onions, chopped
- 1 clove garlic, crushed
- 4 tomatoes, peeled, seeded and thinly sliced
- 3 tablespoons chopped celery leaves
  Pinch of saffron
- ½ teaspoon ground cumin
  Freshly ground black pepper
  Pinch of sugar
- 1 cup rice
- 2 cups simmering fish broth or substitute ½ clam juice and ½ water
- 6 slices lemon, cut in half
- 1 tablespoon finely chopped parsley

Heat the butter in a heavy casserole and sauté the shrimp for about 3 minutes or just until they turn pink. Remove from the pan and sprinkle with salt. Add the onions and garlic to the casserole and sauté 3 minutes. Add tomatoes and celery leaves and sauté 3 minutes more. Add saffron, cumin, pepper, sugar and rice and mix thoroughly. Add the broth, bring to a boil and stir once with a fork. Lower the heat, cover the pan and simmer until the rice has absorbed all the liquid (about 25 minutes). Arrange the shrimp on top of the rice. Place the covered casserole on an asbestos pad over the lowest possible flame and cook 15 minutes more. Garnish with sliced lemon and parsley and serve from the casserole.

Mussel stew

4 servings

- 36 mussels
- 3 tablespoons olive oil
- 2 onions, finely chopped
- 1 carrot, peeled and finely chopped
- 2 small potatoes, peeled and cubed
- ½ cup chopped celery root (optional)
- 3 cloves garlic, crushed
- 5 tomatoes, peeled, seeded and chopped
- 2 teaspoons sugar
- ¼ teaspoon salt
  Freshly ground black pepper
- 2 tablespoons finely chopped parsley

Scrub the mussels with a stiff brush under cold running water. Remove the beards and soak the mussels in cold water for 45 minutes, changing the water every 15 minutes, to remove the sand. Discard any mussels which, if open, do not close their shells when tapped on the back. Discard those which are unusually heavy. Place the mussels in a large pan with only the water clinging to their shells. Cover and cook over high heat about 2 minutes, shaking the pan occasionally, until the shells open. Strain the liquid through several layers of cheesecloth and reserve. Heat the olive oil in a large skillet and sauté the onions until lightly browned. Add the carrot, potatoes and celery root and sauté 2 minutes. Add the garlic, tomatoes, sugar, salt, pepper and reserved mussel liquid and bring to a boil. Lower the heat and simmer, stirring occasionally, for 15 to 20 minutes. Add a tablespoon of water from time to time if the mixture becomes very thick. Add the mussels and simmer 5 minutes. Transfer to a serving bowl and sprinkle with parsley.

Midye dolmasi

Stuffed mussels

4 servings

- 30 to 36 mussels
- 2 tablespoons oil
- 2 onions, finely chopped
- ¼ cup pine nuts
- ⅓ cup currants, soaked
- 1 tablespoon sugar
- ¼ teaspoon salt
  Freshly ground black pepper
- 2 tablespoons finely chopped parsley
- ½ cup rice
- 1 cup fish broth or use half clam juice and half water

Clean and wash the mussels as directed in the recipe for Midye Pilakisi (see page 50). Heat the oil in a skillet and sauté the onions until lightly browned. Add nuts, currants, sugar, salt, pepper and parsley and sauté 2 minutes. Stir in the rice and cook 1 minute. Add the fish broth and bring to a boil. Lower the heat and simmer about 20 minutes or until all the liquid has been absorbed by the rice. Remove from the heat and let cool. Force the mussels open slightly with an oyster knife and stuff each one with a little of the rice mixture. Close the mussels and tie with string. Place them in a heavy pan, add boiling water to cover and simmer 20 minutes. Remove the mussels from the pan with a slotted spoon and let cool to room temperature. Remove the strings before serving.

Kalamarakia me krassi

Squid in red wine

4 servings

- 2 pounds squid
- 2 tablespoons olive oil
- ¾ cup dry red wine
- ½ teaspoon salt
  Freshly ground black pepper
  Pinch of sugar
- 1½ tablespoons finely chopped parsley

Have the fishman clean the squid. Discard the tentacles, wash the bodies and drain thoroughly. Place the squid in a heavy saucepan with the olive oil, wine, salt, pepper and sugar. Bring to a boil reduce the heat and simmer, partially covered, for 1 hour. Remove from the heat and let cool completely. Sprinkle on the parsley before serving.

Samak Mahchi

Stuffed squid

- 1½ pounds squid, cleaned and skinned
  Tentacles of cleaned squid
- 6 tablespoons rice
- 2 medium sized onions, finely chopped
- ½ cup pine nuts, coarsely chopped
- 6 tablespoons oil
- 1 teaspoon salt
- ¼ teaspoon white pepper
  Pinch of saffron
- 4 medium sized onions, thinly sliced
- 4 cups hot water
- 2 tablespoons lemon juice

Wash and drain the cleaned squid. Chop the tentacles and combine with the rice, chopped onions, pine nuts, 3 tablespoons oil, ½ teaspoon salt, ⅛ teaspoon pepper and saffron. Stuff the squid with the mixture. Heat the remaining oil and sauté the squid 5 to 7 minutes turning occasionally. Remove from the pan. In the same oil, sauté the sliced onions until golden brown. Add the remaining salt and pepper and arrange the squid on top of the onions. Pour on the hot water and bring to a boil. Reduce the heat, cover and simmer 15 to 20 minutes. Stir in the lemon juice, remove from the heat and let the squid cool in the liquid before serving.

Kalamaria yemista

Stuffed squid

4 servings

- 12 to 16 small squid
- ¾ teaspoon salt
  Freshly ground black pepper
- 5 tablespoons olive oil
- 4 onions, finely chopped
- ½ cup rice
- 3 tablespoons finely chopped parsley
- 1½ tablespoons finely chopped fresh mint or
  ¾ teaspoon dried mint
- 2 tablespoons water
- 5 tomatoes, peeled, seeded and chopped

Have the fishman clean the squid but reserve the tentacles. Wash the squid and drain thoroughly. Sprinkle inside and out with ½ teaspoon salt and pepper. Chop the tentacles. Heat 3 tablespoons olive oil in a skillet and sauté the onions until lightly browned. Add the tentacles, rice, parsley, mint, remaining salt and pepper and sauté 3 to 4 minutes. Stir in the water and remove from the heat. Stuff each squid ¾ full with the mixture and secure the openings with toothpicks. Place the squid in a casserole. Combine the remaining oil and tomatoes and spoon over the squid. Add enough water to barely cover. Bake in a 350° oven for 1 hour. Serve from the casserole.

Meat dishes

Luleh kebab

Rolled kebab

6 servings

1½ pounds ground lean lamb
1½ medium sized onions, finely
     chopped
 ½ teaspoon salt
     Freshly ground black pepper
 3 egg yolks
     Pinch of saffron soaked in
     1 teaspoon water
     Pinch of cinnamon
     Pinch of cumin

In a bowl, combine the lamb, onions, salt and pepper. Let stand 30 minutes. Add the remaining ingredients and beat with a wooden spoon until the mixture is very light. Divide into 6 portions. Oil 6 skewers and shape the meat in a sausage-like fashion, about 2 inches in diameter, around the skewers. Grill over a hot charcoal fire or under a hot oven broiler for 5 to 10 minutes, depending on the desired degree of doneness. The kebabs should be crisp outside but tender and juicy inside.

Sheep and lambs are the main source of meat in Greece, Turkey, and the other countries of the Eastern Mediterranean. Pastures are too barren and poor to support beef cattle, and pork is forbidden both to Moslems and Orthodox Jews. But the mutton is uniformly of high quality, and young lamb is a superb delicacy in the spring.
Lamb is best when roasted over an open fire and seasoned with spices such as oregano. The smell of lamb roasting over a charcoal fire must be the most characteristic aroma of the Middle East. The best known of these roasted dishes is the shish kebab. 'Kebab' is a common Turkish word which means 'cooked meat', whether roasted, fried, or stewed. The word 'shish' means 'on the skewer'. Thus,

shish kebab, means meat on the skewer. And it is served in all possible forms and variations. Small skewers with small pieces of meat are used for cocktail snacks. These can be bought almost everywhere in Greece, Turkey, and Lebanon, even on the streets, from stalls where there is a small charcoal fire. Children often buy these snacks when they get out of school, the way American children buy ice cream. Larger shish kebabs, to which tomatoes, peppers, or onions have been added between the pieces of meat, are also common. A particularly delicious snack is roast lamb's liver and kidneys on the skewer. In the evening, an incredible variety of kebabs can be ordered in Turkish restaurants. Its not even necessary to order the meal,

just sit still and the waiter will bring what he has. In general, though, a small skewer is served first, then cutlets, followed by a larger skewer, and then the high point of the evening, roast liver and kidneys.

Kolohitia papoutsakia

Zucchini with minced meat

6 servings

  4 *tablespoons butter*
  2 *onions, finely chopped*
1½ *pounds minced lamb or veal*
  1 *teaspoon salt*
     Freshly ground black pepper
  ¼ *teaspoon cinnamon*
  4 *tomatoes, peeled, seeded and chopped*
  6 *small zucchini*
  2 *egg yolks*
1½ *cups thick Béchamel sauce (see page 57)*
  6 *tablespoons grated Parmesan cheese*
  2 *tablespoons butter*

Heat the butter in a pan, add the onions and fry until soft and golden. Add the meat and fry for 2 more minutes. Sprinkle with salt, pepper and cinnamon. Add the chopped tomatoes and simmer for 20 minutes over low heat. Remove the stalk end of the zucchini and cook in salted boiling water for 10 minutes or until tender. Remove, drain and cut in half lengthwise. Scoop out the pulp and combine pulp with the meat mixture. Stuff the halved zucchini with this mixture. Beat the egg yolks in a bowl. Add 6 tablespoons of the Béchamel sauce gradually, beating constantly. Add to the remaining Béchamel sauce. Add 4 tablespoons of the cheese. Place the stuffed zucchini in an oiled baking pan, top with the sauce and sprinkle on the remaining cheese. Bake in a preheated 400° oven until the top is lightly browned.

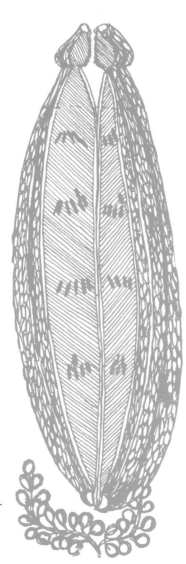

Partsha kushlar

Wrapped lamb mince

4 to 6 servings

  8 *raw lamb slices, 3½ inches square*
  2 *tablespoons butter*
  1 *onion, finely chopped*
  1 *pound ground lamb*
  3 *ripe tomatoes, peeled, seeded and chopped*
  3 *tablespoons chopped parsley*
  1 *teaspoon salt*
     Freshly ground black pepper
  ¼ *teaspoon sugar*
  1 *tablespoon melted butter*
  6 *tablespoons beef broth*
     Juice of ½ lemon

Pound the lamb slices until very thin. Heat the butter in a large skillet. Add the onion and cook 3 minutes until softened. Add ground lamb and fry until lightly browned. Add the tomatoes, 1 tablespoon parsley, salt, pepper and sugar and fry, stirring frequently until all the liquid has evaporated. Remove from the heat and cool to room temperature. Divide mixture into 8 equal portions. Wrap each portion firmly in a slice of lamb, secure with a toothpick and place in a heatproof casserole. Add the melted butter and beef broth and bake in a preheated 325° oven for 30 to 40 minutes until tender. Baste occasionally during cooking. Sprinkle with lemon juice and garnish with remaining parsley.

Kadın budu

Lady's thigh meatballs

4 servings

  1 *pound ground lean lamb*
  1 *onion, grated*
  3 *tablespoons cooked rice*
  3 *eggs*
  1 *tablespoon finely chopped parsley*
  ¼ *teaspoon salt*
     Freshly ground black pepper
     Oil for deep frying
  ½ *cup flour*

In a bowl, combine the lamb, onion, rice, 2 eggs, parsley, salt and pepper and beat until the mixture is light. Form into balls the size and shape of an egg. Poach the meatballs in simmering water for 7 minutes. Remove them with a slotted spoon and drain on paper towels. Heat the oil for deep frying. Beat the remaining egg in a shallow bowl. Dredge the meatballs in flour, dip in the beaten egg and again in flour. Fry in the hot (375°) oil for 3 minutes or until golden brown. Drain on paper towels and serve immediately.

Qa'meh

Minced meat

4 servings

- 6 *tablespoons butter*
- 2 *onions, chopped*
- 1 *pound minced lamb*
    Freshly ground black pepper
- ½ *teaspoon turmeric*
- 5 *small tomatoes, boiled,*
    peeled and forced through
    a sieve
- ½ *cup beef broth*
- ½ *cup yellow split peas*
- 3 *tablespoons lime or lemon*
    juice
- 1 *teaspoon salt*
    Pinch of saffron
- ¼ *cup dried apricots, minced*

Heat 4 tablespoons butter in a
heavy pan. Add the onions and
fry until lightly browned.
Remove the onions. Add the
lamb to the same butter
and fry until lightly browned.
Sprinkle with pepper and
turmeric. Add the tomatoes
and beef broth. Bring to a boil
and simmer for 10 minutes.
Add the split peas, lime juice,
salt and saffron. Cover and
simmer 1 hour. Heat the
remaining butter in a pan, add
the apricots and stir over low
heat for 4 minutes. Add to
the meat and simmer 20 minutes.

Motanjen Khoreshe

Meatballs with fruits and nuts

4 servings

- 1 *pound ground lean lamb*
- 1 *onion, finely chopped*
- ¼ *teaspoon salt*
    Freshly ground black pepper
- 4 *tablespoons oil*
- 2 *cups beef broth*
- ¼ *cup yellow split peas,*
    soaked overnight and drained
- 1 *cup combined almonds and*
    pistachios, chopped
- ½ *pound combined dried*
    apricots and prunes, chopped

In a bowl combine the lamb,
onion, salt and pepper. Form
small meatballs and sauté
in 2 tablespoons oil until nicely
browned on all sides. Add the
broth and split peas and bring
to a boil. Lower the heat,
cover and simmer 40 minutes.
Meanwhile, heat the remaining
oil in a skillet and sauté the
nuts and dried fruits until
lightly browned. Add these
ingredients to the meatballs
and simmer uncovered 40
minutes more. Transfer to a
serving dish and serve with rice.

Kababe barg

Leaf kebab

4 to 6 servings

- 2 *pounds top round of beef*
- 3 *tablespoons onion juice*
- 3 *tablespoons lemon juice*
- ½ *teaspoon salt*
    Freshly ground black pepper

Cut the meat into long thin
slices and pound the slices
until they are even thinner.
Combine the remaining
ingredients in a shallow pan.
Add the meat and let it marinate
overnight in the refrigerator.
Thread the meat on skewers and
cook over a hot charcoal fire
or under the oven broiler for
10 minutes or until nicely
browned. Turn frequently so
that the meat browns evenly.

Tas kebab

Meat with pilaf

6 servings

- 4 *tablespoons butter*
- 2 *onions, thinly sliced*
- 6 *medium sized tomatoes,*
    peeled, seeded and mashed
- 2 *cloves garlic, crushed*
- 1 *teaspoon salt*
    Freshly ground black pepper
- ¼ *teaspoon cinnamon*
- ¼ *teaspoon sugar*
- 1 *bay leaf*
- 2 *pounds veal, cut in 1 inch*
    cubes
- 2½ *cups beef broth*

Heat the butter, add the onions
and fry until soft and golden.
Add the tomatoes, garlic, salt,
pepper, cinnamon, sugar and
bay leaf and fry for 3 minutes.
Add the veal and beef broth and
bring to a boil. Cover, reduce
the heat and simmer for
1 hour. Serve with pilaf rice.

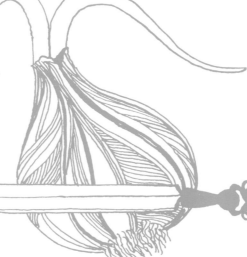

Wholesome yogurt is served everywhere from Greece to regions much farther east. It is also used to prepare fine, slightly sour meat sauces.

Meat with pilaf (recipe page 55, 4th column).

Khoreshe mast

Meatballs with yogurt

4 servings

    1 pound lamb, ground
    1 teaspoon salt
       Freshly ground black pepper
    1 teaspoon turmeric
    3 tablespoons oil
    2 teaspoons ground cumin
    1 teaspoon ground coriander
    ½ teaspoon ground cloves
    1 teaspoon ground cardamom
    ½ teaspoon ground cinnamon
    1 onion, finely chopped
    ¾ cup hot water
 1½ cups yogurt

Combine the lamb with salt, pepper and turmeric and form into small balls. Heat the oil in a heavy pan, add the spices and onion and fry until the onion is soft. Add the meatballs and fry until browned. Add ¾ cup hot water, bring to a boil and simmer gently for about 40 minutes or until the water has evaporated. Add the yogurt, stir and heat without boiling for 5 minutes until heated through. Serve hot.

Moussaka

'Moussaka', Meat and eggplant pie, can be found anywhere the Turks have set foot, from Rumania and Greece to deep into Asia. It is a substantial dish for which a number of different recipes exist. Poor people prepare it with potatoes, those who have more money prepare it with meat.

Meat and eggplant pie

4 servings

- 4 small eggplants
- 1½ teaspoons salt
- 1½ tablespoons oil
- 3 tablespoons butter
- 1½ pounds minced lamb or beef
- 2 onions, chopped
  Freshly ground black pepper
- ¼ teaspoon cinnamon
- 4 ripe tomatoes, peeled, seeded and chopped
- 3 tablespoons chopped parsley
- 2 to 3 tablespoons water
- 6 tablespoons dry breadcrumbs
- 6 tablespoons grated Parmesan cheese
- 3 egg yolks
- 2 cups Béchamel sauce

Peel eggplants and cut into thick slices. Sprinkle with 1 teaspoon salt and set aside for 15 minutes. Wash off excess salt and drain. Heat the oil in a skillet. Add the eggplant slices and fry until lightly browned on both sides. Remove and drain on paper towels. Heat the butter in a frying pan and brown the meat. Add the onions and fry until soft and golden. Season with remaining salt, pepper and cinnamon. Add tomatoes, parsley and water. Bring to a boil and simmer for 20 minutes. Sprinkle ½ the breadcrumbs into a buttered baking dish and cover with ½ the meat mixture. Add ½ the eggplant slices. Sprinkle with ⅓ of the grated cheese. Repeat with layers of remaining meat, eggplant and ½ the remaining cheese. Beat the egg yolks in a bowl. Beat in a few tablespoons of hot Béchamel sauce and add to remaining sauce. Pour sauce over the dish, sprinkle with remaining cheese and breadcrumbs and bake in a preheated 350° oven for 45 minutes or until crust is crisp and brown. Serve with yogurt and a salad.

Béchamel sauce

- 2 tablespoons butter
- 2 tablespoons flour
- 2 cups milk
- ½ teaspoon salt
  Freshly ground black pepper

Melt the butter, stir in the flour and cook over low heat for 1 minute. Add the milk gradually, stirring with a wire whisk to form a smooth medium thick sauce. Season with salt and pepper.

Domates yemistes

Stuffed tomatoes

6 servings

12 medium sized ripe tomatoes
6 tablespoons olive oil
3 small onions, chopped
1½ pounds lamb or veal, minced
½ cup raw rice
3 tablespoons chopped parsley
1 tablespoon chopped fresh
  mint or
  1 teaspoon dried mint
1 tablespoon fresh dill or
  1 teaspoon dried dill weed
1 teaspoon salt
  Freshly ground black pepper
¼ teaspoon sugar
½ cup beef broth

Cut the tops from the tomatoes, scoop out the pulp and force through a sieve. Heat 4 tablespoons of the oil, add the onions and fry until lightly browned. Add the meat and fry for another 2 minutes. Add the rice and fry until transparent. Add all but 3 tablespoons of the tomato pulp. Add the herbs, salt, pepper and sugar and simmer over low heat for 20 to 30 minutes. Stuff the tomatoes with this mixture and replace the caps. Place in an oiled baking dish and brush with remaining oil. Add the reserved pulp and the beef broth and bake in a preheated 375° oven for 20 minutes.

Dolmeh Bademjan

Stuffed eggplants

4 servings

2 large round eggplants
1 tablespoon salt
4 tablespoons oil
½ pound lean ground lamb
1 onion, finely chopped
¼ teaspoon salt
  Freshly ground black pepper
  Pinch of saffron soaked in
  1 teaspoon water
½ teaspoon turmeric
5 tablespoons cooked rice
2 tablespoons finely chopped
  parsley
2 scallions, thinly sliced
4 tablespoons lemon juice
  Pinch of sugar

Cut the tops off the eggplants and reserve. Carefully remove the flesh with the aid of an apple corer. Do not pierce the skin. Sprinkle the inside of the eggplants with salt and let stand 15 minutes. This will drain the bitter juices from the eggplants. Rinse and drain thoroughly. Heat 2 tablespoons oil in a skillet. Add lamb, onion, salt, pepper, saffron and turmeric and sauté until the lamb is nicely browned. Stir in the rice, parsley and scallions and let the mixture cool. Chop the eggplant flesh and sauté in the remaining oil until softened. Combine the eggplant with the meat mixture and stuff the drained eggplant shells. Replace the tops. Place the eggplants in a casserole just large enough to hold them. Add water to come halfway up the sides of the eggplants.

Stir in the lemon juice and sugar. Bring to a boil, lower the heat and cover the pan. Simmer 45 minutes. Place on a serving plate and cut each in half at the table.

Yaprak dolması

Stuffed vine leaves

4 servings

1 (16 ounce) jar vine leaves
5 tablespoons butter
½ cup raw rice
1 cup water
1 pound minced lamb
1 onion, finely chopped
2 tablespoons chopped parsley
½ teaspoon salt
  Freshly ground black pepper
2½ cups water
1 tablespoon lemon juice

Wash the vine leaves under cold running water and drain. Heat 2 tablespoons butter in a pan, add the rice and stir for 4 minutes. Add water and simmer until the rice is tender and almost all the water has been absorbed. Rinse in a colander and let cool. Combine rice with the lamb, onion, parsley, salt and pepper. Stuff the vine leaves as directed in the recipe for Yalanci dolma (page 19) using 1 heaped teaspoon on each leaf. Place some leftover leaves on the bottom of a pan and cover with a tightly packed layer of stuffed vine leaves. Add more layers until all are used. Top with remaining butter. Add the water and lemon juice. Place a plate on top of the rolls to weight them. Bring to a boil, cover, reduce the heat and simmer 30 to 35 minutes. Remove from liquid and drain. Serve hot with yogurt, if desired.

Talash kebab

Meat pastry roll

4 servings

  1 *package (6) frozen patty*
     shells
  4 *tablespoons butter*
  1 *pound ground lean lamb*
  4 *tomatoes, peeled, seeded and*
     chopped
  3 *tablespoons finely chopped*
     parsley
½ *teaspoon salt*
     Freshly ground black pepper
     Pinch of cinnamon

Thaw the patty shells until they
are pliable. Meanwhile, heat 2
tablespoons butter in a skillet.
Sauté the lamb until it has lost
all trace of pink. Add the
tomatoes, parsley, salt, pepper
and cinnamon. Simmer over
moderate heat about 25 minutes
or until almost all the liquid
from the tomatoes has
evaporated. Set the mixture
aside to cool. On a floured
board, knead the patty shells
together into a ball. Roll out the
pastry into an 8 by 14 inch
rectangle. Spoon the lamb
mixture lengthwise down the
middle of the pastry. Fold the
pastry over the lamb so that it
overlaps. Pinch the seam
together with moistened fingers
to seal. Fold the ends over and
seal in the same way. Invert the
roll onto a buttered baking
sheet. Prick the pastry with a
fork to allow the steam to
escape. Melt the remaining
2 tablespoons butter and brush
the pastry with the melted butter.
Bake in a 400° oven for 45
minutes until the pastry is

nicely browned. Transfer to a
serving platter and slice at the
table. A garlic and basil flavored
tomato sauce can be served
separately.

Keftedhes

Meatballs

6 servings

1½ *pounds ground lean meat*
     (use whatever you prefer or
     a combination of meats)
  3 *tablespoons grated onion*
  1 *cup dry breadcrumbs made*
     from dark bread
  1 *tablespoon water*
  2 *eggs*
  3 *tablespoons finely chopped*
     parsley
  1 *teaspoon chopped fresh mint*
     or
  ½ *teaspoon dried mint*
     Pinch of oregano
½ *teaspoon salt*
     Freshly ground black pepper
     Oil for deep frying
½ *cup flour*

In a bowl combine all the
ingredients except the flour and
oil and beat until the mixture is
light. Set aside 1 hour. Form the
mixture into balls the size and
shape of an egg and flatten
slightly. Heat the oil for deep
frying. Dredge the meatballs in
flour and fry in the hot oil for
5 to 10 minutes until nicely
browned. Drain on paper
towels and serve immediately.

Vothino stifado

Beef stew

4 servings

- 4 *tablespoons olive oil*
- 2 *pounds beef, cut in 1 inch cubes*
- 2 *cloves garlic, crushed*
- 1 *teaspoon salt*
  Freshly ground black pepper
- ¼ *teaspoon oregano*
- 4 *medium sized tomatoes, peeled, seeded and chopped*
- ¾ *cup dry white wine*
- 1¼ *cups beef broth*
- 1 *bay leaf*
- 1 *pound small white onions*
- 3 *tablespoons finely chopped parsley*

Heat 3 tablespoons of oil, add the beef and brown it on all sides. Add garlic, salt, pepper and oregano and continue frying for another 2 minutes. Add tomatoes and fry 1 minute. Add the wine, broth and the bay leaf. Bring to a boil and simmer gently for 1 hour or until the meat is tender. Heat the remaining oil in a frying pan. Add the onions and fry, stirring until well browned. Add to the beef, sprinkle with parsley and cook over low heat for 20 minutes.

Stifado

Meat stew

6 servings

- 2 *pounds stewing beef, cubed*
- ¼ *cup olive oil*
- 1 *teaspoon salt*
  Freshly ground black pepper
- 1 *bunch whole scallions*
- 1½ *cups red wine*
- 2 *tablespoons wine vinegar*
- 2 *bay leaves*
- 2 *cloves*
- 1 *cinnamon stick*
- 2 *cups water*
- 3 *carrots, sliced*
- 3 *large potatoes, cut in large cubes*

Brown the beef in the olive oil for 5 minutes. Add the salt, pepper, scallions, wine, vinegar, bay leaves, cloves, cinnamon stick and water. Bring to a boil and simmer, covered, for 1½ hours. Add the carrots and potatoes and continue cooking for 30 minutes or until the vegetables are tender. Remove the bay leaves and cinnamon stick and serve with rice.

Chingana pilav

Kidneys, liver and rice. Gypsy style

6 servings

    4   lamb or calves kidneys
    6   slices calves liver or beef liver
    2   cups boiling water
    ½   teaspoon salt
        Freshly ground black pepper
    2   tablespoons oil
    1   onion, finely chopped
    ¼   teaspoon dried mint
    1   tablespoon finely chopped
        parsley
    ½   cup rice
    1   cup boiling beef broth

Place the kidneys and liver in a saucepan. Add the boiling water, salt and pepper. Cover and simmer over moderate heat for 10 minutes. Drain and cut the kidney and liver into small pieces. Heat the oil in a clean saucepan. Add the onion and fry for 3 minutes. Add the kidneys and liver and sauté for 5 minutes. Stir in the mint, parsley and beef broth. Cover and simmer over low heat for 20 minutes. In the meantime cook the rice. Serve with the rice and a tossed salad.

Moscari stifado

Veal ragout

4 servings

    3   tablespoons olive oil
    2   pounds veal, cut into 1 inch
        cubes
    4   onions, finely chopped
    2   cloves garlic, crushed
    4   tomatoes, peeled, seeded and
        chopped
    ½   cup dry white wine
    ¼   teaspoon salt
        Freshly ground black pepper
  1½   to 2 cups chicken broth

Heat the oil in a casserole and sauté the veal until lightly browned. Add the onions and garlic and sauté until brown. Add tomatoes, wine, salt and pepper and simmer 5 minutes. Add the broth and bring to a boil. Reduce the heat to the lowest possible point and cover the casserole. Place an asbestos pad under the casserole and cook for 2½ to 3 hours. Check from time to time to see if the liquid is evaporating too quickly and add more broth if necessary. Serve from the casserole.

Kufteh mo'alla

Big meatballs

4 servings

1 pound ground lean lamb
1 onion, finely chopped
½ cup yellow split peas, cooked
1 cup rice, cooked
4 scallions, sliced
3 tablespoons finely chopped
    parsley
½ teaspoon salt
    Freshly ground black pepper
2 tablespoons combined
    currants and raisins, soaked
½ cup pitted prunes, soaked
    and chopped
3 hard boiled eggs, chopped
½ cup pistachio nuts
3 tablespoons chopped walnuts
1 onion, chopped and sautéed
4 cups beef broth
3 tablespoons rice, pounded
    between 2 sheets of waxed
    paper
3 tablespoons lemon juice
    Pinch of saffron soaked in
    1 teaspoon water
    Pinch of sugar
1 tablespoon oil
1 tablespoon finely chopped
    fresh mint or
    1½ teaspoons dried mint
1 tablespoon finely chopped
    fresh basil or
    1½ teaspoons dried basil

In a bowl, thoroughly combine
the lamb, onion, split peas, rice,
scallions, parsley, salt and
pepper. Divide the mixture in
half. Shape one of the halves
into a ball with a large hollow
in the center. Combine the
currants and raisins, prunes,
2 eggs, pistachio nuts, walnuts
and sautéed onion and fill the

hollow with half the mixture.
Repeat with remaining meat and
stuffing to form a second
meatball.
Carefully place the meatballs in
a casserole just large enough to
hold them. Pour in enough broth
to just cover the meatballs. Add
the rice and bring to a boil.
Lower the heat, cover and
simmer 1 hour. Add the lemon
juice, saffron and sugar and
simmer 10 minutes more. Heat
the oil in a small skillet and
sauté the mint and basil for 2
minutes. Carefully lift out the
meatballs and place on a
serving dish. Top with the fried
mint and basil and the remaining
hard boiled egg. Serve the broth
separately.

Kufteh Tabrizi

Stuffed meat Tabriz style

6 servings

1 cup rice, cooked
½ cup yellow split peas, soaked
    and cooked
1 pound ground lamb
3 medium sized onions, finely
    chopped
½ teaspoon salt
    Freshly ground black pepper
½ teaspoon turmeric
¼ teaspoon cinnamon
¼ teaspoon ground cloves
½ cup dried pitted prunes,
    chopped
¼ cup chopped almonds
1 tablespoon butter
1 tablespoon chopped parsley
1 teaspoon crushed dried mint
½ cup beef broth

Combine the rice, split peas,
lamb, 2 onions, salt, pepper,
turmeric, cinnamon and cloves
until well blended. Place ½ this
mixture in a buttered 9 inch
square baking dish. Fry the
prunes, almonds and remaining
onion in 1 tablespoon butter for
5 minutes. Add parsley and mint.
Spread this stuffing over the
rice mixture and cover with
remaining rice. Add the beef
broth and bake in a preheated
350° oven for 45 minutes.

Yogurtlu kebab

Meat with yogurt

4 servings

1½ to 2 pounds boneless leg of
    lamb
2 tablespoons olive oil
1 small onion, grated
½ teaspoon salt
    Freshly ground black pepper
6 tablespoons yogurt
2 to 3 tablespoons butter
2 medium sized tomatoes,
    peeled, seeded and mashed
4 thin slices whole wheat or
    any brown bread, toasted
1½ cups yogurt, heated
1½ teaspoons paprika

Cut the lamb into ½ inch cubes.
In a bowl, combine the olive oil,
onion, salt, pepper and yogurt.
Add the lamb cubes and
marinate 12 hours. Drain the
lamb and dry it thoroughly.
Heat the butter in a skillet and
sauté the lamb over high heat
until well browned on all sides.
Remove with a slotted spoon
and keep warm. Spread the
tomatoes over the toasted bread,
top with the lamb and pour on
the heated yogurt. Reheat the
butter remaining in the skillet.
Add the paprika and cook,
stirring, 2 minutes. Pour the
mixture over the lamb and serve.

Fillet wusach Matsadah

Fried fillet of beef in puff pastry

6 servings

>   2 *pounds fillet of beef, cut into*
>   *1 inch steaks*
>   4 *tablespoons butter*
> 1¾ *cups mushrooms*
>   ½ *pound chicken livers*
>   1 *teaspoon salt*
>   *Freshly ground black pepper*
>   1 *package frozen individual*
>   *patty shells, thawed*
>   1 *egg, beaten*

Sauté the beef for 2 minutes in hot butter. Remove from the pan. Wash the mushrooms and slice thinly. Cut the chicken livers into small pieces. Add salt and pepper and sauté mushrooms and livers in the same butter in which the meat was browned. Remove and cool. Roll each patty shell to a ⅓ inch thick round. Put each piece of meat in the middle of the pastry. Cover with the mixture of livers and mushrooms. Pinch the pastry closed around the fillet and brush with beaten egg. Bake in a preheated 400° oven for 20 to 25 minutes. Serve with baked tomatoes.

Patlıcan kebabı

Lamb with eggplants

4 servings

>   4 *small eggplants, sliced*
>   1 *tablespoon salt*
>   4 *tablespoons butter*
>   2 *onions, thinly sliced*
> 1½ *pounds lean lamb, cut into*
>   *1 inch cubes*
>   4 *tomatoes, peeled, seeded and*
>   *chopped*
>   ½ *teaspoon salt*
>   *Freshly ground black pepper*
>   1 *cup water*
>   1 *tablespoon finely chopped*
>   *parsley*

Sprinkle the eggplant slices with salt and set aside on a rack for 15 minutes. (This will drain the bitter juices from the eggplants.) Heat ½ the butter in a casserole and sauté the onions until soft. Add the lamb and sauté until well browned on all sides. Add tomatoes, salt and pepper and simmer 15 minutes. Meanwhile, rinse the eggplant slices and pat dry with paper towels. Heat the remaining butter in a skillet and sauté the slices over low to medium heat about 2 minutes on each side. Place on top of the lamb and add water and parsley. Cover the pan and simmer 50 minutes. Serve from the casserole.

Arni me domates

Lamb and tomatoes

4 servings

> 1½ *pounds lamb*
>   1 *teaspoon salt*
>   *Freshly ground black pepper*
>   4 *tablespoons butter*
>   6 *ripe tomatoes, peeled,*
>   *seeded and chopped*
>   ¼ *teaspoon cinnamon*
>   ½ *teaspoon sugar*
>   ¾ *cup beef broth*

Cut the lamb into 4 pieces, rub with salt and pepper and set aside for 20 minutes. Heat the butter in a pan, add the lamb and brown on all sides. Add the tomatoes, cinnamon and sugar and 2 tablespoons beef broth. Simmer for 10 minutes. Continue cooking for 1 hour or until the meat is tender. Add the beef broth as needed during the cooking period, keeping only a small quantity of liquid in the pan. Serve with noodles.

Pilav kuzulu

Lamb pilaf

4 servings

>   4 *tablespoons butter*
>   1 *onion, finely chopped*
>   1 *pound lamb, cut in small*
>   *cubes*
>   1 *teaspoon salt*
>   *Freshly ground black pepper*
>   ¼ *teaspoon cinnamon*
>   3 *ripe tomatoes, peeled, seeded*
>   *and chopped*
>   2 *tablespoons pine nuts*
>   2 *tablespoons raisins*
>   1 *green pepper, seeded and*
>   *sliced*
> 1½ *cups raw rice*
>   2 *tablespoons chopped parsley*
>   *Pinch of saffron soaked in*
>   *3 cups beef broth*

Heat the butter, add the onion and fry until soft and golden. Add the lamb and brown it on all sides. Add salt, pepper and cinnamon. Add the tomatoes, pine nuts, raisins and green pepper, cover and simmer for 10 minutes. Add the rice and stir for 2 minutes. Add parsley, saffron and broth. Cook over moderate heat until all the liquid has been absorbed and small holes appear on the surface of the rice. Reduce the heat to low, cover, put an asbestos pad under the pan and cook for 20 to 30 minutes until the rice is tender.

Meat casserole (photo below)

There is very little liquid called for in this recipe, though some juices will be formed by the vegetables. This is intended to be an extremely thick stew.

Güvec

Qormeh sabzi

Meat casserole

6 servings

- 2 small eggplants, sliced
- 2 teaspoons salt
- 4 tablespoons butter
- 2 pounds lamb, cut in 1 inch cubes
- 2 onions, sliced
- ½ pound green beans, broken in half
- 3 small zucchini, cut in thick slices
- 4 medium sized tomatoes, peeled and quartered
  Freshly ground black pepper
- 1 teaspoon paprika
- 2 tablespoons chopped parsley

Sprinkle the eggplant slices with 1 teaspoon salt and set aside for 15 minutes. Rinse and drain. Heat the butter in a casserole and fry the lamb until browned. Add the onions and fry for another 2 minutes. Arrange all the vegetables on top and sprinkle with the remaining salt and pepper. Add water to almost cover the vegetables. Sprinkle with paprika and bring to a boil over moderate heat. Transfer to a preheated 350° oven and bake for 50 to 60 minutes. Sprinkle with parsley and serve.

Meat and vegetable stew

4 servings

- 5 tablespoons oil
- 1½ pounds shoulder of lamb, finely diced
- 1 onion, chopped
- ½ teaspoon salt
  Freshly ground black pepper
- ½ teaspoon turmeric
- ⅓ cup lemon juice
- ½ cup water
- 10 scallions, thinly sliced
- 3 tablespoons finely chopped celery leaves
- ½ pound spinach, chopped
- 3 tablespoons chopped parsley
- ⅔ cup canned chick peas (garbanzos), drained

Heat 2 tablespoons oil in a heavy casserole and sauté the lamb until well browned on all sides. Add the onion and sauté until soft. Add salt, pepper, turmeric, lemon juice and water and bring to a boil. Lower the heat, cover and simmer very slowly 15 minutes. Heat the remaining oil in a skillet and sauté the scallions, celery leaves, spinach and parsley for 2 minutes, stirring constantly. Add these vegetables and the chick peas to the meat and combine thoroughly. Bring to a boil and lower the heat. Cover and simmer very slowly another 20 minutes.

The lack of wood for fuel in the eastern Mediterranean countries may well have inspired the practice of making stews. By cutting meat finely with *vegetables or fruit and cooking the mixture all together in one pan, only a single fire is needed.*

Khoreshe Sib

Mosamma bademjan

Meat and apple stew

4 servings

    4 *tablespoons oil*
    1 *onion, finely chopped*
 1½ *pounds lean lamb, cut into*
       1 inch cubes
    ½ *teaspoon salt*
       Freshly ground black pepper
       Pinch of cinnamon
 1½ *cups water*
    4 *small cooking apples, peeled,*
       cored and chopped
       Juice of 1 lemon

Heat 2 tablespoons of the oil in a casserole and sauté the onion until soft. Add the lamb and sauté until nicely browned on all sides. Add salt, pepper, cinnamon and water and bring to a boil. Reduce the heat, cover and simmer 45 minutes. Heat the remaining oil in a skillet and sauté the apples 3 minutes. Add the apples and lemon juice to the stew and simmer 30 minutes more.

Meat and eggplant stew

4 servings

    1 *small eggplant, sliced*
    2 *teaspoons salt*
    ½ *cup oil*
    2 *onions, sliced*
    1 *pound lamb, cubed*
       Freshly ground black pepper
    1 *teaspoon turmeric*
    ¼ *teaspoon cinnamon*
    ½ *cup water*
       Juice of 1 lemon
    3 *tomatoes, peeled, seeded*
       and chopped
    ⅓ *cup yellow split peas,*
       soaked overnight and drained

Sprinkle the eggplant with 1 teaspoon of the salt and set aside for 15 minutes. Wash off excess salt and drain thoroughly. Heat ½ of the oil, add the onions and fry until lightly browned. Add the lamb and fry for another 5 minutes. Sprinkle with the remaining salt, pepper, turmeric and cinnamon. Stir in the water and lemon juice. Simmer for 15 minutes. Add the tomatoes and split peas and simmer for another 30 minutes. Heat the remaining oil in a skillet, add the eggplant and fry for about 5 minutes. Add to the stew and simmer for 20 minutes.

In Greece, this dish is prepared using a whole baby lamb and the liver, kidneys, heart and tripe are added to the stuffing.

Arni me spanaki avgolemono

Lamb with spinach, egg and lemon sauce

4 servings

      6 *tablespoons butter*
      2 *onions, chopped*
   1½ *pounds lamb, cut in 1 inch
          cubes*
      1 *teaspoon salt*
          Freshly ground black pepper
      ¾ *cup beef broth*
   1½ *pounds spinach*
      2 *egg yolks*
      2 *tablespoons lemon juice*

Heat 4 tablespoons of the butter and fry the onions until soft and golden. Add the lamb and fry for 5 minutes over high heat. Add salt, pepper and beef broth, reserving 2 tablespoons of the broth. Simmer gently for 45 minutes or until the meat is tender. Simmer the cleaned spinach in its own juice in a covered saucepan for 5 minutes or until tender. Drain and chop coarsley. Season, if necessary, with salt and pepper. Spread the spinach on top of the meat, dot with remaining butter and simmer for 15 minutes. Beat the egg yolks until creamy and light. Add the lemon juice and reserved beef broth and pour over the meat and spinach. Cook over very low heat for 10 minutes, being careful not to let the mixture boil. Serve immediately.

Arni me kolokitia

Lamb with zucchini

4 servings

      5 *tablespoons butter*
   1½ *to 2 pounds leg of lamb, cut
          into 1 inch cubes*
      2 *onions, finely chopped*
      4 *tomatoes, peeled, seeded and
          chopped*
      2 *cloves garlic, crushed*
      ½ *teaspoon salt*
          Freshly ground black pepper
      2 *tablespoons finely chopped
          parsley*
      6 *small zucchini*

Heat 2 tablespoons butter in a casserole and sauté the lamb until well browned on all sides. Add the onions and sauté until softened. Stir in the tomatoes, garlic, salt, pepper and parsley. Cover and simmer 1 hour. Check from time to time to see if the mixture is becoming too dry and add broth or water, 1 tablespoon at a time, if necessary. Cut the ends off the zucchini and slice lengthwise. Cut crosswise to make 4 sections. Heat the remaining butter and sauté the zucchini 5 minutes over medium heat. Add to the lamb, cover and simmer 30 minutes more. Serve from the casserole.

Arnaki yemisto

Stuffed Easter lamb

8 servings

      1 *(4 pound) boned leg of lamb*
      1 *teaspoon salt*
          Freshly ground black pepper
      4 *tablespoons melted butter*
          Juice of 1 lemon
      ½ *pound ground lean lamb*
      1 *medium sized onion, finely
          chopped*
      ⅓ *cup rice*
          Pinch of cinnamon
      2 *tablespoons finely chopped
          parsley*
      1 *tablespoon finely chopped
          fresh mint or*
      1 *teaspoon dried mint*
      2 *cups beef broth*

Lay the lamb out flat on a board and sprinkle all over with ½ teaspoon salt and pepper. Brush with 2 tablespoons butter and the lemon juice. Heat the remaining butter in a skillet and sauté the ground lamb until it has lost all trace of pink. Add the onion, rice, remaining salt, pepper and cinnamon and sauté 5 minutes more. Stir in the parsley, mint and ⅔ cup broth and simmer 15 minutes. Remove from the heat and let cool. Spread the mixture on the leg of lamb, roll up tightly and tie securely in several places. Place the lamb on a rack in a roasting pan. Pour the remaining broth into the pan. Roast the lamb in a 450° oven for 15 minutes. Reduce the heat to 350° and continue cooking 1½ to 2 hours depending on the desired degree of doneness. Baste the lamb occasionally with the broth.

Arni me bamiès

Lamb with okra

4 servings

      3 *tablespoons butter*
      1 *onion, chopped*
   1½ *pounds lamb, cut in 1 inch
          cubes*
      1 *clove garlic, crushed*
      2 *medium sized tomatoes,
          peeled, seeded and sliced*
      1 *teaspoon salt*
          Freshly ground black pepper
          Juice of ½ lemon
      1 *large can okra, drained*
      1 *cup water*

Heat the butter, add the onion and fry 3 minutes until soft and golden. Add the lamb and brown on all sides. Add the garlic, tomatoes, salt and pepper and fry for another 5 minutes. Add lemon juice, okra and water. Bring to a boil, reduce the heat and simmer for 1 hour or until the meat is tender.

Küzü Hashlama

Lamb with leeks

4 servings

    4   tablespoons butter
 1½   pounds lamb, cut in 1 inch
        cubes
 1½   pounds leeks or onions
    8   scallions
    1   tomato, peeled, seeded and
        chopped
    1   tablespoon freshly chopped
        dill or
    1   teaspoon dried dill weed
    3   potatoes, peeled and sliced
    2   tablespoons chopped parsley
    1   teaspoon salt
        Freshly ground black pepper
 1½   cups water

Heat the butter in a casserole.
Add the lamb and brown it
well on all sides. Wash the leeks
and cut into 4 inch long pieces.
Remove the top green part of the
scallions. Place the leeks,
scallions and tomato on top of
the lamb. Add the dill and cover
with potato slices. Sprinkle with
parsley, salt and pepper. Add
the water, bring to the boil and
simmer gently for 1½ hours.
Serve hot.

Arni psito me kastana

Roast lamb with chestnuts

6 servings

    1   (4 to 5 pound) leg of lamb
    4   cloves garlic, slivered
        Sprigs of fresh rosemary or
    1   teaspoon dried rosemary
        Juice of ½ lemon
    2   tablespoons olive oil
 ½   teaspoon salt
        Freshly ground black pepper
    1   cup beef broth
    2   pounds chestnuts, peeled

Make incisions in several places
in the lamb and stuff with garlic
slivers and rosemary leaves. Rub
with lemon juice and oil and
sprinkle with salt and pepper.
Place the lamb in a roasting pan
and add the broth and chestnuts.
Roast the lamb in a 375° oven
for 1½ hours or until it reaches
the desired degree of doneness.
Transfer the lamb to a platter
and surround with the chestnuts.
Serve with a green salad.

Ciger tavasi

Fried liver

4 servings

 ¾   pound lamb's liver
    1   teaspoon paprika
    2   tablespoons flour
    2   tablespoons finely chopped
        parsley
 ½   teaspoon salt
 ¼   teaspoon freshly ground
        black pepper
    3   tablespoons olive oil
    1   tablespoon chopped parsley

Wash and dry the liver with a
paper towel and cut into slices
¼ inch thick. Sprinkle with
paprika. Combine flour, parsley,
salt and pepper and roll liver in
this mixture until evenly coated.
Heat the oil, add the liver slices
and fry 5 to 8 minutes until
brown and tender. Garnish with
parsley and serve.

Mi'laaq mashwi bitoum

Grilled liver with garlic

6 servings

 1½   pounds calves' liver
    3   cloves garlic, crushed
 1½   teaspoons salt
        Freshly ground black pepper
 1½   teaspoons crushed dried mint
        leaves
    2   tablespoons olive oil
    2   large onions, cut into cubes
        Juice of 1 lemon

Remove the tough outer skin
and veins from the liver and slice
into thick strips. Combine the
garlic, salt, pepper and mint in a
bowl and toss the liver strips in
the mixture. Sprinkle the liver
with olive oil and set aside for
30 minutes. Thread the liver
strips on skewers alternately
with the onions. Grill over a
charcoal fire or under the
broiler for 15 minutes, turning
occasionally, until nicely
browned. Sprinkle the liver and
onions with lemon juice and
serve.

Poultry and game dishes

The tender, young spring chicken is a rarity in the countries along the Mediterranean coast for economic reasons. But starting with a somewhat aged chicken, *and using imaginative and refined preparation, cooks in these countries can provide a priceless dish. Chicken stew.*

The fact that chicken livers and wine make a good combination has long been known in the eastern Mediterranean as well as the kitchens of France.

Kotopoulo kapama

Chicken stew

4 servings

½ teaspoon salt
 Freshly ground black pepper
 Pinch of cinnamon
 Juice of ½ lemon
1 (3 to 3½ pound) chicken,
 cut into serving pieces
2 tablespoons butter
1 tablespoon olive oil
6 tomatoes, peeled, seeded and
 chopped
2 cups chicken broth
 Pinch of sugar

In a bowl, combine the salt, pepper, cinnamon and lemon juice. Brush the chicken pieces on all sides with the mixture and let stand 10 minutes. Pat the pieces dry with paper towels and reserve any excess marinade. Heat the butter and oil in a casserole and sauté the chicken pieces until nicely browned on all sides. Remove from the pan and keep warm. Add the tomatoes and sauté 1 minute. Add any excess marinade, the broth and sugar and bring to a boil. Simmer vigourously 7 minutes. Return the chicken to the pan, reduce the heat, cover and simmer 45 minutes until chicken is tender.

Sikotakia tis kottas me saltsa

Chicken livers in Madeira

6 servings

1½ pounds chicken livers
3 tablespoons butter
2 tablespoons flour
1 cup chicken broth
½ medium sized onion, finely
 chopped
1 clove garlic, crushed
1 tablespoon finely chopped
 parsley
¼ teaspoon salt
 Freshly ground black pepper
⅓ cup Madeira

Wash the chicken livers and dry them thoroughly. Heat the butter in a skillet and sauté the livers 5 minutes over high heat, turning them gently with a wooden spoon. Remove the livers with a slotted spoon and keep warm. Add the flour to the butter in the skillet and cook, stirring, 1 minute. Add the broth gradually, stirring constantly with a wire whisk until a thick sauce forms. Add the onion, garlic, parsley, salt and pepper and simmer 3 minutes, stirring constantly. Add the Madeira and simmer 5 minutes. Return the chicken livers to the pan and cook just long enough for them to heat through.

Kotopoulo me hilopites

Itsch pilav

Since the bird's name is 'turkey', many people think its home was originally the country of that name. But of course the turkey is American in origin. The Spanish conquistadores brought this bird back with them to Europe. When the French first saw it, they thought it came from the West Indies and called it 'coq d'Inde', bird of India, which later became 'dinde', which it remains to this day. In Turkey, the bird was called 'India' or 'hindi'. But since the English confused the East with the West Indies, and even thought Turkey and India were the same place, this bird of western origin was given the name of an eastern country, Turkey. Although turkey is not, then, indigenous to Turkey, it has become a favorite dish there, especially for New Year's Eve. Chicken is also popular in Turkey. It is roasted over a charcoal fire, or, in small villages, taken to the baker's to be baked in his oven. A popular dish with chicken is rice pilaf. It is one of the commonest and most fundamental dishes throughout the Middle East. The first duty of a housewife is to be able to make a good rice pilaf, with separate rice grains, not too dry and not too wet, tasty and full-flavored. It can be difficult to make an absolutely perfect rice pilaf the first time. It takes practice, as well as the right spices and herbs – saffron, garlic, onion, cardamon, almonds, and raisins.

Chicken and noodles

4 servings

1 (3 pound) chicken, cut into serving pieces
4 tablespoons butter
½ teaspoon salt
Freshly ground black pepper
1 onion, chopped
2 cloves garlic, crushed
2 tomatoes, peeled, seeded and chopped
1 teaspoon tomato paste
1 stalk celery, finely chopped
1 cup white wine
3 tablespoons finely chopped parsley
1 tablespoon cornstarch dissolved in
2 tablespoons cold water
1 pound noodles
3 tablespoons grated Parmesan cheese or Greek goat cheese

Brown the chicken in hot butter in a large skillet. Remove the chicken pieces and season with salt and pepper. Add onion and garlic to the same hot butter and fry for 3 minutes until softened. Add tomatoes, tomato paste and celery. Return the chicken to the skillet and add the wine and parsley. Cover and simmer for 50 minutes until the chicken is tender. Stir cornstarch paste into the pan juices and cook for 2 minutes until thickened into a sauce. In the meantime, cook the noodles in plenty of boiling salted water for 8 minutes until just tender. Place the noodles on a serving plate. Pour the sauce over the noodles and arrange chicken pieces on top. Sprinkle chicken with Parmesan cheese and serve immediately.

Pilaf with liver

4 servings

1 pound chicken livers
5 tablespoons butter
1 teaspoon salt
Freshly ground black pepper
1½ cups thinly sliced scallions
2 medium sized tomatoes, peeled, seeded and chopped
2 tablespoons pine nuts
2 tablespoons chopped almonds
2 tablespoons raisins
1 cup rice
2 cups water
2 tablespoons chopped parsley

Wash the chicken livers and dry them thoroughly. Heat 3 tablespoons butter in a skillet and sauté chicken livers. Remove from the pan and sprinkle with ½ teaspoon salt and pepper. Add ¾ cup of the scallions to the skillet and sauté until lightly browned. Remove the scallions from the pan with a slotted spoon. Heat the remaining butter in a 3 quart casserole or saucepan and sauté remaining scallions. Add the tomatoes, pine nuts, almonds and raisins and sauté 2 minutes, stirring constantly. Add the rice, water, remaining salt and pepper and bring to a boil. Stir once with a fork, reduce the heat so the mixture just simmers and cook 25 minutes or until the rice has absorbed the liquid. Place the reserved livers and scallions on top of the rice and cover the pan tightly. Place an asbestos pad under the pan and cook 15 minutes. Sprinkle with parsley and serve from the casserole.

Shorabat khodar bidshash

Chicken with vegetable stew

4 servings

    1 *(2½ pound) chicken, cut in
       8 pieces*
    6 *tablespoons butter*
    1¾ *cups chicken broth*
    ½ *teaspoon salt*
       Freshly ground black pepper
    ¼ *teaspoon cinnamon*
    6 *small white onions*
    1 *small zucchini, cut in ½ inch
       thick slices*
    1 *carrot, cut in 1 inch pieces*
    2 *medium sized potatoes,
       peeled and cubed*
    3 *medium sized tomatoes,
       peeled, seeded and coarsely
       chopped*

Brown the chicken in 4
tablespoons of the butter in a
large casserole for about 10
minutes. Add the chicken broth,
salt, pepper and cinnamon.
Simmer gently for 30 minutes.
Sauté the vegetables in the
remaining butter for 10 minutes
and add to the chicken. Simmer
15 minutes more until the
vegetables are tender.

Riz bidshash u banadura

Chicken with rice and tomatoes

4 servings

    1½ *cups raw rice*
    1 *(3½ pound) frying chicken,
       cut in serving pieces*
    4 *tablespoons butter*
    2 *large tomatoes, peeled,
       seeded and chopped*
    1 *tablespoon tomato paste*
    1½ *cups chicken broth*
    1½ *teaspoons salt*
       Freshly ground black pepper
    ¼ *teaspoon cinnamon*

Cover the rice with hot water
and let stand 30 minutes. Fry
the chicken pieces in the butter
over a moderately high heat
for 15 minutes or until browned.
Add the tomatoes, tomato paste,
chicken broth, salt, pepper and
cinnamon. Bring to a boil,
cover, reduce the heat and
simmer for 35 minutes until
tender. Remove the chicken
and reserve ½ cup of the sauce
from the pan. If necessary, add
enough water to the remaining
sauce to make 3 cups. Add the
rice and cook for about 20
minutes until tender. Transfer
the rice to a serving dish, top
with the chicken and pour on
the reserved ½ cup of sauce.

Dshash mashi

Stuffed chicken

4 servings

    1 *(3 pound) chicken*
    ½ *pound sausage meat*
    ½ *cup rice, cooked for 10
       minutes*
    1 *onion, finely chopped*
    ¼ *cup pine nuts, coarsely
       chopped*
    ¼ *cup almonds, coarsely
       chopped*
    ½ *teaspoon salt*
       Freshly ground black pepper
       Few strands of saffron
    ¼ *teaspoon cinnamon*
    1 *tablespoon finely chopped
       parsley*
    3 *tablespoons melted butter*

Wash and dry the chicken.
Combine the sausage meat,
rice, onion, nuts, salt, pepper,
saffron, cinnamon, parsley and
2 tablespoons of butter. Stuff
the chicken with this mixture
and truss. Brush with the
remaining butter and roast in a
preheated 350° oven for 1¼
hours until tender.

Kotopoulo yemisto

Stuffed chicken

4 servings

    1 *(3½ pound) chicken*
    2 *slices bacon, diced*
    2 *tablespoons butter*
    ¾ *cup finely chopped onions*
    ¾ *cup toasted breadcrumbs*
    ½ *cup ground walnuts*
    ¼ *cup ground filberts*
    3 *tablespoons finely chopped
       parsley*
    ¼ *teaspoon salt*
       Freshly ground black pepper
       Pinch of cinnamon
    2 *eggs*
    1 *tablespoon softened butter*

Wash and dry the chicken.
Reserve the liver. Fry the bacon
until crisp. Remove with a
slotted spoon and drain on
paper towels. Add the butter to
the rendered bacon fat and sauté
the liver until nicely browned.
Remove, drain on paper towels
and chop. Add the onions to the
pan and sauté until lightly
browned. In a bowl, combine
the bacon, chicken liver, onions,
breadcrumbs, walnuts, filberts,
parsley, salt, pepper, cinnamon
and eggs. Stuff the chicken with
the mixture and truss. Rub the
chicken with softened butter and
place on a rack in a roasting
pan. Roast the chicken in a 350°
oven for 1½ hours, basting
occasionally with the
accumulated pan juices. Remove
the trussing strings and place on
a serving platter.

Ta'am V'reah

Stuffed drumsticks baked in wine

6 servings

    6 *large chicken drumsticks*
    2 *medium sized onions, finely chopped*
    2 *tablespoons butter*
  ½ *pound chicken livers, finely chopped*
    1 *cup blanched almonds, toasted and chopped*
  ½ *teaspoon salt*
     Freshly ground black pepper
    2 *cups dry white wine*

Cut lengthwise along the inside of the thigh and leg of each drumstick. Remove the bone, taking care to preserve the shape of the leg. Sew the leg closed, leaving a small opening at the top. Sauté the onions in the butter until softened. Remove from the pan with a slotted spoon. Combine half the onions with the chicken livers, ½ cup almonds, salt and pepper. Fill the drumsticks with the mixture using a pastry bag. Sew up the opening. Arrange the drumsticks in a buttered baking pan. Let them brown in a 400°oven for 10 minutes. Reduce the oven heat to 350°. Pour the wine into the baking pan and bake the drumsticks 1 hour, basting occasionally with the wine. Arrange the drumsticks on a heated platter and sprinkle with the remaining almonds.

Roast duck with orange sauce.

Although turkey comes from the New World, the dish received quite an enthusiastic welcome in the Old World, and particularly in the countries around the Mediterranean. Stuffed turkey breast. (recipe page 75, 1st column)

Barvas wusach Yafo

Roast duck with orange sauce

8 servings

    2 (4 pound) ducks
    2 teaspoons salt
       Freshly ground black pepper
    6 oranges
    2 tablespoons sugar
    4 tablespoons cornstarch
       dissolved in
       ¼ cup water

Season the cavity of the ducks with salt and pepper. Truss the ducks. Prick the skin with a fork and place on a rack in a large roasting pan. Roast uncovered in a 350° oven for 1¼ hours. Squeeze 5 oranges. Heat the sugar in a pan until melted and brown. Add the orange juice. Stir the cornstarch mixture into the sugar and orange juice and simmer 3 minutes, stirring constantly. Cut the ducks into serving pieces and arrange on a heated platter. Cover with the orange sauce and garnish with slices from the remaining orange. Serve with steamed cabbage, green peas tossed in butter and roast potatoes.

Pilitsh güveci sebzeli

Chicken with vegetables

4 servings

- 1 (2½ pound) chicken, cut into serving pieces
- 2 teaspoons salt
  Freshly ground black pepper
- 2 tablespoons flour
- 1 pound eggplant, peeled and sliced
- 4 tablespoons olive oil
- 2 onions, thinly sliced
- 2 small green peppers, seeded and cut into strips
- 2 small zucchini, thinly sliced
- 4 ripe tomatoes, peeled, seeded and sliced
- 1 (8 ounce) can okra, drained and sliced
- ¾ pound string beans, cut in 1½ inch long pieces
- 1½ cups chicken broth

Dredge chicken pieces in combined ½ teaspoon salt, pepper and flour. Sprinkle the eggplant with remaining salt and set aside for 15 minutes. Rinse eggplant slices and pat dry on paper towels. Fry the chicken in the hot oil for 15 minutes until golden brown. Remove from pan and keep warm. Add the onions, peppers and eggplant and fry for 3 minutes. Add zucchini, tomatoes, okra and string beans and fry 1 minute longer. Transfer all the vegetables to a casserole. Place the chicken pieces on top of the vegetables. Add chicken broth, cover and bake in a preheated 350° oven for 40 minutes, basting the chicken occasionally. Serve from the casserole.

Tsherkes tavugu

Circassian chicken

4 servings

- 1 (2½ to 3 pound) chicken
- 1 onion, coarsley chopped
- 2 tablespoons parsley leaves
- ½ teaspoon salt
  Freshly ground black pepper
- 2 slices day-old bread, crusts removed
- 2 tablespoons grated onion
- 1 clove garlic, crushed
- ½ cup finely ground walnuts
- 1 teaspoon paprika
- 1 tablespoon walnut oil
  Parsley sprigs for garnish

Place the chicken, onion, parsley leaves, salt and pepper in a pan and barely cover with water. Bring to a boil and skim the broth. Lower the heat, cover the pan and simmer 45 minutes. Remove the chicken from the broth and let cool to room temperature. Meanwhile, strain the broth, return it to the pan and boil over high heat until reduced to 1½ cups. Soak the bread in ½ cup of the broth, squeeze it dry and crumble into a saucepan. Add the grated onion, garlic, walnuts and broth. Bring to a simmer, stirring constantly until the sauce is thickened. Taste for seasoning and add salt and pepper if necessary. Remove the skin from the chicken and slice the meat thinly. Combine the meat with half of the sauce and place in a serving dish. Pour the remaining sauce on top. Combine the paprika with the walnut oil and sprinkle over the chicken. Garnish with parsley sprigs and serve.

Pilitsh yahnisi

Chicken casserole

4 servings

- 1 (3 pound) chicken, cut into serving pieces
- 1 teaspoon salt
  Freshly ground black pepper
- ½ cup flour
- 3 tablespoons olive oil
- 2 onions, sliced
- 1 cup chopped celery root (optional)
- 1½ cups sliced mushrooms
- 4 tomatoes, peeled, seeded and sliced
- 2 cloves garlic, crushed
- ½ teaspoon rosemary
- 2 tablespoons finely chopped parsley
- ¾ cup water

Sprinkle the pieces of chicken with salt and pepper and set aside 5 minutes. Dredge the pieces in flour and sauté in hot olive oil until nicely browned on all sides. Transfer to an ovenproof casserole. Sauté the onions, celery root and mushrooms in the same oil for 3 minutes stirring frequently. Add the tomatoes, garlic, rosemary, parsley and water and pour over the chicken. Cover the casserole and bake in a 350° oven for 1 hour or until chicken is tender. Taste for seasoning and add salt and pepper if necessary. Serve from the casserole.

Pilav tavuklu

Chicken pilaf

4 servings

- 1 (2½ pound) chicken
- ½ teaspoon salt
  Freshly ground black pepper
- 3 tablespoons butter
- 1 onion, sliced
- 3 tablespoons chopped walnuts
- ¾ cup fresh or frozen green peas
  Pinch of saffron
- 1 tablespoon chopped parsley
- 1 cup rice
- 2 cups simmering chicken broth

Remove the skin from the chicken and cut the meat into strips. Sprinkle with salt and pepper. Heat the butter in a heavy casserole and sauté the onion until lightly browned. Add chicken and sauté 1 minute. Add walnuts, peas, saffron and parsley and sauté 2 minutes, stirring constantly. Add the rice and stir 30 seconds. Add the simmering broth and bring to a boil. Stir once with a fork, lower the heat, cover and simmer until the rice has absorbed all the liquid (about 25 minutes). Place the casserole on an asbestos pad over the lowest possible heat and cook another 15 minutes. Transfer to a serving dish and serve immediately.

Merchavia

Stuffed turkey breast

6 servings

1¾ *pounds turkey breast*
  1 *cup pitted green olives*
  1 *egg*
  ½ *teaspoon salt*
    Freshly ground black pepper
  ½ *teaspoon ground ginger*
    Flour
  2 *tablespoons butter*
  2 *tablespoons oil*
  ¾ *cup sweet white wine*
  1 *cup orange juice*
  ½ *cup chicken broth*
  ½ *cup pitted black olives*

Cut 6 slices from the turkey breast and arrange on a flat surface. Chop the remaining turkey meat with half of the green olives and place in a bowl. Add the egg, salt, pepper and ginger and combine thoroughly. Spread some of the mixture on each slice of turkey breast. Roll up each piece beginning at one long side and secure with toothpicks. Dredge each roll in flour and sauté in hot combined butter and oil until golden brown on all sides. Transfer the rolls to an ovenproof baking dish. Add the wine, orange juice and broth to the pan in which the rolls were browned. Bring to a boil and let boil 5 minutes. Chop the remaining green olives with the black olives and sprinkle over the turkey rolls. Pour on the sauce and bake in a 350° oven for 25 minutes. Slice the rolls, place on a heated serving platter and spoon a little of the sauce over the meat. Serve with boiled cauliflower in white sauce, baked eggplant or fried mushrooms.

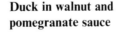

Fesenjan

Duck in walnut and pomegranate sauce

4 servings

  1 *(4 pound) duck, cut into*
    serving pieces
  ¾ *teaspoon salt*
    Freshly ground black pepper
  1 *cup fresh pomegranate juice*
    or
    ¼ *cup pomegranate syrup*
  4 *tablespoons butter*
  2 *medium sized onions, finely*
    chopped
  1 *teaspoon turmeric*
  ½ *cup ground walnuts*
  2 *cups chicken broth*
    Pinch of sugar
  1 *tablespoon finely chopped*
    parsley
  8 *whole walnuts*

Sprinkle the pieces of duck with ½ teaspoon salt and pepper. If using fresh pomegranate juice, boil it over high heat until reduced to ¼ cup. Heat 2 tablespoons butter in a skillet and sauté the onions 2 minutes. Add the remaining salt, pepper and turmeric and sauté 5 minutes more. With a slotted spoon, transfer the onions to a casserole and add the ground walnuts and chicken broth. Cover and simmer 20 minutes. Meanwhile, heat the remaining butter in the skillet and sauté the pieces of duck over medium heat until well browned on all sides. Transfer to the casserole and cook 45 minutes. Stir in the reduced pomegranate juice or syrup and the sugar and simmer, uncovered, 10 to 15 minutes. Place the duck pieces on a serving dish and pour the sauce over. Garnish with chopped parsley and whole walnuts and serve.

Vegetable dishes

Just as Sheherazade managed to survive by telling a new story for a thousand and one nights, there are a thousand and one recipes in the Near East for preparing the omnipresent eggplant. (recipe page 78, 1st column)

Sebze bastısı

Vegetable stew

4 servings

    1 medium sized (1 pound)
       eggplant
    1 teaspoon salt
    4 tablespoons butter or oil
    2 onions, sliced
    2 green peppers, seeded and
       cut into strips
    2 zucchini, sliced ¼ inch thick
    1 cup string beans, cut into 1½
       inch pieces
    2 cloves garlic, crushed
    2 tablespoons chopped parsley
    ½ teaspoon sugar
       Freshly ground black pepper
    1 cup beef broth
    2 tablespoons chopped parsley
       for garnish

Cut the eggplant into ¼ inch slices, sprinkle with salt and set aside for 15 minutes. Wash off salt, drain and pat dry with paper towels. Heat 2 tablespoons butter in a skillet. Add the eggplant slices and fry until lightly browned on both sides. Transfer to a baking dish. Fry the onions and peppers in the remaining butter 3 minutes. Add the zucchini and beans and fry for 2 more minutes, stirring frequently. Place the vegetables on top of the eggplant. Add garlic, parsley, sugar, pepper and beef broth. Cover and place in a preheated 350° oven for 1 hour. Garnish with parsley and serve hot.

The people of the Eastern Mediterranean are very fond of vegetables, especially of the so-called 'fruit vegetables', such as eggplants, zucchini and cucumbers. Most popular of all is the cucumber. In the old quarters of Istanbul and of other Eastern cities, stalls along the sidewalks sell cucumbers as a cheap and refreshing treat during the hot, humid days of summer. Cucumber salad is also a favorite during the summer months, especially if it is served with yoghurt.
Eggplant is another vegetable very much appreciated.
Eggplants have been grown throughout the Middle East since ancient times, but they probably originated in Persia. The original Persian word for 'eggplant' was 'badindjan'. The Arabs added an

article in front of it to make 'al-badindjan', and the word entered most European languages as 'aubergine'. During the summer, stacks of shiny, dark-purple eggplants are highlights of markets from Athens to Tel Aviv. Eggplants are fried, baked, stewed, stuffed or eaten in salads; they can also be roasted, pickled or finely crushed. The eggplant is in fact a universal vegetable, and with its subtle flavor it can be combined with a variety of other tastes.
In Greece, zucchinis, the oblong, yellow-green vegetables so loved in ancient Rome, are still especially popular. There is a great deal to be said on a hot day for a Greek salad made of slices of zucchini in olive oil with a lot of lemon juice and pepper.

Patlızcanlı pilav

Pilaf with eggplant

4 servings

 3 *small eggplants*
 1 *tablespoon salt*
 3 *tablespoons olive oil*
 2 *tomatoes, peeled, seeded and chopped*
 1 *clove garlic, crushed*
 ¼ *teaspoon salt*
   Freshly ground black pepper
 1 *cup rice*
 2 *cups simmering chicken broth*

Cut the eggplants in half lengthwise and cut each into ½ inch thick slices. Sprinkle with salt and set aside on a rack for 15 minutes. (This will drain the bitter juices from the eggplants.) Wash off the excess salt and pat dry with paper towels. Heat the olive oil in a large casserole and sauté the eggplant slices until lightly browned on both sides. Add the tomatoes and garlic and simmer over low heat for 5 minutes, stirring occasionally. Add salt, pepper and rice and combine thoroughly. Pour in the simmering broth and bring to a boil. Lower the heat, cover and simmer until the rice has absorbed all the liquid (about 25 minutes). Place the casserole on an asbestos pad over the lowest possible heat and cook 15 minutes more. Serve hot or cold and pass a bowl of yogurt separately.

Patlıcan tavası

Fried eggplant with yogurt

4 servings

 2 *to 3 eggplants, depending on size*
 1 *tablespoon salt*
 4 *tablespoons olive oil*
 1 *medium sized green pepper, seeded and cut into strips*
 3 *tomatoes, peeled, seeded and sliced*
 1¼ *cups yogurt*
 1 *clove garlic, crushed*
 ¼ *teaspoon salt*
 1½ *tablespoons finely chopped fresh mint or*
 ¾ *teaspoon dried mint*

Cut the eggplants into ½ inch thick slices, sprinkle liberally with salt and set aside on a rack for 15 minutes. (This will drain the bitter juices from the eggplants.) Wash off the excess salt and pat dry on paper towels. Heat the oil in a large skillet and sauté the eggplant slices until lightly browned on both sides. Remove and drain on paper towels. Add the green pepper to the skillet and sauté 3 minutes. Add tomatoes and continue cooking 2 minutes. In a bowl, combine the yogurt with the garlic and salt. In a serving dish layer the eggplant slices and tomato mixture, spreading each layer with a little of the yogurt mixture. Sprinkle with mint and serve hot or chill and serve cold.

Patlıcan salatası

Eggplant salad

4 servings

 2 *large eggplants*
   Juice of 1 lemon
 1 *tablespoon oil*
 ½ *cup yogurt*
 2 *cloves garlic, crushed*
 ½ *teaspoon salt*
 ⅛ *teaspoon white pepper*
 3 *tomatoes, peeled, seeded and sliced*
 ½ *cup black olives, pitted and halved*
 3 *scallions, sliced*

Place the eggplants in a baking pan in a 350° oven for 1 hour or until they are very soft to the touch. Scoop out the pulp and purée in a blender. Add the lemon juice, oil, yogurt, garlic, salt and pepper and blend until the mixture is smooth. Place in a serving bowl and garnish with tomatoes, olives and scallions. Chill 1 hour before serving.

Patlıcan kebabı

Eggplant purée

4 servings

 2 *eggplants*
   Juice of 1 lemon
 1 *tablespoon olive oil*
 2 *cloves garlic, crushed*
 ½ *teaspoon salt*
 2 *tablespoons yogurt*
 ½ *(3 ounce) package cream cheese*
   Lettuce leaves
 8 *black olives, pitted and halved*
   Parsley sprigs

Place the eggplants on a baking sheet in a 350° oven for 1 hour until very soft to the touch. Cut in half, scoop out the pulp and purée in a blender. Add the lemon juice, olive oil, garlic, salt, yogurt and cream cheese and continue blending until the mixture is smooth and thoroughly combined. Transfer the purée to a bowl and chill several hours. To serve, arrange several lettuce leaves on a plate. Mound the eggplant purée in the center and garnish with olives and parsley sprigs.

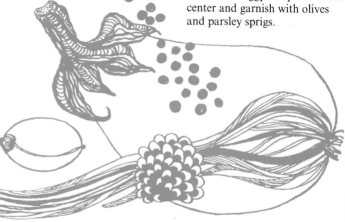

Karnı yarık

Stuffed eggplant

6 servings

- 6 *very small eggplants*
- 1½ *teaspoons salt*
- 6 *tablespoons olive oil*
- 3 *large onions, thinly sliced*
- 4 *ripe tomatoes, peeled, seeded and chopped*
- 2 *cloves garlic, crushed*
- 1½ *tablespoons chopped parsley*
- ½ *teaspoon sugar*
   Freshly ground black pepper
   Juice of 1 lemon
- 1 *cup beef broth*

Wash the eggplants and make a deep incision lengthwise without cutting through the underside or both ends. Sprinkle with 1 teaspoon salt and set aside for 5 minutes. Heat 2 tablespoons oil in a skillet and fry the onions until soft and lightly browned. Remove from the heat, add the tomatoes, garlic, ½ the parsley, sugar, ¼ teaspoon salt and pepper and combine thoroughly. Wash the eggplants to remove the salt and pat dry. Heat 2 tablespoons oil in a pan and fry the eggplants over medium heat for 10 minutes or until softened. Transfer the eggplants to a baking dish. Spread them open and stuff with the tomato-onion mixture. Sprinkle with the remaining oil, salt, pepper and lemon juice. Add the beef broth and bake in a preheated 350° oven for 45 minutes. Remove from the oven. Allow to cool completely. Garnish with remaining parsley and serve cold.

Pirincli ispanak

Spinach with rice

4 servings

- 2 *pounds spinach*
- 1 *cup raw rice*
- 4 *tablespoons butter*
- 1 *onion, thinly sliced*
- ½ *cup tomato purée*
- 4 *medium sized tomatoes, peeled, seeded and chopped*
- 1¼ *cup water*
- 1 *teaspoon salt*
   Freshly ground black pepper

Wash and drain the spinach and chop finely. Soak the rice in hot water for 10 minutes and drain. Heat the butter and fry the onion about 3 minutes until soft and golden. Remove from heat and place onion in a heatproof casserole. Cover with the chopped spinach and then an even layer of rice. Mix the tomato purée, tomatoes, water, salt and pepper and pour over the rice. Place over moderate heat and cook until all the liquid has been absorbed. Cover, place an asbestos pad under the casserole and steam over the lowest possible heat until the rice is tender and fluffy.

Domatesli fasulye

Kidney beans with tomatoes

4 servings

- ½ *pound kidney beans, soaked overnight*
- 3 *cups cold water*
- 1 *teaspoon salt*
- 2 *tablespoons olive oil*
- 2 *onions chopped*
- 6 *medium sized tomatoes, peeled, seeded and chopped*
- 2 *cloves garlic, crushed*
- ½ *teaspoon salt*
   Dash cayenne pepper
- ½ *tablespoon chopped fresh basil or*
   ½ *teaspoon dried basil*
- 1 *bay leaf*
- ¼ *teaspoon paprika*
- 2 *tablespoons chopped parsley*

Place the beans in a saucepan and add water and salt. Bring to boiling point and simmer for about 2 hours until tender and soft. Drain the beans. Heat the oil in a skillet. Add the onions and fry until soft and golden. Add the tomatoes, garlic and salt and cook, stirring occasionally, until mixture is reduced to a smooth purée. Add the pepper, basil, bay leaf and paprika. Place the beans in a casserole, add the tomato sauce, cover and simmer for 20 minutes. Remove the bay leaf, sprinkle with parsley and serve either hot or cold.

Pancar salatası

Beet salad

4 servings

- 1½ *tablespoons olive oil*
- 1 *tablespoon lemon juice*
- 1¼ *cups yogurt*
- 1 *clove garlic, crushed*
- ¼ *teaspoon salt*
- ⅛ *teaspoon white pepper*
- ½ *pound cooked beets, diced*
- 2 *tablespoons finely chopped parsley*

In a bowl, beat the olive oil and lemon juice together with a wire whisk. Add the yogurt, garlic, salt and pepper and stir until thoroughly blended. Fold in the diced beets and transfer to a serving bowl. Sprinkle with parsley and serve.

During the hot, dusty Turkish summer there is nothing so refreshing as to be seated on a terrace under the shade of a plane tree with a large bowl of cucumber and yogurt.

Beet salad (recipe page 79, 4th column)

Cacık

Cucumbers in yogurt

6 servings

> 3 cucumbers, peeled and cubed
> 3 cups yogurt
> 2 cloves garlic, crushed
> ½ teaspoon salt
>   Freshly ground black pepper
> 1 tablespoon melted butter
> 1 tablespoon oil
> 1 tablespoon wine vinegar
> 2 tablespoons chopped fresh dill or
>   1 tablespoon dried dill weed
> 2 tablespoons chopped parsley
> ½ cup walnuts, chopped
> 2 hard boiled egg yolks, crumbled

Mix all the ingredients together in a bowl and chill in the refrigerator for 1 hour. Serve with coarse brown bread.

The poetic Arabic language has a number of quaint expressions for stuffed eggplant, for example, 'the sheik of the eggplants' or, 'the sultan was delightful'.

Mahshi Batindshan bi zayt

Stuffed eggplant

6 servings

    6 small or 3 medium-sized
      eggplants
    1 cup cooked rice
    ¼ cup chopped walnuts
    4 tablespoons chopped parsley
    3 tablespoons chopped onion
    2 medium sized tomatoes,
      peeled, seeded and chopped
    ½ cup olive oil
    ½ large red or green pepper,
      seeded and chopped
    1½ teaspoons salt
      Freshly ground black pepper
    2 firm ripe tomatoes, sliced

Remove the stalks from the eggplants and cut each in half lengthwise. Hollow out each half with a sharp knife. Mix rice, walnuts, parsley, onion, tomatoes, oil, red or green pepper, 1 teaspoon of the salt and pepper until well combined. Stuff the eggplant ¾ full with this mixture. Place the sliced tomatoes in a heavy saucepan and arrange the eggplants on top. Sprinkle with ½ teaspoon salt and add enough water to half cover the eggplant. Cover, bring to a boil, reduce the heat and simmer for about 45 minutes until tender. Uncover after cooking 30 minutes to allow the sauce to thicken. Transfer to a serving dish, let cool and serve.

Kousa Qablama

Stuffed zucchini

6 servings

6 small zucchini
½ cup butter
1 cup chopped onion
2½ cups ground lamb
½ cup pine nuts
1 teaspoon salt
Freshly ground black pepper
¼ teaspoon cinnamon
2 cups tomato juice
1 cup Béchamel sauce
(recipe page 57)
3 tablespoons dry breadcrumbs
6 tablespoons grated cheese,
preferably goat cheese
2 tablespoons butter

Wash the zucchini, cut off the stalk ends and hollow out with a teaspoon. Heat ¼ cup of the butter in a skillet and cook the onion for 5 minutes until browned. Add the lamb, pine nuts, salt, pepper and cinnamon and fry until the meat is lightly browned. Set aside to cool and stuff the zucchini with the mixture. Seal with the scooped out pulp. Heat the remaining butter in a casserole, add the zucchini and fry over high heat until browned. Add the tomato juice, bring to a boil, reduce the heat and simmer for 20 minutes or until tender. Drain the zucchini and cover with Béchamel sauce. Combine breadcrumbs with grated cheese and sprinkle over the sauce. Dot with the butter and place in a preheated 400° oven until the cheese has melted and a golden crust has formed.

Kousa Mahshi

Meat stuffed zucchini

6 servings

6 small zucchini
1½ cups ground lamb
1 cup cooked rice
4 tomatoes, peeled, seeded and
chopped
1 teaspoon salt
Freshly ground black pepper
¼ teaspoon cinnamon
1½ cups tomato juice
1 cup beef broth

Cut off the stalk end of the zucchini. Cut each zucchini in half lengthwise and hollow out the inside with a spoon. Combine the ground lamb, rice, half of the tomatoes, ½ teaspoon of the salt, pepper and cinnamon. Stuff the zucchini with this mixture. Place the remainder of the tomatoes in a heavy pan, cover with the zucchini and add the tomato juice, beef broth and remaining salt. Bring to the boil, reduce the heat and simmer in a covered pan for 40 minutes. Uncover and continue cooking for about 10 minutes or until the sauce has thickened. Serve either hot or cold.

Mercimek köftesi

Lentil cakes

6 to 8 servings

½ cup red lentils
2 cups water
1 cup bulgar (cracked wheat)
2 tablespoons butter, melted
2 onions, finely chopped
1½ teaspoons cumin
½ teaspoon paprika
½ teaspoon powdered fenugreek
1 tablespoon finely chopped
celery leaves
1 tablespoon finely chopped
parsley
½ teaspoon salt
Freshly ground black pepper

Wash lentils, place in a pan and add water. Bring to a boil, lower the heat, cover and simmer 30 minutes. Remove from the heat, stir in the bulgar and let stand 1 hour. Drain off any liquid, add all the remaining ingredients and combine thoroughly. Shape the mixture into flat cakes. No further cooking is needed. Serve cold with chilis marinated in vinegar and sour pickles.

Mahshi Malfouf

Hummus bi Tahini

Charshofay Natseret

Stuffed cabbage rolls

6 servings

   1 *medium sized white cabbage*
1½ *cups ground lamb*
   1 *cup cooked rice*
   3 *tomatoes, peeled, seeded and chopped*
1½ *teaspoons salt*
       Freshly ground black pepper
       Pinch of cinnamon
   8 *cloves garlic, crushed*
   1 *tablespoon lemon juice*
   1 *cup tomato juice*
       Water
   1 *teaspoon crumbled dried mint leaves*

Discard the tough outer leaves of the cabbage. Cook the cabbage in plenty of boiling, salted water for a few minutes, just until the leaves can be easily removed from the stalk. In a bowl, combine the lamb, rice, 1 tomato, 1 teaspoon salt, pepper and cinnamon. Cut the cabbage leaves into 5 inch triangles. Place 1 tablespoon of the lamb mixture on a leaf and fold as illustrated on page 19. Tie securely with a thread. Continue until all the filling is used. Place the remaining tomatoes and 2 cloves garlic on the bottom of a casserole. Arrange the cabbage rolls on top. Sprinkle with lemon juice and ¼ teaspoon salt. Pour in the tomato juice and enough water to barely cover the rolls. Bring to a boil, lower the heat, cover and simmer 20 minutes. Combine the remaining garlic, salt and mint and spread over the cabbage rolls. Simmer

uncovered 15 minutes more. Serve from the casserole.

Chick pea salad

4 servings

2½ *cups canned chick peas, drained*
   3 *tablespoons light sesame oil or olive oil*
   4 *tablespoons lemon juice*
   2 *cloves garlic, crushed*
   ½ *teaspoon salt*
   1 *tablespoon chopped parsley*

Rub the chick peas through a strainer. Add the oil and lemon juice alternately, 1 tablespoon at a time, until all is blended. Add garlic and salt and stir until a thick, smooth mixture is formed. Refrigerate for 3 hours before serving. Sprinkle with parsley. This salad may be decorated with whole chick peas and lemon slices.

Artichokes with meat mixture

4 servings

   2 *tablespoons oil*
   2 *cloves garlic, crushed*
1½ *pounds fillet of beef*
   1 *cup beef broth*
   8 *canned artichoke hearts*
   ½ *cup pine nuts*
   ¼ *teaspoon salt*
       Freshly ground black pepper
   ¼ *teaspoon cumin*

Heat the oil in a casserole. Add the garlic and the beef and sauté over high heat until the beef is well browned on all sides. Add all the remaining ingredients and bring to a boil. Lower the heat, cover the pan and simmer 10 to 15 minutes or until the beef reaches the desired degree of doneness. Slice the beef and arrange on a serving plate. Garnish with the artichoke hearts and pour on the sauce. Serve immediately.

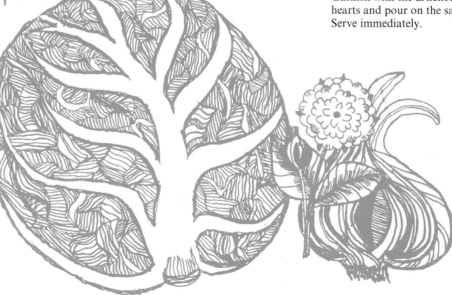

Desserts

The Turks learned to make the finest and crispest dough from the Arabs: it is so fine and thin that you can see through it.

Baclava

Pastries with nuts and syrup

8 to 10 servings

- 1 pound filo leaves (about 24 sheets)
- 16 tablespoons butter, melted
- 2½ cups walnuts or almonds, chopped
- 2 cups sugar
- ½ cup water
- 1 tablespoon lemon juice

Brush a 9 × 12 × 2 inch dish with melted butter. Fold a sheet of filo in half and carefully lay in the pan. Brush with melted butter. Repeat until there are 6 layers of filo. Sprinkl ⅓ of the nuts on the last layer. Add 6 more filo leaves, brushing each one with melted butter. Add ⅓ more nuts. Repeat this procedure until all ingredients are used ending with a pastry layer. Brush the top layer with butter and cut into diamond shapes 2 inches wide. Bake in a preheated 350° oven for 30 minutes. Reduce the heat to 300 and continue baking for 30 minutes longer. Add the sugar to the water. Add lemon juice and boil the syrup for 5 minutes Pour over the warm pastry and let cool before serving.

The rose is the symbol of love and tenderness in the Near East, and this flower has a very important place in daily life. Only someone who is a total stranger to these countries would find it curious that a traffic policeman in Athens, Istanbul, Ankara or Beirut will be carrying a rose behind his ear. When the traffic is quiet for a moment he removes the rose and smells it elegantly. If you are invited to dinner by a Greek, Turkish, or Arab family, they will immediately go to the garden and pluck a fresh rose for you as the honored guest. From the very fragrant rose, the damascena, the Turks make a sweet marmalade they eat at breakfast. On the Greek island of Chios, the people prepare candied rose petals, which are offered on a small dish with a spoon, a cup of black coffee and a glass of water as a sign of welcome. And Turkish cakes with such fancifully romantic names as lady's slip and lady's navel, all float in sweet syrup and are flavored with rose water. They always add a drop of rose water to the simplest rice or semolina puddings to give a soft aroma. Even jet black Turkish coffee ('as black as night, hot as fire and sweet as love', as the Turks say) has a few drops of rose water.

Turkish and Arab cakes are incredibly sweet, made with honey and molasses. But they are also very delicate in taste, with almonds, hazelnuts, candied orange peels and fruit all going into them. The Eastern Mediterranean is a land of many different fruits: cherries, peaches, plums and apricots, all of which were brought to Europe by the Romans.

In February the almond trees bloom with whitish-pink flowers on the hills of Israel. And in May the first soft, white, but not yet completely ripe almonds appear.

These are perfect for preparing almond milk and almond mousse.

Melon with almond cream (recipe page 86, 1st column)

Maadan Hasultan

Almond mousse with apricot sauce

6 servings

    5 egg yolks
    8 tablespoons sugar
    2 cups milk
 ½ cup heavy cream, whipped
 ½ cup roasted almonds, ground
 ½ teaspoon vanilla extract
 ½ teaspoon almond extract
    2 egg whites
    2 teaspoons gelatin
    1 cup hot water

Sauce:

    1 pound can apricots, drained
       and pitted
    2 tablespoons sugar
    1 teaspoon lemon juice
    6 strawberries or cherries

Beat the egg yolks with 4 tablespoons of the sugar in the top of a double boiler. Heat the milk to boiling point. Add milk to the yolks and cook until thickened into a custard, stirring constantly. Combine the whipped cream with the ground almonds, vanilla, almond extract and custard. Beat 2 egg whites with the remaining 4 tablespoons sugar until stiff. Dissolve the gelatin in hot water and allow to cool slightly. Fold gelatin and egg whites into the whipped cream mixture. Fill serving glasses ¾ full. Chill in the refrigerator for 4 hours. Place the apricots in a blender with 2 tablespoons sugar and lemon juice and blend until smooth. Pour over the mouse and decorate with strawberries or cherries.

Haroun Alrashid

Melon with almond cream

6 servings

    5 eggs, separated
    8 tablespoons sugar
    2 cups milk
    ½ cup heavy cream
    ½ cup raw pistachio nuts
    ½ teaspoon vanilla
    ½ teaspoon almond extract
    2 egg whites
    2 teaspoons gelatin
    1 cup hot water
    3 cantaloupes
    2 pints strawberries
    1 cup heavy cream, whipped

Prepare Almond mousse
(see page 85) eliminating
the apricot sauce and
using whole pistachio nuts in
place of ground almonds. Cut a
slice about ¼ inch thick from
the top and bottom of each
melon. Carefully scoop out the
seeds from the top. Rinse out
with cold water and drain. When
dry, fill each melon with
alternate layers of custard and
strawberries and refrigerate for
at least 4 hours but preferably
overnight. Cut each melon
lengthwise into 2 halves before
serving. Decorate with
additional strawberries and
whipped cream. This dessert is
unique but its preparation is
simple and quick. It is advisable
to prepare it the day before
serving so the flavor will be fully
developed.

Amygdalo

Almond pears

16 pears

    4 (4 ounce) packages slivered
      blanched almonds
 1¼ cups sugar
    1 cup freshly made
      breadcrumbs
    3 egg whites
    1 teaspoon vanilla
   16 cloves
      Orange flower water
      Powdered sugar

Grind the almonds in a blender
until very fine and place in a
mixing bowl. Add the sugar,
breadcrumbs, egg whites and
vanilla and knead the ingredients
together until thoroughly
combined. Divide into 16
portions and form each into a
small pear shape. Insert a clove
in the top of each "pear" to
resemble the stem. Place pears
on a buttered baking sheet and
bake 20 to 25 minutes in a 350°
oven. Let cool completely. Dip
in orange flower water and dust
with powdered sugar.

Murabba mhashee batindshan

Eggplant jam

Makes 2½ cups

    1 pound ripe eggplant
    2 cups sugar
    2 cups water
    6 cloves (tied in a cheesecloth
      bag)
    2 tablespoons lemon juice

Cut the stalks off the eggplants,
peel and cut the eggplant into
½ inch cubes. Cover with water,
bring to the boil and cook for
10 minutes. Drain. Dissolve the
sugar in 2 cups water and add
the cloves. Bring to a boil, add
the eggplant and remove from
the heat. Allow to stand for 24
hours. Remove the eggplant
with a slotted spoon and boil the
syrup for 20 minutes. Add the
eggplant to the syrup and boil
for a further 30 minutes. Remove
the cloves, add the lemon juice
and pour into hot sterilized jars.
Let cool completely, cover with
transparent wrap and store in a
cool dark place.

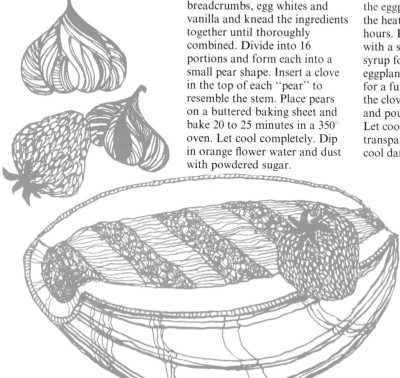

Lokum

Turkish delight

2½ cups water
4 cups sugar
1 cup cornstarch
¾ cup grape juice or orange
  juice
1 teaspoon cream of tartar
  Few drops liquid red food
  coloring (optional)
  Oil
  Powdered sugar

Bring the water to a boil, add
the sugar and stir until
thoroughly dissolved. Mix the
cornstarch with the grape juice
and cream of tartar. Gradually
pour into the boiling syrup,
stirring constantly. Continue
cooking for 20 minutes, stirring
frequently to prevent sticking.
Add food coloring. Oil a 7 inch
square cake pan with sides
1 to 1½ inches high. Pour in the
mixture and let stand until cool
and set. Cut into 1 inch squares.
Dust with powdered sugar and
serve.

Hanim parmagi

Ladies' fingers

8 servings

1¾ cups water
½ cup butter
1¼ cups flour
4 eggs
  Oil for deep frying
1 cup sugar
1 cup water

Pour the water into a saucepan
and bring to a boil. Add the
butter and stir until melted.
Sift the flour and add all at
once, stirring constantly. Stir
vigourously until the mixture
forms a ball around the spoon
and leaves the sides of the pan.
Remove from the heat and cool
slightly. Add 1 egg at a time,
beating thoroughly after each
addition. Continue beating until
the mixture is thick and shiny.
Chill the mixture for 1 hour.
Form tablespoons of the
mixture into fingers 2 to 2½
inches long. Deep fry in
preheated 375° oil until puffed
and golden brown. Drain on
paper towels. Dissolve the sugar
in the water, bring to a boil and
cook for 15 minutes until a
thick syrup is formed. Pour over
the ladies' fingers and serve hot.

Kadın gögbegi

Ladies' dimple cakes

½ cup butter
½ cup sugar
4 eggs
4 cups flour
½ cup milk
  syrup
¾ cup sugar
¾ cup water
1 cup heavy cream, whipped

Beat the butter until creamy.
Add the sugar and beat until
the mixture is light and fluffy.
Add the eggs 1 at a time, beating
well after each addition. Add
the flour and milk alternately
and stir until the ingredients are
thoroughly combined. Flour
your hands and form the dough
into balls the size of small
apples. Place on a buttered
cookie sheet and make a deep
depression in each cake. Bake in
a 350° oven for 40 minutes.
Prepare a syrup as directed in
the previous recipe for Ladies'
fingers, using ¾ cup sugar
and the water and pour over the
cakes. When the syrup has been
absorbed, place a spoonful of
whipped cream into each
"dimple" and serve.

Melopita

Honey pie

6 to 8 servings

3 cups flour
¾ teaspoon salt
1½ teaspoons baking powder
10 tablespoons butter
6 tablespoons cold water
3 cups cottage cheese
¾ cup sugar
1½ teaspoons cinnamon
1 cup honey
5 eggs

Sift the flour, salt and baking
powder into a bowl. Cut in the
butter with a pastry blender until
the mixture is crumbly. Stir in
the water gradually, using only
enough to make the dough stick
together. Roll out the pastry and
fit into a 10 inch pie plate. Beat
the cottage cheese and sugar
until well combined and fluffy.
Add 1 teaspoon cinnamon and
the honey. Add the eggs, one at
a time, beating well after each
addition. Fill the pastry shell
with this mixture. Bake in a
preheated 300° oven for 40
minutes. Raise the oven heat to
375° and bake an additional 10
to 15 minutes. Turn off the heat
and leave the pie in the oven
until completely cooled. Sprinkle
with the remaining cinnamon
and serve.

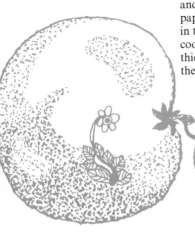

88

Pistachios are light apple-green colored nuts in a beige-brown shell which bursts open when roasted. Most pistachios come from Syria. They are used unsalted for ice cream and pastry; when lightly salted they are served as appetizers with the aperitif.

Date rolls stuffed with nuts. (recipe page 89, 2nd column)

Glida fistoor halabi

Ice cream with pistachio nuts

10 servings

- 6 eggs, separated
- ¾ cup sugar
  Pinch of salt
- 2 cups shelled pistachios
- 2 cups heavy cream
  Few drops green food coloring
  Shelled pistachios for garnish (optional)

Beat the egg yolks with 6 tablespoons sugar and a pinch of salt until very thick and lemon colored. Do not underbeat. Fold in the pistachio nuts. Beat the egg whites until soft peaks form. Add 2 tablespoons sugar and continue beating until stiff. Stir ⅓ of the egg whites into the yolk mixture and carefully fold in the remainder. Beat the cream until it thickens slightly. Add the remaining ¼ cup sugar and beat until stiff. Fold the cream and food coloring into the egg mixture gently but very thoroughly. Spoon into individual serving dishes, garnish with pistachios and freeze 6 hours before serving. Alternatively, you may transfer the mixture to a large plastic container. Cover tightly and freeze overnight until firm.

Mishlahat Haneger

Date rolls stuffed with nuts

40 servings

- 2 egg yolks
- 2 tablespoons whipping cream
- 1 cup milk
- 5 tablespoons sugar
- 1 tablespoon almond essence
  Green food coloring
- 7 tablespoons butter
- 5 tablespoons flour
- 1 cup ground roasted almonds
- 80 dates
- 2 pounds filbert nuts
- 80 half almonds

Beat the egg yolks lightly with the cream and leave to one side. Pour the milk into a saucepan. Add the sugar, almond essence and a few drops of food coloring. The mixture should be light green in color. Bring to boiling point. In the meantime, heat the butter and stir in the flour. Cook over low heat for 1 minute but do not allow the flour to turn brown. Add the boiling milk mixture gradually, stirring constantly to form a smooth sauce. Add the egg yolks and cream. Stir in the ground almonds. Place the mixture in the refrigerator for 4 hours. It will become a firm dough. Remove the pits from the dates and stuff each date with 2 or 3 whole filberts. Roll the dough into a rectangle and cut into 80 strips 2½ inches long and ½ inch wide. Wrap the strips lengthwise around the stuffed dates. Decorate each date with ½ almond. Serve in portions of two for dessert or with Turkish coffee or liqueurs.

Sholleh zard

Yellow rice

8 servings

- 9 cups water
- 2 cups rice
- 2 drops yellow food coloring
- 2 tablespoons butter
- 1 cup rosewater
- 2 cups sugar
  Pinch of saffron soaked in
  1 teaspoon water
- 1 teaspoon cinnamon
- ½ teaspoon cardamom
- ¼ cup slivered almonds

Bring 6 cups water to a boil. Add rice and stir once with a fork. Lower the heat, cover and simmer 30 minutes until the rice has absorbed most of the liquid. Heat the remaining water and add to the rice. Stir in the food coloring and butter and simmer 2 hours, stirring frequently. Add rosewater, sugar, saffron, cinnamon and cardamom and simmer 5 more minutes. Stir in the almonds and remove from the heat. Pour into a serving dish and let cool to room temperature before serving.

Ugat pereg

Pastry with poppy seeds

8 to 10 servings

Pastry:
- 1 package dry yeast
- ¼ cup lukewarm water
- 1 tablespoon sugar
- 1 teaspoon salt
- 3 cups flour
- 2 eggs, lightly beaten
- ¾ cup butter, melted

Filling:
- ¾ cup poppy seeds
- ⅓ cup water
- ⅓ cup sugar
- 1 teaspoon vanilla
- 2 tablespoons fruit preserves

Pastry: Dissolve the yeast in water and add the sugar and salt. Place the flour in a bowl and add the eggs, butter and yeast mixture. Knead to form a smooth elastic dough and set in a warm place until doubled in bulk.
Filling: Place the poppy seeds, water and sugar in a pan and cook over medium heat until the mixture has thickened slightly. Add the vanilla and preserves. Roll the pastry into a rectangle ¼ inch thick. Spread with the filling and roll up. Bake in a preheated 350° oven for 45 minutes.

Yaourtopita

Yogurt cake

1 cup butter
1 cup sugar
5 eggs, separated
Grated rind of 1 lemon
4 cups flour
Pinch of salt
2 teaspoons baking powder
1¼ cups yogurt
Powdered sugar

Beat the butter until creamy.
Add the sugar gradually and
beat until the mixture is light and
fluffy. Add the egg yolks 1 at a
time, beating well after each
addition. Finally, beat in the
lemon rind. Sift together the
flour, salt and baking powder.
Add to the butter mixture
alternately with the yogurt,
beating after each addition just
until combined. Beat the egg
whites until stiff. Stir ⅓ of the
whites into the batter and
carefully fold in the rest. Pour
the batter into a well buttered
and floured 9 inch cake pan and
bake in a 350° oven 1¼ hours
or until a cake tester comes out
clean. Cool 10 minutes in the
pan before removing to a wire
rack. Before serving, sprinkle
the top of the cake with sifted
powdered sugar.

Halva

Semolina sweet

4 servings

2 cups water
1½ cups sugar
½ cup butter
*1 cup semolina or cream of
wheat*
2 tablespoons chopped almonds
½ teaspoon cinnamon

Heat the water, add the sugar
and stir until dissolved. Bring to
a boil and cook for 15 minutes
until the syrup thickens. In
another saucepan, melt the
butter, stir in the semolina and
continue stirring until the butter
is absorbed. Add the syrup and
stir until smooth. Place the
mixture in a baking dish in a
preheated 325° oven for 20
minutes until the syrup has been
absorbed. Stir in the almonds
and pour into a serving dish.
Dust with cinnamon and chill in
the refrigerator before serving.

Halvas tou fournou

Semolina cake

8 to 10 servings

¾ cup butter
1¼ cups sugar
4 eggs, separated
*2½ cups semolina or cream of
wheat*
2 teaspoons baking powder
2 teaspoons cinnamon
*2 cups coarsely chopped
almonds*
¼ cup brandy

1½ cups water
1½ cups sugar
¼ teaspoon cinnamon
1 teaspoon lemon juice

Beat the butter until soft and
creamy. Add the sugar and beat
until light. Add the egg yolks,
1 at a time, beating well after
each addition. Stir in the
semolina, baking powder,
2 teaspoons cinnamon, almonds
and brandy. The mixture will be
stiff. Beat the egg whites until
stiff and fold into the batter.
Place in a 9 inch square buttered
baking pan. Bake in a preheated
350° oven for 10 minutes.
Reduce the heat to 275° and
bake for 50 minutes. Bring the
water to a boil, add the sugar
and stir until dissolved. Simmer
for 10 minutes. Add the
cinnamon and lemon juice and
keep warm. Remove the cake
from the oven, transfer to a
serving dish and, while still
warm, pour over the hot syrup
until all is absorbed. Cool before
serving.

Irmik helvası

Semolina with almonds

6 to 8 servings

4 tablespoons butter
1¼ cups whole blanched almonds
⅔ cup semolina
3½ cups milk
½ cup sugar
1 teaspoon vanilla

Heat the butter in a saucepan
over low heat. Add almonds and
sauté a few minutes. Add
semolina and continue cooking
slowly 15 minutes, stirring
frequently, until the mixture is
nicely browned. Meanwhile,
place the milk and sugar in a
saucepan and bring to a boil,
stirring until the sugar dissolves.
Pour the hot milk slowly into the
semolina and almonds, stirring
constantly. Simmer until very
thick. Stir in the vanilla, spoon
into individual serving dishes
and serve warm.

Rizogalo

Rice pudding

4 servings

2½ cups milk
1 teaspoon grated lemon rind
½ cup raw rice
½ cup sugar
2 egg yolks
1 tablespoon milk

Heat 2½ cups milk in a saucepan. Add the lemon rind and bring to a boil. Stir in the rice and cook for 5 minutes, stirring frequently. Add the sugar and stir until dissolved. Cook over a very low heat until the rice is tender. Remove from heat. Beat the egg yolks with the remaining milk and stir into the rice mixture. Return to the heat and cook 2 minutes without letting it boil. Pour into a heatproof serving dish. Let cool to room temperature and then chill in the refrigerator.

Loukoumades

Honey puffs

2½ cups flour
½ teaspoon salt
½ package dry yeast
1 cup lukewarm water
Oil for deep frying
½ cup honey
¾ cup sugar
1¾ cups water
2 teaspoons lemon juice
2 teaspoons cinnamon

Sift the flour and salt together into a bowl. Sprinkle the yeast over the lukewarm water and stir to dissolve. Add the yeast mixture to the flour and beat or knead 5 minutes until the dough is smooth and elastic. Cover the bowl with a damp cloth and let rise 1 hour or until the dough has doubled in bulk. Heat the oil for deep frying. Pinch off small pieces of dough and fry in the hot oil for about 3 minutes until golden brown. Drain on paper towels and keep warm. In a saucepan, combine the honey, sugar, water and lemon juice and bring to a boil. Cook, stirring, until the sugar dissolves and the mixture is syrupy. Pour over the hot puffs and sprinkle with cinnamon.

Kourabiedes

Almond cakes

1 cup butter
½ cup sugar
1 egg yolk
2 cups flour
1 teaspoon baking powder
Pinch of salt
1 cup finely ground almonds
½ teaspoon almond extract
Orange flower water or rose water (optional)
Powdered sugar

Beat the butter until creamy. Add the sugar and continue beating until the mixture is light and fluffy. Beat in the egg yolk. Sift together the flour, baking powder and salt. Gradually beat the flour mixture, almonds and almond extract into the butter mixture. Unless you have a very strong mixer, you will probably have to beat in the last of the flour and almonds by hand. Knead the dough 5 minutes. Roll pieces of the dough into small egg shaped balls and place on buttered baking sheets. Bake in a 350° oven 25 minutes. Remove to a wire rack and let cool a few minutes. Sprinkle with orange flower water or rosewater if desired and roll in powdered sugar.

Bagaleh

Sesame pastries

6 to 8 servings

- 1 package dry yeast
- ¼ teaspoon sugar
- 1 cup lukewarm water
- 4 cups flour
- ½ cup butter, melted
- 1 teaspoon salt
- 1 egg, beaten
- ¼ cup sesame seeds

Stir the yeast and sugar into the warm water and allow to stand for 10 minutes. Combine the flour, butter, salt and yeast mixture and knead until a smooth dough is formed. Cover with a towel and let rise in a warm place for 2 hours. Form walnut sized pieces into strips 4 inches long and join the ends to form bagels. Brush each with beaten egg, coat with sesame seeds and place on a buttered baking sheet, leaving a space between each pastry. Bake in a preheated 375° oven for 20 minutes.

Cafe

Turkish coffee

4 servings

- 4 heaping teaspoons pulverized coffee (use Turkish coffee or expresso)
- 4 teaspoons sugar
- 4 demitasse cups cold water
- 8 drops rosewater

Place the coffee, sugar and water in a small saucepan. Bring to a boil and, when the foam rises, remove from the heat and stir. Repeat this 2 more times but do not stir the last time. Sprinkle on the rosewater, pour into demitasse cups and serve.

Aryan

Yogurt drink

4 servings

- 1 cup yogurt
- 3 cups ice water
- ½ teaspoon salt
- 1 teaspoon finely minced fresh mint (optional)

Beat the yogurt and gradually add the ice water. Stir in the salt and mint, if desired, and chill in the refrigerator for ½ hour before serving. Instead of yogurt and ice water, buttermilk may be used.

Conversion tables

Liquid measures

American
standard cup

metric equivalent
(approximately)

1 cup = ½ pint	= 8 fl. oz. (fluid ounce)	= 2,37 dl (deciliter)
1 tbs. (tablespoon) = ½ fl. oz.		= 1,5 cl (centiliter)
1 tsp. (teaspoon) = ⅙ fl. oz.		= 0,5 cl
1 pint	= 16 fl. oz.	= 4,73 dl
1 quart = 2 pints	= 32 fl. oz.	= 9,46 dl

British
standard cup

metric equivalent
(approximately)

1 cup = ½ pint	= 10 fl. oz.	= 2,84 dl
1 tbs.	= 0.55 fl. oz.	= 1,7 cl
1 tsp.	= ⅕ fl. oz.	= 0,6 cl
1 pint	= 20 fl. oz.	= 5,7 dl
1 quart = 2 pints	= 40 fl. oz.	= 1,1 l (liter)

1 cup = 16 tablespoons
1 tablespoon = 3 teaspoons

1 liter = 10 deciliter = 100 centiliter

Oven temperatures

Centigrade	Fahrenheit	
up to 105° C	up to 225° F	cool
105–135° C	225–275° F	very slow
135–160° C	275–325° F	slow
175–190° C	350–375° F	moderate
215–230° C	400–450° F	hot
230–260° C	450–500° F	very hot
260° C	500° F	extremely hot

Solid measures

American/British

metric equivalent
(approximately)

1 lb. (pound)	= 16 oz. (ounces)	= 453 g (gram)
	1 oz.	= 28 g
2.2 lbs.		= 1000 g = 1 kg (kilogram)
	3½ oz.	= 100 g

Kitchen terms

Aspic
A stiff gelatine obtained by combining fish or meat bouillon with gelatine powder.

Au gratin
Obtained by covering a dish with a white sauce (usually prepared with grated cheese) and then heating the dish in the oven so that a golden crust forms.

Baste
To moisten meat or other foods while cooking to add flavor and to prevent drying of the surface. The liquid is usually melted fat, meat drippings, fruit juice or sauce.

Blanch (precook)
To preheat in boiling water or steam. (1) Used to inactivate enzymes and shrink food for canning, freezing, and drying. Vegetables are blanched in boiling water or steam, and fruits in boiling fruit juice, sirup, water, or steam. (2) Used to aid in removal of skins from nuts, fruits, and some vegetables.

Blend
To mix thoroughly two or more ingredients.

Bouillon
Brown stock, conveniently made by dissolving a bouillon cube in water.

Broth
Water in which meat, fish or vegetables have been boiled or cooked.

'En papillote'
Meat, fish or vegetables wrapped in grease-proof paper or aluminum foil (usually first sprinkled with oil or butter, herbs and seasonings) and then baked in the oven or grilled over charcoal. Most of the taste and aroma are preserved in this way.

Fold
To combine by using two motions, cutting vertically through the mixture and turning over and over by sliding the implement across the bottom of the mixing bowl with each turn.

Fry
To cook in fat; applied especially (1) to cooking in a small amount of fat, also called sauté or pan-fry; (2) to cooking in a deep layer of fat, also called deep-fat frying.

Marinate
To let food stand in a marinade usually an oil–acid mixture like French dressing.

Parboil
To boil until partially cooked. The cooking is usually completed by another method.

Poach
To cook in a hot liquid using precautions to retain shape. The temperature used varies with the food.

Reduce
To concentrate the taste and aroma of a particular liquid or food e.g. wine, bouillon, soup, sauce etc. by boiling in a pan with the lid off so that the excess water can evaporate.

Roast
To cook, uncovered, by dry heat. Usually done in an oven, but occasionally in ashes, under coals or on heated stones or metals. The term is usually applied to meats but may refer to other food as potatoes, corn, chestnuts.

Sauté
To brown or cook in a small amount of fat. See Fry.

Simmer
To cook in a liquid just below the boiling point, at temperatures of 185°–210° Bubbles form slowly and collapse below the surface.

Skim
To take away a layer of fat from soup, sauces, etc.

Stock
The liquid in which meat or fish has been boiled together with herbs and vegetables.

Whip
To beat rapidly to produce expansion, due to incorporation of air as applied to cream, eggs, and gelatin dishes.

Alphabetical index

Index by type of dish